FLIGHT FROM THE REPUBLIC

Also by North Callahan

ROYAL RAIDERS:
The Tories of the American Revolution

DANIEL MORGAN:
Ranger of the Revolution

HENRY KNOX:
General Washington's General

SMOKY MOUNTAIN COUNTRY

THE ARMED FORCES AS A CAREER

THE ARMY

FLIGHT
FROM THE
REPUBLIC

The Tories
of
The American Revolution

NORTH CALLAHAN

GREENWOOD PRESS, PUBLISHERS
WESTPORT, CONNECTICUT

Library of Congress Cataloging in Publication Data

Callahan, North.
    Flight from the Republic.

    Reprint of the ed. published by Bobbs-Merrill, Indiana-
polis.
    Bibliography: p.
    Includes index.
    1. American loyalists. I. Title.
[E277.C25 1976]   973.3'14   75-42359
ISBN 0-8371-7428-7

The author expresses his appreciation for the assistance given by P. J. Johnson, Director, Municipal Tourist and Convention Bureau, Saint John, New Brunswick, Canada, in securing illustrative material.

Originally published in 1967 by The Bobbs-Merrill Company, Inc., Indianapolis

Reprinted with the permission of The Bobbs-Merrill Company, Inc.

Reprinted in 1976 by Greenwood Press, a division of Williamhouse-Regency Inc.

Library of Congress Catalog Card Number 75-42359

ISBN 0-8371-7428-7

Printed in the United States of America

To North, Jr.

CONTENTS

FOREWORD

In the title of this book, the word "Republic" is used to convey an idea rather than an entity, since it is realized that the republic as embodied in the United States of America came into definite being in 1789. Years before this, however, a *de facto* state of the same type was emerging.

Appreciation is expressed for valuable assistance in the preparation of this book from the Penrose Fund of the American Philosophical Society and from the Arts and Science Research Fund of New York University. My colleagues at the latter institution, as well as in the American Revolution Round Table and elsewhere, have been exceedingly heartening in their warm and helpful encouragement.

Many individuals gave important support to this project and though it would be fitting to name them here were space available, the organizations with which they are identified are set forth in the notes of reference. In every principal place the author visited in search of material, he found gratifying cooperation and aid. Descendants of the American Tories, especially, expressed gratitude that their long-neglected phase of history was being further explored and expressed in this companion volume to the earlier *Royal Raiders*.

Retracing the odyssey of the Tory exiles was an adventure in itself. A recent journey to Canada from Boston, a route the first sizable group of them took, helped in visualizing the contrast in natural surroundings, even though modernization has greatly softened the change. Government officials of Nova Scotia showed commendable interest and helpfulness in facilitating the use of the archives at Halifax. A tour by atuomobile down through the picturesque province to the little town of Shelburne brought one face to face with the site of a considerable American Tory community which sprang up quickly but soon virtually died, as did the hopes of many of its founders. Back northward by way of the peaceful town of Annapolis Royal and then along the beautiful Annapolis Valley, the land of "Evangeline," gave added inspiration to one in quest of the atmosphere in which the refugees settled. This New Scotland also afforded new hope to the weary exiles ousted from their American homes.

Across the wide Bay of Fundy and its swiftly reversing tides, Saint John, New Brunswick, furnished further evidence of Tory fortunes or lack of them in the beginning of their sojourn in Canada. Officials of Saint John were enthusiastically cooperative in this project which involved the residents of almost two hundred years ago. A search among the fading tombstones of a midtown Tory cemetery at twilight brought not only some gems of obituary tribute but grimly humorous wordings as well. Here in New Brunswick the infamous but always controversial Benedict Arnold, who might be called a turn-coat Tory, held forth for several years after the war and showed the same strangely interesting characteristics which got him into trouble in the states below. The University of New Brunswick at Frederick revealed the current commendable progress of Canadian higher education and in its archives is rich Tory material.

Ottawa is, of course, the main source of manuscript materials in Canada, and at its Public Archives, research goes on 24 hours a day. Staff members were alert to each specific need and showed real dispatch in finding requested Tory documents, as well as spotting newly arrived collections which added to the author's research. Canada seems conscious of need for more original work in its history, and the government is assisting in this important regard. To the south, at the sites of settlements of the Loyalists—as they are duly called in that neighboring country—were found stories and bits of information which help to round out the general account. Examples such as the story of the Tory ancestors of Charles Lindbergh proved fascinating. As one approaches the boundary of the United States and Canada, the unfolding story of the Revolutionary exiles who crossed northward makes an American of today realize even more vividly that there is really no dividing line between the cardinal interests of these neighbors. Much of modern Canada may be said to have been founded by these exiles.

The migration of Tories to Canada began from adjoining New York state in 1774 and continued in varying degrees until 1789, eight years after the virtual close of the American Revolution and six years after the formal signing of the peace treaty —an agreement which most Tories considered a travesty upon the tenets of justice. By the terms of this treaty, it was vaguely stipulated that creditors on each side should "meet no lawful impediment" in recovering all debts in sterling money and that the Congress of the United States should "earnestly recommend" to the states the restoration of the rights and possessions of the "real British subjects" and of Loyalists who had not borne arms. All other Loyalists were to be given twelve months in which to adjust their affairs and recover confiscated property. It was further provided that no future confiscations should be made, that imprisoned Loyalists should be released and that no more prosecutions should be permitted. Acting with collective tongue in cheek, the Congress accordingly sent recommendations to the states concerned, but with no significant effect. Instead of due restitution, petty annoyance and persecution followed, severe ordinances and statutes were passed against the Loyalists, and an exodus from the new United States was the only relief open to most of them. This exodus has been compared with that of the Moors from Spain and the Huguenots from France.

In England, a Tory haven of importance second only to Canada, there was a mixed reception. As the man who might be called "Mr. Tory himself" stated, "The terms, Whig and Tory, had never been used much in America. The Massachusetts people in general were of the principle of the ancient Whigs, attached to the Revolution and to the succession of the crown in the house of Hanover. A very few who might have been called Tories in England, took the name of Jacobites in America. All of a sudden, the officers of the crown and such as were keeping up their authority, were branded with the name of Tories, always the term of reproach; their opposers assuming the name of Whigs, became the common people, as far as they had been acquainted with the parties in England, all supposed the Whigs to have been in the right and the Tories in the wrong."

So there was an official welcome for such prominent Tories as Thomas Hutchinson, King George III himself giving them personal greetings and assurances of English hospitality and lasting care. Enticed at first by such promises, these important Tories found the British scene, especially London, a haven of hope and refuge. But this was an ephemeral impression. It was not long before the loyal Americans were forgotten and penury as well as loneliness replaced the early satisfactions. Fortunately, for the present purpose, journals and diaries were kept by some of the refugees, as well as letters written to friends and relatives in America, many of which have been preserved, and utilized in this volume.

Re-visiting England in quest of the American Tory heritage is a rather nebulous thing. But the spacious old Public Record Office in London still holds an eighteenth-century aura, emitted from the mellowed manuscripts reposing there. Claims of the Loyalists for the losses they suffered, lists of persons and property, handbills, pamphlets and old newspapers as well as letters and memoranda are part of such records. There is more bulk than substance in these archives, as far as the Tories are concerned, but as in all research, the body of the material must be gone through in order to determine what, if anything, useable is therein.

The British Museum proved to be the next best source of Tory history, although it was so far behind in its orders for copying that months were required before reproductions of the desired materials could be obtained. The modernization of its manuscript room is a welcome innovation of convenience and comfort as compared to the former days of musty alcoves there. Repositories at English universities and colleges were found to contain some information in original form, while from the local libraries and government offices were extracted bits and pieces. Even collections stored in English and Scottish castles over two centuries old hold some remnants of the Tory saga, as the notes and bibliography of this book show. But in the general munificence of eighteenth-century Britain, most of the refugees were soon overlooked and their records tell a sad but exciting tale of disillusionment which at times was as dank and cold as the climate.

As far as the Atlantic islands are concerned, it has been an obvious pleasure to visit them. Bermuda was a convenient stopping-off place for some not bent on England, and while not many of the Loyalists lingered there, those who did made themselves importantly felt. Still standing are a few homes of the Tories, as illustrated in this book, and in the official records are numerous documents of the refugees, especially those of an early governor and chief justice of Bermuda, two Tories from America. On the tip of this resort island stands a sturdy fortress with guns of the colonial period. Within the cavernous recesses of the fort, one can almost envision the dramatic theft of 100 barrels of powder which were taken from under the very noses of the British authorities and conveyed to the United States where they were used by George Washington. Ironically, a framed letter from Washington about the daring incident is on the wall of the historical society in St. Georges, once the capital of Bermuda.

Southwestward in the Bahamas, the Tories settled in clusters. Nassau gleams with relics of the Revolution, and the local telephone directory might, for a considerable part of it, be a list of those who once graced Boston or some other city of the United States, but who chose the royal cause and exile. Although there is little historical material in the Nassau archives about American Tories, there is much in the minds of its people. One female descendant, when queried about the matter, sounded forth in a strong tirade against "that rascal, George Washington, and the accursed Continental Congress."

It is in the islands lying out from Nassau where most Tory descendants of this region are, as described in the following pages. Some of the islands, such as storied Spanish Wells, have a utopian type of community, the tranquillity and goodness of which soothe the modern soul. As far away as Antigua and Jamaica, American Tory descendants keep alive the spirit of their ancestors, in whose hearts, for a time, it failed.

NORTH CALLAHAN
New York University, October, 1966

FLIGHT FROM THE REPUBLIC

THE COMING OF THE LOYALISTS, 1783

(From a painting by Hy Sandham, a print of which is in the Public Archives of Canada in Ottawa.)

[I]

A CITY THAT WAS

OUTWARD TO THE GULF STREAM sailed the Loyalists in a fleet of eighteen square-rigged vessels on the bright day of April 27, 1783, leaving New York Harbor with feelings more buoyant than sad. For unlike the crew in *Moby Dick*, they sought a haven ahead which they felt in their hearts must be much better than the homeland astern. Eastward, then north, they skirted the coast of New England and made straight for a promised land which most of them knew only by the euphonious name of Nova Scotia.

On board the vessels, which were joined by several sloops and schooners as well as two ships of war, were almost 500 families, bereft of a homeland they once had thought always would be theirs. But now with the flag of Great Britain at the mastheads, they were returning to the fold of the mother country as refugees from the ending American Revolution. Their sovereign and his government had promised them a new home; they were joyously on their way to find it, determined to hold it so close that they would never lose it again.

The planning had been precise. Five years before, when the war was still young, Lord North had with remarkable perspicacity foreseen the problem. He expressed a strong desire of "permanently providing for the American sufferers who will soon be too numerous to be provided for as they hitherto have been. Cannot a practicable and advantageous plan be devised," he asked, "of settling them in the provinces which still remain connected with England and of granting them lands and other encouragements to induce them to settle there?"

Astute and kindly Sir Guy Carleton, the Irish-born British general who had kept Canada loyal to the Crown and set a sharp example by twice defeating Benedict Arnold when the latter was on the American side, had high hopes for the Nova Scotian expedition. "The provision which it is necessary should be made for those Loyalists who have sacrificed their properties and exposed themselves to hazards of every kind in supporting the union of the Empire, has induced me to look for a resort on the behalf of many in the province of Nova Scotia," Sir Guy had written from New York to Provincial Governor John Parr. But becoming all too fanciful, he added, "I am in hopes, Sir, that the post, thus established by an industrious body of men, inured to hardships, accustomed to danger, and acquainted with fisheries and trade, will bring a great accession of strength and wealth to the province and give it suddenly that importance which it is now of the highest consequence that it should obtain." [1]

Appointed by Carleton to survey and supervise the laying out of Roseway Harbor, as Shelburne was then called, were Loyalists Joseph Durfee of Newport, Rhode Island, James Dole of Albany, New York, Peter Lynch and Thomas Courtney of Boston, and William Hill, Joseph Pynchon and Joshua Pell of New York. They were enjoined to make an "equitable distribution" of the land. Perhaps the general had in mind a communal society similar to the later Brook Farm or New Harmony; but if he did, this earlier experiment in the kindness of human nature was to suffer the same ill fate. Even so, for part of its early period the settlement did carry the name of "New Jerusalem." Here, it was urged that "every inhabitant or settler be obliged to perform the due cultivation of his lands," but just who was to stand over all of them and administer this obligation was not stated. [2]

Such questions do not seem to have disturbed the minds of the exiles approaching Shelburne, however; entering the picturesque harbor, even though they could see no spot where even a tent could be set, they remained sanguine about the prospects. To their inexperienced eyes, it looked as if this were the place to build a second New York. Indeed, Shelburne did become the largest town in British North America, and was later seriously considered by Governor Parr to replace Halifax as the capital of Nova Scotia. Many professions were to be found there: jurists and bakers, wine merchants, wig makers, dealers in snuff and hair powder, gunsmiths, silversmiths, carvers and artisans of all kinds. [3]

Among the first to land was Benjamin Marston of Marble-head, Massachusetts, "a Tory of the olden time, and in the Revolution, a sturdy adherent to the royal cause." He had been appointed to survey and superintend the laying out of the new site at Port Roseway and was a fitting, if at times irascible, man for the purpose. To his diary we owe our knowledge of much of what went on in the infant days of the struggling town of Shelburne, both in its physical development and in the minds of its people. Marston was a Harvard graduate and had been a prosperous merchant and one of those who signed the loyal address to Thomas Hutchinson, the last royal governor of the Massachusetts Bay Colony. Marston seems to have been a man of generous spirit and sanguine disposition, possessed of a vigorous constitution, an active mind and habits; he was a lover of good society and a devoted admirer of the ladies, and a bit of an artist and poet.[4] To escape tarring and feathering, he had fled from a Marblehead mob in the night. His young and pretty wife had died soon afterward.

He found the land around Shelburne better than had been believed. It was to be free of quitrents, to be laid out and surveyed at the cost of the government, the settlers to have fishing and fowling rights. As if to enhance the prospects, Marston kept a detailed record of the weather at this time, with much of it being fair with moderate winds, though he did not hesitate to record fog and drizzle. When the exiles took a long second look at the scene, they found that between water and sky were a rocky shore and dense masses of forest. Nothing had been done in the way of clearing and making ready for the new colony, this perhaps being due to the lack of cooperation between the Nova Scotia authorities and Sir Guy Carleton, commander-in-chief in New York.

Based upon the report of the surveyor, it was decided that the actual site of the city would be on the northeast portion of the harbor. Many objected on the grounds that the land was too rough and uneven. The group had been divided into companies for the purpose of organization, and now their leaders proposed that three men be selected from each company to "do the matter over again," as Marston put it. "That is to commit to a mob of sixty what a few judicious men found very difficult to transact with a lesser mob. . . . This cursed republican, town meeting spirit has been the ruin of us already," he continued in bitter reminiscence of the strife in New England, "and unless checked

3

by some stricter form of government will overset the prospect which now presents itself of retrieving our affairs." [5]

It was agreed, however, that the town should consist of five long parallel streets, crossed by others at right angles, each square containing 16 lots, 60 feet in front and 120 feet in depth. One of the thoroughfares was appropriately named "Water Street," and the space between it and the shore was to be cut up by small lanes and divided into little lots, so that each settler might have a town and water lot as well. Outside the city, each was to have a 50-acre farm either on the shore or nearby. At either end of the township, a reservation was made for a common. It was a utopian dream born of the sadness of bidding farewell to the homeland.

Some of the newcomers were socially prominent and had been important business people in the colonies. Most of them had had military service during the Revolution, had received rough treatment from the victors and now undoubtedly retained a desire for retaliation, which might fall upon neighbors as well as enemies. Probably the most prominent family was that of Captain Gideon White, son of a colonel of Marshfield, Massachusetts, and a descendant of one of the Mayflower Pilgrims. Ironically, he and his family now made another landing on a "stern and rockbound coast" and were to try again to find that freedom of thought and action which their forefather had sought and thought he had found at Plymouth. Through all the fortunes, good and bad, which Shelburne was to experience, the Whites were faithfully to remain and carry on, their descendants figuring prominently down into modern times.

"As soon as we had set up a kind of tent," wrote the Reverend Jonathan Beecher in his journal, "we knelt down, my wife and I and my two boys, and kissed the dear ground and thanked God that the flag of England floated there, and resolved that we would work with the rest to become again prosperous and happy."

Now that the pretty pattern was laid out, men from the various vessels hurried ashore and started cutting down trees, "very cheerfully," Marston noticed, then added acidly, "a new employment to many of them." As soon as the land was sufficiently cleared, tents were pitched and huts erected on the clearings, one shelter with a supply of ammunition being allotted to each family. Helping also were slaves brought by their owners, Andrew Barclay having brought 57, Stephen Shakespeare 20

4

and Charles Bruff 15, among others.[6] The tent of Benjamin Marston was put up just in time, for it began raining hard, the frequent showers being followed by fog.

On Monday, May 12, the settlement suffered its first casualty, a Mr. Mason dying after an illness of only three days. This was offset somewhat, however, by the arrival in port of one of the fishing sloops with 800 codfish which had been caught by only five men in the space of 24 hours, an encouraging omen. Had all the settlers been so industrious and fortunate as these anglers the outcome might have been better. But Marston, who went to work as early as five a.m., observed that some of the newcomers, particularly those of the lower classes, were not at work until 11 a.m. During the war these men apparently had been engaged in work which did not entail much labor but brought good pay, a not unusual wartime situation. Now that they were required to buckle down to hard work with uncertain rewards, they balked. "They began to be clamorous and to have a thousand groundless rumors circulating among them to the prejudice of those to whom they ought to submit," the surveyor observed. But they did not agree with such submission, especially since real authority was at first a nebulous thing and thus easy to evade. The former military officers and the captains of the transports had no binding control over the people, nor were all these leaders themselves very capable. With the government giving out subsistence, they could not invoke the effective rule of John Smith at Jamestown, that "those who do not work shall not eat." Some were even inclined to be mutinous, but this threat did not grow to serious proportions.

A deputy collector and impost officer, Stephen Binney, arrived from New York and held a meeting. The people responded well to him, especially when he allowed them to seize a quantity of privately owned lumber boards and convert them to their own use. But Binney ran into a personal difficulty when, after he had put up his bed in Ben Marston's tent, he spent a whole Sunday morning trying to find a barber to shave him. When at last he found one, the fellow was so clumsy that he cut Binney rather badly on the face, until "he was all the rest of the day at times examining the wounds." [7]

The people of Port Roseway drew for their lots, keeping the officials busy apportioning the various parcels of land. It was an exciting distribution, and there was dissatisfaction as well as gratification. Some of them grumbled, some were pleased, but to those in charge of the process, the people presented a rather unfavorable aspect—as least to Marston, who seems to have been the closest observer who made a record of his opinions. Viewing their bent for comfort, he philosophized, "Nothing so easy as to bear hardships in a good house by a good fireside, with good clothes, provisions etc. Seneca, with some thousands per annum, wrote very learnedly in praise of poverty. Master Stephen Binney thinks with a good house he could be very well content to stay here a little while and endure hardships." [8]

Two days later, the embryo city experienced a harbinger of one of those problems which all municipalities must face. A fire broke out which was suspected to have been set by some dissatisfied person, and burned up the personal effects of a few of the families before it was brought under control. In spite of difficulties, though, it was observed that there was something about the idea of owning land which was exceedingly agreeable to the human mind. Each man could now pilot his family through the rocks, stumps and swamps, point to some combination of these and say, "This is ours."

On the king's birthday, June 4, there was a celebration that included a ball to which most of the populace went. But the *feu de joie* that was to be performed in the streets was dampened by showers. Two days later, the Reverend William Black, a Methodist preacher, arrived. He repaired to the tent of a "Brother Barry," who insisted that the parson lie down while he sat up all night, since it was raining and room was lacking. On the following Sunday, Black put notices on some of the tents, announcing preaching for 11 o'clock, three in the afternoon and six in the evening. On Monday he preached again, but by this time met with some opposition from non-believers. Three men came at him "like to mad bulls of Bashan, their mouths full of blasphemy and awful imprecations." A stone was thrown at him by one of them. [9]

As the summer wore on, the appetite for land and shelter was sharpened by the thoughts of the approaching cold of winter. Seeing that all the settlers were properly taken care of proved no easy job, especially where there were mean dispositions coupled with greedy natures and lack of manners. Also, the heat vied with the black flies in the woods to harass those laying out the lots. But by the middle of July, some two months after the newcomers had sailed up the harbor, they drew for their 50-acre lots; the town had been separated into northern and southern divisions, the streets had received their names, the lots were numbered, and insofar as possible, each of the original settlers was assigned a town and farm lot. But according to Marston, there were many who were left out who were equally entitled to lots. He blamed this on the people as a whole, saying that "They want government, more knowledge and a small portion of generosity." He believed that those who came in the first fleet wanted to grab up the whole grant of land, "hoping the distresses of their fellow Loyalists who must leave New York, will oblige them to make purchases"—thus the earlier ones would profit from speculation.

As evidence of Port Roseway's importance, Governor John Parr of Nova Scotia arrived there on Sunday, July 20, 1783, in the ship *Sophia*. Salutes were fired as he disembarked, and he made a rather grand entrance into the young city by proceeding up King Street, both sides of which were lined by the inhabitants. The leading citizens greeted the governor, and in answer he mounted the steps of a house and read a proclamation naming the town "Shelburne" in honor of Lord Shelburne, a member of the British cabinet (afterwards Marquis of Lansdowne and Secretary of State for the colonies) who had wisely opposed some of the British government measures such as the Stamp Act. The proclamation was followed by cheers and toasts and the naming by the governor of justices of the peace and other officers and the administering of the oath of office to them. Then came a festive dinner aboard the *Sophia*, with more toasts, these to the king's health, to the new town of Shelburne, and to the general settlement of the Loyalists in Nova Scotia. But a considerable number of those present objected to naming their community after Shelburne, who they felt had "sold them out" by being too generous with Canadian boundaries and in other phases of the peace negotiations after the Revolutionary War.

Governor Parr seemed on this occasion a sort of one-man chamber of commerce for the new town. He wrote Sir Guy Carleton that "From every appearance I have not a doubt but that it will in a short time become the most flourishing town for trade of any in this part of the world, and the country will for agriculture." At the same time, the governor expressed grave doubts about the soil along the River St. John, now in New Brunswick; yet if the present appearance of the two places is an indication, somewhat the reverse of this statement is true.

Prior to this, one of the new settlers had written to a friend in New York and expressed similar sentiments: "I am happy in having this opportunity of testifying the great satisfaction I enjoy in coming to this place; the prospects of happiness for a set of Loyal people are so many, that without great neglect in the civil departments and other matters prejudicial to the internal policy of the settlement, they must be a flourishing people. The situation is abundantly provided by nature with one of the finest harbors on the continent of America, and the soil is by far the most preferable of any in the Province." [10]

As if to emphasize these ardent if premature encomiums, even while Parr was there, 90 more families from New York arrived at Shelburne, as well as others from New England. All were provided with shelter, but those who readied it were hard put to get the job accomplished in time, 183 arriving in one day. Strong efforts were made to distinguish the actual settlers from the speculators, for quite a number of the latter appeared from time to time in hopes of staking off property and then making quick money out of it. Now a large number of additional Negro emigrants landed under the supervision of Colonel Stephen Black, a trusted mulatto. These people were located together on the northwest side of the harbor in a community called Birchtown, named after the British commandant of the city of New York. Many of them were claimed as slaves in New York, but Carleton had declined to give them up to their old masters, on the ground that they had been declared free by a proclamation of Sir Henry Clinton.

That some of the applicants were not above offering emoluments for a choice selection of property can be believed from the August 9 entry in the diary of Ben Marston: "At home all day, it being rainy all the morning and remaining part of the day blew exceedingly hard at N.W. A Capt. McLean has this evening sent me a green turtle, about seven pounds. I am obliged to him. He is to have a house lot, but this must not blind my eyes. He must run the same chance as his neighbors who have no turtles to send."

More honest than polite at times, the busy surveyor a few days later noted that he had received a billet from a Captain Christian inviting him to breakfast on board the ship *Cyclops*. Marston accepted verbally, adding, "I was too tired, too dirty, too hungry to sit down and write an answer to his billet. He may think me an odd fellow: he is welcome to the opinion."

But Marston did not accept an invitation to meet with some of the group captains, because he understood that the business to be transacted concerned trespassing on some of the lots already set aside for the colored people. Particularly was he incensed about a Mr. Sperling who "with a pocket compass and cod line ran over the western side of the harbor as far as Cape Negro, laying out 50-acre lots. He has taken into his survey, Birchtown," Marston continued, "which will utterly ruin it, for that will shift the niggers at least two lots." It was understood that Sperling was being paid two dollars apiece for all the white people who were to settle on this property, which Marston felt was a "piece of villainy." Also he was alarmed at reports that a number of minors were included in the lists of those who were to draw for lots.

Though Marston kept busy, he often seems to have been bored, judging from his entry of "Dined on board the *Cyclops* in the Gun Room—noise and nonsense." But the next day, he dined again on the ship, this time in the "Great Cabin," and he described the occasion as being one of "decency and agreeableness." Nothing is said of his family back home, but he must have been lonely, for on a Sunday after he had dined in town, he said in his diary, "Home at dark to lonesome, solitary tabernacle." But this was apparently soon remedied when Colonel Abraham Van Buskirk, formerly of the Third Battalion of the New Jersey (Loyalist) Volunteers, and his family moved into Marston's house. His vivid comment about this was, "They live down cellar." [11]

By the autumn of 1783, the town of Shelburne was beginning to take definite shape. It was now laid out in five major divisions with a burying ground at the southern border, the entire municipal area being about a mile and a half long and half a mile wide. Barracks with a sizable garrison attached was on the tongue of land at the end of the harbor opposite the town. The population had grown to 5,000, which appeared to be about right for the preparations that had been made. What did not seem to be right was the arrival of about 5,000 more exiled souls, just when those already on hand were settling down for the rapidly approaching winter. This was probably the most portentous event of the early history of the town which was fast becoming a city; the best-laid schemes for the place were thrown out of gear, and a strain was placed upon the meager resources which was to prove in the long run disastrous. Coupled with the unexpectedly large number was the dubious quality of the new arrivals, who proved on the whole to be inferior to those already there. The second group was made up largely of disbanded soldiers, unfit for steady, laborious work and with little initiative. With them came many civilians and followers of a somewhat undesirable type, prone to grumbling and mischief and to accepting as much as possible for a minimum of labor in return.

Even so, they were better off than the unfortunate Tory brothers left behind in the United States. Carleton had written to George Washington that the disregard of the articles of peace shown by the newspapers and by threats from committees formed in various towns (even in Philadelphia where the Congress was in session) was such that he felt obliged by his national duty and by humanity itself to remove all who should wish it. New York was soon to be evacuated by the British, so the move had to be made in haste. Therefore 8,000 persons left New York in September, most bound for Shelburne. One of the ships bound for Saint John was wrecked on a ledge near Cape Sable, but all the Shelburne ships arrived safely.[12]

Carleton was not unaware of the risks his people would run by being sent to Nova Scotia at the very brink of the winter season. He had proposed to furnish every man, woman and child of the exiles with a complete suit of clothes, two pairs of shoes, hose and two shirts, a competent supply of farming utensils and twelve months' provisions from the date of their landing. Even so, the number of those who decided to go to Shelburne from America greatly exceeded the expectations of the authorities of the province, who had agreed upon a plan for a smaller settlement; so that in order to provide for the late arrivals, modifications of the original plan were necessary. Those who first had charge of the operations—that is, the captains of the various companies into which the settlers were divided—were generally unfitted for more than temporary control. In the emergency, the local and provincial officials probably did as much as they could. Two new divisions were run out on the reservations intended for the north and south commons, and the long streets were increased in number.

Ben Marston, caught in the middle of this mess, left no doubt as to how he felt about the newcomers. "These people," he penned in his ever more vitriolic diary, "are the very worst we have had yet; they murmur and grumble because they can't get located as advantageously as those who have been working hard these four months. They seem to be the riffraff of the whole." There does seem to have been ground for some dissatisfaction, however. James Dole, one of the original agents, wrote to General Carleton complaining that "Governor Parr furnished us with three surveyors at the public cost to lay out the town lots and to our great surprise has reserved two miles length of the best ground" and had otherwise pre-empted land which the people from New York had thought was to be theirs. Carleton then wrote to Parr stating that he had "had many complaints of the conduct of the Deputy Surveyors," possibly meaning Marston among them, "who though they demand no fees, are said to expect *presents* for the performance of their duty, which many of the settlers are not able to afford, but without which, I am credibly informed, their applications are nevertheless neglected." The general also reported that "partialities in the general distribution of lands are much complained of." [13]

The matter of providing food and other necessities naturally was of utmost importance, and fortunately this was in charge of a capable man, Commissary Edward Brinley. From three storehouses built on the island in front of Shelburne, daily provisions were doled out to all. For these 10,000 hungry souls, 70,000 barrels of flour were purchased for distribution, and the amount of farm implements and materials was huge also. Millions of nails and spikes, a large number of hammers, axes, locks and tools of all sorts were among them, and 18,000 saws, for example, were distributed. This generous arrangement was to continue for at least three years, with the amount gradually diminishing from full rations for the first year for the Loyalists, to two-thirds for the second and one-third for the third year. But according to the records, the government dealt liberally with all needy applicants, regardless of the planned allowances. Disbanded soldiers and officers had full rations for a somewhat longer period.

Rough shelters were hurriedly erected for the late-comers, but many had to live as best they could. Some spent the winter on vessels in the cove while others had only tents as their houses. Of course there was a great deal of suffering among the people who had been used to the milder winters and the sturdy homes of New England and New York, but fortunately at Shelburne the winter of 1783–84 was comparatively mild. This was not the case in neighboring New Brunswick. Especially at Saint John and at Fredericton, the winter was severe and the exiles who had gone there were living in tents as well as in log houses and bark camps. A number of them died of exposure. These conditions were further aggravated by the failure of supplies to arrive on time, unlike the regular system worked out at Shelburne.[14]

Early in 1784, a muster report was made of those at Shelburne. In addition to the types of persons already described, there was now an unusually large group of disbanded military men. The list of Loyalist regiments represented there reads likes a citation for those most distinguished in America. The famous British Legion of Tories, commanded by the fiery and able Colonel Banastre Tarleton and finally defeated by Daniel Morgan, was partly disbanded at Shelburne. So were the King's American Regiment; those of the Prince of Wales and the Duke of Cumberland; the Nova Scotia Volunteers; the 1st, 2nd and 3d New Jersey Volunteers; 1st and 2nd De Lancey's Volunteers, as well as the Queen's Rangers and other units. Of the 41 military organizations represented at Shelburne, 24 were British regulars, 16 were Loyalist corps, and a few were Hessians. Most of the Loyalist troops were disbanded in New Brunswick. During the summer of 1783, there had been a considerable garrison stationed at Shelburne for protection and for use in preserving order. Fifty-one guns were mounted at Point Carleton, on the edge of the city.

By the end of the first year, about 1,400 buildings had been erected, many of them roomy and even elegant; and 3,000 house lots, 1,000 store and wharf lots, as well as 1,000 farm lots of from 50 to 500 acres had been allotted. An estimated $7,000,000 was spent in building the town. Beautiful gardens were laid out, fronting on graceful avenues. Stately edifices were erected with "magnificent appointments, all forming a fitting setting for the wealth and aristocracy that made up the population of Shelburne." At about this time, the citizens received from King George III a gift of a fire engine, a much appreciated offering. But despite the assurance that it was "the most modern and very latest thing in fire-fighting appliances," water first had to be carried to it in buckets, which it then pumped out to quench the flames.

Commissary Edward Brinley was so busy mustering and enrolling the Loyalists on their arrival that on one occasion after he had confined a man for breaking the regulations, the man brought suit against him for false prosecution. The commissary was about to proceed to nearby Liverpool to defend himself against the suit, when about 2,000 more exiles arrived from New York and two ships loaded with supplies arrived. Not having an assistant, Brinley felt he could not leave his post. As a consequence, the plaintiff was awarded 42 pounds damages for an hour's confinement. Brinley, however, refused to pay it.

During the first part of the second year, additional parties of exiled Tories continued to arrive but not in such large numbers as previously. In general, most of the settlers farmed, made gardens or fished. Apparently no manufacturing was established except for several sawmills. Those who did not take up farming or clearing of land often became idle and indolent. In July, such conditions resulted in a riot waged by discharged soldiers against the Negroes, and a number of their houses were destroyed. The riot occurred mainly because the Negroes were willing to work for lower wages than the veterans.[15]

Several causes now began to contribute to the retardation of the new city in Nova Scotia. In many instances, the lots drawn were not suited to the business or aptitudes of their owners, and it was a slow and difficult process to purchase or exchange them for other ones. Skilled labor for building was scarce, as was an adequate supply of building materials. But more detrimental than these were the internal dissensions and the general feeling of dissatisfaction with the provincial government. For some inexplicable reason, the province chose to lay heavy duties on the imports of Shelburne at a time when the city should have been aided as much as possible. Some of the inhabitants demanded that such excessive imposts be at least postponed until the city could be incorporated and properly represented in the legislature. But Governor Parr only expressed his regrets at his inability to relieve them of the taxes and added his hopes for better conditions in the future.

Indicative of the falling off of ardor for Shelburne within the United States was this paragraph in a Philadelphia newspaper:

"Many of the refugees who have settled at Port Roseway have wrote to their friends in New York, by no means to come to that place."

Further uncertainty existed in a neighboring state, as shown by a parody in the *Jersey Journal:*

To go or not to go; that is the question
Whether it were best to trust the inclement sky
That scowls indignant; or the dreary Bay
Of Fundy and Cape Sable's rocks and shoals,
And seek our new domains in Scotia's wilds,
Barren and bare, or stay among the rebels,
And by our stay rouse up their keenest rage.[16]

Printing was first introduced into Canada at Halifax in 1752, but presses were established nowhere else in that province until the American Revolution brought two printing establishments and three newspapers to Shelburne. The *Royal American Gazette* made its appearance there early in 1784. It was a transplanted continuation of a Loyalist journal in New York City published by James and Alexander Robertson and Nathaniel Mills. All three of these men came to Shelburne, opened a printing office on King Street and issued the weekly for several years. In October, 1784, a second newspaper made its appearance in Shelburne. This had the extended name of *The Port Roseway Gazette and General Advertiser* and was printed by J. Robertson, Jr., for T.&J. Swords on King Street. Still a third journal was established in the new city, *The Nova Scotia Packet and General Advertiser,* which was published by James Humphreys, a Tory who had been driven from Philadelphia by a patriot mob during the Revolution. His office was at the corner of George and Water Streets in Shelburne, where he also sold "Spirits and all kinds of merchandise." A notice in the last-named newspaper dated July 27, 1786, is edifying:

To be Sold
By VALENTINE NUTTER
In Water Street opposite the Court House

Mess pork in barrels
Ditto beef in ditto
Fish by the quintal
Ship bread by the tierce
Crackers by the cag
Rum by the hogshead
Cherry rum in barrels
Orange juice by the gallon
London manufactured tobacco
Snuff in bladders

A City That Was

Fishermen's boots
Cod lines and hook
Mackerel ditto
Powder and shot
A general assortment of stationery
And many other articles.

There was considerable interest in religion, and during the first two years of the town's development, progress was made along these lines. Most of the Loyalists were members of or adherents to the Church of England and it would seem logical that this church should have flourished from the start. It doubtless would have, had there not been rival claimants for the honor of leading the local flock. One was Reverend William Walter, formerly of Trinity Church, Boston, and later chaplain of the 3rd Battalion of De Lancey's Brigade; the other was Reverend George Panton, formerly rector at Trenton, New Jersey, and subsequently chaplain of the Prince of Wales Volunteers. Both of these highly esteemed ministers stated that they had been asked to join the Tory exiles, and each felt that he should be the official head of the church at Shelburne. Both had devoted followers there, and these refused for a long time to compromise, thus retarding the success of the religious cause itself. Two separate parishes were formed, that of the Reverend Walter being called Trinity, the Reverend Panton's organization being called the Parish of St. Patrick. There was no bishop to settle the problem and Governor Parr appeared to favor Panton. Regular services were held by both groups in temporary places of worship, baptism, burials and other rites being conducted by both clergymen. This schism so delayed the erecting of a church building that it was not until 1788 that the two factions agreed to unite. From this grew Christ Church, opened on Christmas Day, 1789, which was to become a memorable institution in Shelburne. The Church of Scotland was represented in the community, and had many members among the early settlers. Its first minister was the Reverend Hugh Fraser, who during the Revolution had been chaplain of the British 71st Regiment of Highland Light Infantry. Methodists likewise flourished to some extent, the Reverend William Black being their first pastor. Baptists in Shelburne were few in number. The Quakers made some headway in the community but their influence was comparatively minor. As to education, by 1791 there were 12 one-room public schools in Shelburne and one in the Negro suburb of Birch-town. Nine were taught by men and three by women, that of the Negro section being headed by Colonel Black personally. An advertisement in the *Port Roseway Gazette* of June 27, 1785, informed the readers that the local youth would be instructed in reading, writing, arithmetic, bookkeeping, navigation, mensuration, the use and construction of maps and sea charts, Greek, Latin and other languages. Dancing was also offered as a diversion.[17]

Punishment for offenses in the new settlement was harsh but was according to the laws and customs of that day. People were put to death for such acts as stealing or even attempted robbery. The lash was freely used and if this was not effective enough, the culprit was sent to the workhouse, where scarce food and plentiful work were designed to cure him of criminal tendencies. Apparently the first person to be publicly whipped in Shelburne was a Negro woman named Diana who was sentenced to receive 200 lashes at the cart's tail on a Saturday and 150 lashes on the following Saturday. A whipping post was constructed on Stanhope Hill and here the cat-o'-nine-tails was copiously applied. The last sentence of this kind on record also pertained to a Negro woman. She received 21 lashes with the "cat" in 1826. At the corner of Water and Ann streets a pillory was built and was in use by November, 1784. The hapless victims placed therein suffered physical discomfort and were struck by garbage thrown by the jeering passersby.

As to the personalities of those who took a leading part in the community, Ben Marston has left some vivid impressions. In regard to the local courts, he commented, "Abraham Van Buskirk is a gentleman and a man of good understanding, has been in service all the war and yet is more the soldier than the lawyer. J. Pyncheon does not want understanding, but is very timorous and, as timorous creatures generally are, cunning; he shows the New England man very plainly in his manner . . . a Mr. Justice Thomson, an old white oak chip; a Mr. Justice Brewer, bred a merchant, has good natural parts which have been improved by education, calculated to make a conspicuous figure in his own line and he has ambition and capacity to make a useful and judicious magistrate, but at present rather coxcombical . . . a dismounted dragoon officer of Tarleton's, his acquirements in law knowledge not much below the surface." [18]

That Shelburne was becoming a difficult place, at least for

some of its leaders, is borne out in Marston's comments. Writing to a friend, he stated, "I am in as perfect good health as a reasonable mortal can wish for, but almost dimmed to death for town lots and water lots, for 50-acre lots and 500-acre lots. My head is so full of triangles, squares, parallelograms, trapezias and rhomboids, that the corners do sometimes almost put my eyes out. However, I thank God they are there. Had it not been for them, I should by this time have starved to death, or what is ten times worse, have been the burden and pity of my friends." [19]

Such a mood apparently grew worse, for when Marston heard that New Brunswick was to be settled by New England Loyalists, he decided to go there if he could be employed, for he expected to find more old friends than he had in Nova Scotia. "Shelburne is composed of such a mixed multitude, so very few people of education among them," he wrote in his diary, "that it will take me all the rest of my life to get myself well accommodated to their ways of acting and thinking; and unless one can give in to the general mode of thinking and acting of those he lives with, he can have but little enjoyment."

There were those who were having but little enjoyment with Marston, too. One of these was Governor Parr, who visited Shelburne again to try to settle the disturbances there. Apparently he felt that Marston was involved in some of the difficulty, for the latter understood that Parr blamed him. "But I have the satisfaction to know that the best people of that settlement are my friends," stated the indomitable Marston, "and what a Rabble thinks of me is never my concern—though a Governor may be among them."

The governor was among them, and he evidently believed that Marston had been too partial in the granting of land. This charge was answered by the statement that Shelburne had had no more difficulty than other such new settlements; that the greatest difficulty they had to encounter was living in less roomy and comfortable habitations; that fishing and shipping had prospered on the whole; but that a few vessels which were supposed to be employed in bringing Loyalists from New York were, instead, smuggling in gin and brandy.

Despite his arguments and attempts to see the governor and placate him, Marston was dismissed abruptly from his post as chief surveyor of Shelburne. Although he was obviously too outspoken—if his diary is any indication of his verbal expression —and although Governor John Parr, a military hero, has been described as "the ideal governor" for the times, it does appear that Benjamin Marston was treated unfairly. If he showed partiality, it seems to have been his judgment rather than his integrity that was at fault. There is no evidence of corrupt conduct on his part, for he left Shelburne for Halifax as he had come, a poor man. Marston was highly esteemed by Sir John Wentworth, Parr's successor as governor of Nova Scotia, who appointed him a deputy surveyor of the King's Woods. Later, Marston was made sheriff of the county of Northumberland, his headquarters being at Miramichi in New Brunswick. He found the people to be mostly "illiterate and given to drunkeness." Later, he went to England to apply for compensation for his losses in the United States, but was disappointed in the small amount he received. In 1792, Marston was appointed surveyor for a company organized in England to make a settlement in West Africa. Unfortunately, he along with others was seized with a fever, and died there on August 10, 1792. He had hoped to the last to return to his homeland, Massachusetts, from which he had been absent for seventeen years.[20]

With the exit of Benjamin Marston, the spirit of Shelburne seemed also to ebb away. As early as 1784, there were hints of what was to come. Marston along with James McEwen and Joseph Pynchon, magistrates of Shelburne, and other officials wrote to Lord North, the genial, able but pliant prime minister under George III, that "Notwithstanding the utmost exertions of the people, which have had very great, unavoidable difficulties from the state of the country, the deficiencies of materials and the vast additional numbers exceeding all expectation and amounting in the whole to near ten thousand, that were constantly arriving at an advanced season of the year, from the want of earlier means of conveyance, have prevented their establishing themselves either in such personal accommodations or circumstances of public utility as we ardently wished; and one numerous and important body of the people who wish to cultivate the lands, and are qualified to become efficient settlers, and immediately beneficial to government, claim particular attention. From the difficulty of penetrating an embarrassed country to obtain locations, and the lateness of the season which entirely prevents any exertions for subsistence, they must, without a continuation of support from Government, experience not only the greatest distress, but their settlement be rendered in a great measure impracticable."[21]

This call of distress was echoed by Mather Byles, Jr., son of
the colorful Tory pastor of Boston, in a communication from
Halifax to Edward Winslow, a Massachusetts Tory who became
a colonel in the British service and afterward judge of the
Superior Court of New Brunswick. Byles stated that he had had
"an abundance of distressful stories from Shelburne" and other
places in Nova Scotia, and that the people of the settlements
were in danger of starving.[22]

A crisis was developing in the burgeoning city but there
was still hope. From a social and economic standpoint, Shelburne reached a high point in the years 1786 and 1787. Log
huts had followed tents and then came the new and promising
frame buildings. Streets were well defined. Inspiring the settlers,
as it does those who see it now, was a harbor of rare beauty and
usefulness. Wharves had been built along the water front, but
instead of using the good white oak and other such fine timber
at their very doors, the exiles bought their vessels in Britain.
Attractive ships arriving from the West Indies were purchased
in the local port. But this situation was improved by the passage
of an act by Nova Scotia in 1785 offering a bounty of ten
shillings per ton on all vessels of more than 40 tons built in the
province. As a result of this impetus to shipbuilding at home,
eight vessels of 80 and 90 tons were built during the following
summer and autumn for Shelburne merchants. The ship
Roseway, 250 tons, was launched from a shipyard in the northern part of the city on December 22, 1786. It is believed to have
been the first British ship launched in the province. Another,
the little *Roseway Yacht* of only eight tons, crossed from Halifax to London in 1786 in 28 days. The ship *Minerva* was built
in 1789 for George and Robert Ross, who were Shelburne merchants, traders and fish dealers, and whose old store on Charlotte Lane, with their house against its southern wall, is now
used as a museum. Its shingled length stretches back into the
overgrown garden which ends at Maiden Lane. This place oc-
cupies what were once four of the small water lots of Shelburne.

The lumber business flourished fairly well during the early
years of settlement. A cargo of squared timber was shipped to
London in 1785 and was said to be the first full shipload of
Nova Scotia products sent to England. Business was also carried
on in dry goods, wet goods, "ironmongery," potash, rum, books,
candy and jewelry. There were four hostelries in Shelburne, the
British Coffee House, King's Arms Tavern, the Merchant's

Coffee House, and Steele's Tavern, furnishing festivity at times and reasonably good accommodations. So much rum was available and so cheap that drunkenness was all too common and crime thereby increased. Early in May, 1785, a "Loan Bank" was projected by certain local merchants who advertised for subscribers, but the idea did not materialize.[23]

By early 1786, the sum of 1,500 pounds had been voted by the provincial legislature for construction of a road from Halifax to Shelburne and thence to Yarmouth. Prior to this time, a road had been started from Shelburne to Annapolis, a picturesque town northwestward across the peninsula on St. Mary Bay, a wide inlet from the Bay of Fundy. This highway was then known as "Pell's Road" because of the fact that the construction of it and the allotment of land on its borders were under the direction of Joshua Pell II, a New York Tory who was forced to flee from his large estate in Pelham, and was one of the original group to come to Shelburne. He had been a "very rich man" and a lieutenant of militia in New York when the war broke out, but later joined the British and scouted for them on Long Island. Later he fled with his wife, Abigail, to Nova Scotia along with their eight children and four servants. He also served as one of the group captains, having under his supervision 162 of the people who came to Shelburne. The stone remains of his once fine house may still be seen there. He later went to Niagara Falls and eventually returned to New York City, where he prospered in business.

The building of such a Nova Scotian road had been attempted back in 1783, but many difficulties were encountered. After repeated efforts to cut through the wilderness, a sort of road was opened between the towns and was used occasionally. Apparently, it was never completed or at least made good enough for general travel, for in spite of further money grants from the province and assistance from the military department, the Annapolis road was finally abandoned. The soil along it was found to be too rocky for profitable farming. Today a smooth highway connects the two localities and travel over it is a pleasure, at least in summer. Obviously, access to and from the outside world was of importance to Shelburne, and the lack of it contributed to its decline. What roads did exist all too often offered handy egress to discontented folks. Even so, a chamber of commerce was established there in 1785 for the encouragement of trade and the bringing in of helpful measures and men.

A City That Was

What seemed to many to be the most promising aspect of Shelburne commerce was fishing. But instead of developing the shore and bank fisheries which have succeeded in more recent times, the Shelburne merchants went in for a much bigger thing—whale fishing. A whaling company was established in 1784 and its success was about equal to that of the Moby Dick expedition. Nine firms comprised the company, one in London, two in Halifax and six in Shelburne. An agent was sent to England, where he purchased a brig and schooner, and with these, whaling operations were begun. Several other vessels were added to the fleet, but the venture failed after five years with the threat of the loss of the capital invested. But some shore and bank fishing enterprises did manage to succeed and to last through these trying years into the present day. In 1788, for example, dry codfish, pickled fish, smoked salmon, fish oil and sperm oil were exported from Shelburne. Three years later, Shelburne shipowners tried the shipping trade between the United States and Newfoundland. But again, obstacles arose. The operations along this line were not exactly legal, because British law forbade entry into the ports of ships coming directly from the United States. Resourceful Shelburne shipowners, however, evaded this law by loading their vessels in the United States and then entering and clearing at Shelburne for New-foundland. But even this scheme was thwarted after a couple of successful seasons. Fisheries to the north of Saint John failed; Newfoundland was too near to Quebec, where harvests had been unusually good and were available for export; and the English merchants, discovering that they were being undersold, drove the Shelburne ships from the new route by commercial and political pressure.

Crime increased in Shelburne and so did the severity of court sentences. For example, a Michael Burke, convicted of stealing two jackets, was sentenced to spend one month in the house of correction, and was to receive ten lashes upon entry, ten every Monday during the month and ten lashes on leaving, as a farewell souvenir. That even this was not effective was borne out by the fact that a few months later, Burke was convicted of a similar offense and ordered to receive five lashes at the corner of every street in the city. Prince Frederick was given 39 lashes for stealing shoes, Daniel Anderson the same punishment for taking towels, as was Thomas Lloyd for obtaining timber fraudulently. John Russell was sentenced to 100 strokes of the cat-o'-nine-tails for stealing a bed quilt. James Walsh, who was an indentured servant of Patrick Wall, petitioned for release from service. Instead, the court held that his request was based upon frivolous and unsatisfactory grounds and ordered him to jail for one week, then to receive ten lashes and make up to his master the time lost by his imprisonment. Margaret Tallant and Elizabeth Brown were given the following sentence: "You, Margaret Tallant and Elizabeth Brown, having this day been convicted of publishing a scandalous and malicious libel, from hence you both are to be put into a cart, with the following inscriptions on your breasts and backs; viz: *Convicted of a Scandalous and false Libel* and to be led to the pump in King Street, and then to proceed through Water Street, as far as the middle to George Street and from thence to proceed back to the corner of John Street and Water Street, and from thence to be conducted to your respective abodes. To prevent any abuse to the Culprits, all the Constables to attend." There is a legend in Shelburne that when the elder of the two gossips descended from the cart, she thanked the driver for the pleasant ride and for the view of the city from the top of the conveyance.[24]

Magdelon Hay appeared in court in August, 1786, and charged one William Summers with defaming her character. According to her, he met her at one of the public wells in Shelburne and she accused him of not paying anything toward the cost of the pump at the well, and of therefore being a thief. He retorted that she had been drummed out of a regiment in New York, that she was a faggot. He was fined ten shillings and cost for defamation; apparently she benefited from feminine prerogative and got off scot free.[25]

As can well be imagined, amusements were limited in early Shelburne because of the very nature of the situation. Masonic dinners are recorded as frequent and festive. The king's birthday and other national holidays were the occasions for sizable military and naval displays, flag flying, band playing, and salutes fired from both batteries and ships in the harbor. In the evening, the barracks would be brightly illuminated, as well as many of the houses in the city.

One of the more serious problems of Shelburne, and one which no doubt worked against its progress, was the growing acrimony between the settlers who went there from 1749 to 1775 and the exiles who arrived later. Much jealousy also developed between the two groups and this resulted in a great deal of private and public criticism. Prominent figures, especially those involved in elections, felt the brunt of these opposing viewpoints.

One binding factor among the exiles was the misfortune which came upon so many upon arrival in Shelburne. For example, Robert Appleby, one of the captains in charge of part of a group of Loyalists who came on the ship *Williams* in 1783, had been a man of considerable means in Philadelphia. He brought with him to Nova Scotia a family of six and a servant, among the 142 in his charge. Appleby went into the mercantile business in Shelburne, but it dwindled, and within three years, and in accordance with the law and custom of that day (he owed more than 100 pounds), he was imprisoned for debt. He remained in custody for months until an act of the provincial legislature set him free.

Efforts had been made to bolster and sustain such business enterprises, but "the times were out of joint," it seemed. There was a depression following the American Revolution and this reached into Nova Scotia. Commerce tended to become constricted, and the laws of the province which were meant to deal with the conditions were themselves crude and inadequate and not too well administered. Shelburne was remote from other settlements and needed but could not get good roads. The harbor was partially frozen over in winter. The people themselves were drawn largely from cities or substantial towns or were fresh from long military service, so were unaccustomed to the new and stringent requirements of a pioneer community where fishing and farming were necessarily the chief vocations. The soil in general proved not very suitable for successful farming, and free issue of British government foodstuffs ended in 1787, forcing the erstwhile recipients to search for remunerative work, which was not plentiful.

A reverse exodus began. Even by 1785, notices of houses for sale made up a good part of the advertisements in the Shelburne newspapers, which at the same time ironically contained articles describing the place as an earthly paradise. But by 1787, "men were treading on the heels of their fellows as they hastened away." The sheriff's records of auction sales show that furniture, household goods and merchandise brought fair returns but that land and houses sold for a fraction of their real value. A house and town lot in the south division belonging to

William Hill sold for four pounds and ten shillings. The town lot of Kenneth Reach brought three pounds, while his 200 acres of land in the country brought only four and one half pence per acre. James Robertson's town lot and water lot both netted slightly over one pound.[26]

Often it was impossible to sell the property, in which case the owner simply abandoned it and went away to greener fields. Many went to Halifax, Lunenburg and other towns in Nova Scotia, while others journeyed to Great Britain, the West Indies or back to their former homes in the United States. Several of the most prominent Shelburne settlers sought to return to New York, but many were disappointed in not being able to reclaim their former property.

Certainly, though, the cost of living locally was not an important contributing factor to the exodus. A price scale established in 1784 by the Court of Quarter Sessions—a kind of forerunner of our government price-fixing—was reasonable. A night's lodging in a tavern was six pence per person; stabling for a horse, one shilling; for "a man or woman's dinner of good wholesome meat, with bread and vegetables, ten pence"; pasture for a horse one night, three pence. Flour sold for 20 to 30 shillings a barrel, potatoes for two shillings a bushel, butter nine pence a pound, and rum or brandy could be had in plentiful quantities for four shillings a gallon. "A certain amount of temporary happiness to the worried citizen was available at small cost." [27]

Provincial Revenue Reports show that from March, 1786, to June, 1787, customs revenue in Shelburne amounted to 906 pounds, while that of Halifax, by comparison, was 8,168 pounds, Shelburne being second in amount in the province. Next year, Shelburne rose in revenue to 1,380, while that of Halifax declined slightly from the year before. But by 1789, Shelburne had only 431 pounds of revenue while Halifax had 5,302 pounds, and even tiny Annapolis showed a revenue return of 393 pounds, thus indicating the decline of Shelburne, for which so many bright hopes had existed. One explanation has been that "The main difficulty was in the fact that it was born too soon—came into being before there were proper means to support its existence." Another commented: "Never did a city rise so grandly and fall so miserably. . . . Boys wandered through the streets and amused themselves with stoning out the windows, with no one to chide them—for there were windows to spare. Some of the houses were torn down and carried away to other towns to build again, and others of these stately mansions . . . were pulled down and used for firewood." [28]

Not even the war between England and France which broke out in 1793 helped Shelburne survive, as wartime conditions sometimes do. Actually, it worked against the progress of the city. Privateers captured some of the already dwindling fleet of ships. Serious damage was also done to the city by a tremendous storm which struck the Nova Scotian coast on September 25, 1798. It swept away a number of Shelburne wharves which were never replaced, the total damage amounting to an estimated 100,000 pounds. By the end of the century, Shelburne was almost a deserted city, its fine houses vacant, its streets grown up in weeds. A visitor passing through about this time wrote, "The houses were still standing though untenanted. It had all the stillness and quiet of a moonlight scene. It was difficult to imagine it was deserted. The idea of repose more readily suggested itself than decay. The houses which were originally built of wood, had severally disappeared. Some had been taken to pieces and removed to Halifax or Saint John; others had been converted into fuel, and the rest had fallen prey to neglect and decomposition. The chimneys stood up erect and marked the spot around which the social circle had assembled; and the blackened fireplaces, ranged one above another, bespoke the size of the tenement and the means of its owner. In some places they had sunk with the edifice, leaving a heap of ruins; while not a few were inclining to their fall, and awaiting the first storm to repose again in the dust that now covered those who had constructed them. Hundreds of cellars with their stone walls and granite partitions were everywhere to be seen, like uncovered monuments of the dead. Time and decay had done their work." [29]

In the three decades from 1785 to 1815, the estimated population of Shelburne fell from 10,000 to 300 people. Even with the foregoing explanations of the abandonment, it is still hard to comprehend how such a city could be built so auspiciously and so soon virtually disappear. For many years it was the tendency of old-timers to bemoan eloquently the loss of this once promising community, to dream of its erstwhile prosperity, to miss their warm friends who had once lived there and to stir up sentiment in general for what was and what might have been.

Happily the picture is not entirely dark. Shelburne did not

disappear. A few sturdy souls stayed on and built for the future; the harbor remains as good and beautiful as ever; schools, churches, good roads and other transportation facilities now exist where once they were only visions. Shipbuilding came into its own. A prominent shipbuilder, Donald MacKay, was born in Shelburne, grandson of a Scottish officer who was one of the first Loyalist grantees. In addition to shipbuilding, furniture making and fishing became the leading industries of Shelburne, which looks to tomorrow rather than yesterday. But the saga of the exiles had hardly begun.

[2]

THE EXODUS SPREADS

The Tories with their brats and wives
Have fled to save their wretched lives.

So RAN A BIT OF DOGGEREL of the day. And it was all too true, especially when British General Sir William Howe and his army left Boston in a hurry in the boisterous month of March, 1776. Boston was at the time a town of some 16,000 people, and of these 1,000 accompanied Howe in his inglorious exit to the sea. "Neither Hell, Hull nor Halifax can afford worse shelter than Boston," exclaimed one of the refugees, and acted accordingly. Even though the waves were tempestuous, they presented less hazard to these benighted Loyalists than the irate patriots themselves.

The refugees were told to take nothing with them but what was necessary, but this order was not followed. Hopeless confusion marked the exit. Carts, trucks, wheelbarrows and coaches hastened to the wharves where every available vessel awaited the exodus. Several of the ships, badly needed for transporting the people, were soon filled with the private property of a few. How crowded the cabins soon became may be gathered from the situation in Benjamin Hallowell's, where 37 persons, men, women, and children, huddled together on the floor.

Outwardly, the fleet made an imposing appearance. Composed of 170 sailing vessels, mostly small schooners top-heavy with their cargoes, and protected by three men-of-war, it resembled a forest of canvas gliding across the water. Hidden in the midst of such haste, thieving members of the British crews piled plunder on board wherever they could and thus added to the danger and confusion. Isaac Smith wrote to John Adams that "Commodore John Manley's fleet has taken a brig bound to Halifax, on board of which is Bill Jackson and all his effects, and it's said she has a large quantity of the stolen goods—and there is on board likewise, one, Greenbrush, receiver general of the stolen goods and has distinguished himself in that way by demanding people's property from them." [1] Looking down from Penn's Hill, sprightly Abigail Adams observed that this was "the largest fleet ever seen in America."

Among those who sailed there was fear that the motley fleet would never arrive in Nova Scotia. But arrive it did, after six days of tossing about on the choppy seas beset by March winds. Abigail Adams took note of the arrival in one of her numerous and colorful letters to her husband. "We have intelligence of the arrival of some of the Tory fleet at Halifax," she penned, "that they are much distressed for want of houses, obliged to give six dollars per month for one room, provisions scarce and dear. Some of them with six or eight children round them sitting upon the rocks crying, not knowing where to lay their heads. Just Heaven has given them to taste of the same cup of affliction which they one year ago administered with such callous hearts to thousands of their fellow citizens, but with this difference that they fly from their injured and enraged country, whilst pity and commiseration received the sufferers whom they inhumanely drove from their dwellings." [2]

No wonder, then, that some of the exiled Tories accompanied General Howe to New York City when he went there in June, while most of those who had gone to Halifax took passage to England. Only a few of this company remained in Nova Scotia, but they had led the way. From 1776 to 1783, small bands made their way to Halifax. But it was not until the final evacuation of New York by the British at the end of the Revolution that the full tide of Tories flowed into Nova Scotia, which by this time had been contemptuously labeled by the patriots as "Nova Scarcity." [3]

As the war progressed, the Tories remaining in the United States became more and more anxious about their eventual fate. Already, as shown in the preceding volume, *Royal Raiders*, they had been persecuted by the patriots, who, to charges related to such persecution, retorted that they were but giving an eye for an eye. When the able but unfortunate Lord Cornwallis surrendered at Yorktown, the fears of the Tories reached a high state. Again they looked to Mother England and hoped and prayed that their good King George would not let them down and leave them in the hands of this upstart, George Washington, and his rebel forces. The Tories knew that they probably were listed on the patriot records as traitors, that their property was recorded as available, and they feared that it was just a matter of time until they would be harried until destitute. But still they hoped. . . .

As soon as it was known that terms of the Treaty of Paris in 1783 were far from favorable to the loyal American subjects, and it became increasingly plain that the animosity against the Tories was not abating, those in New York began discussions about some country in which they could start their weary lives afresh. They were not encouraged by the situation described by Colonel Beverly Robinson in a letter to General Clinton: "Oh my dear sir, what dreadful and distressing tidings does she bring us—the independence of America given up by the king without any conditions whatever, the Loyalists of America to depend upon the mercy of their enemies for the restoration of their possessions. . . ." [4]

So irate became some of the Tories at the king that they stuck posters up in many parts of New York City railing against what they felt had been a royal abandonment of their cause. Some even expressed the sentiment that the English who had earlier encouraged them had now actually treated them worse than the American patriots.

Wishing to leave was one thing; being able to afford such a serious undertaking was another. Looking over the map, Loyalist leaders concluded that the region of Nova Scotia offered the most inviting aspects for settlement. An association aimed at aiding those who desired to go there was formed in 1782, having as its president the Reverend Samuel Seabury, one of the ablest of all Tories; and as its secretary Sampson Salter Blowers, who later became the chief justice of Nova Scotia. Sir Guy Carleton approved of the plans of this group, and it was arranged that about 500 exiles would go northward in the autumn, under the leadership of three agents, Amos Botsford, Samuel Cummings and Frederick Hauser. These agents had no other instructions than what were dramatically delivered to them in a parting moment by Brook Watson, Commissary General in New York:

"You are to provide an asylum for your distressed countrymen. Your task is arduous, execute it like men of honor. The season of fighting is over—bury your animosities and persecute no man. Your ship is ready and God bless you."

The party set sail from New York in nine ships on October 19, 1782, and within a few days was disembarking at the village of Annapolis Royal, located on the western fringe of Nova Scotia and on a picturesque inlet touching the Bay of Fundy. In those last hectic days of peace, it seemed that "everybody, all the world, moved to Nova Scotia." The hundred unsuspecting inhabitants of Annapolis Royal were almost overrun by the influx, and the Reverend Jacob Bailey, a Tory who was already there, reported that all the houses were crowded and many incomers were unable to procure any lodgings. This minister, who became rector of St. Luke's Church at Annapolis Royal, knew what hardship meant. A graduate of Harvard, he had been an Episcopal clergyman at Dresden, Maine. According to his own report, his single offense was continuing divine service, but he was threatened, insulted and told to leave. He had a family consisting of a wife, a young infant and two girls of about 11 years of age. In the summer of 1779, he had fled to Halifax, and according to his description, his feet were adorned with shoes which sustained the marks of rebellion and independence. His legs were covered with a pair of thick blue woolen stockings which had been so often darned and mended that little of the original parts remained. His breeches, "which just concealed the shame of his nakedness, had been formerly black, but the color being worn out by age, nothing remained but a rusty gray, bespattered with lint and bedaubed with pitch."

Besides the regular duties of his parish, Bailey had a regiment of soldiers to serve as chaplain, though he received no extra pay for this. All this, he reported, "while those who grow opulent . . . unattended either with labor or expense reproach me with officiousness, ridicule my indigence and pursue me with the most unabating malice. . . . Though disappointed in my expectations and deprived of my just perquisites, yet I am happy amidst my struggles to support an increasing family with decency, and in having no altercations with my people." The minister wrote to London to Dr. Samuel Peters, another Tory clergyman who had left America after fantastically cruel mistreatment, saying that the latter had no idea of what it was to travel in such a new country as Nova Scotia. Apparently Peters had advised Bailey to keep a dignified appearance.[5]

Liberality in the granting of land induced many Tories to

go to Nova Scotia. In the distribution to disbanded military personnel, field officers were promised 5,000 acres each, captains 3,000 acres, lieutenants 2,000 acres, and enlisted men 300 acres. Other Tories were to receive at least 200 acres, although there were special instances, such as that of William Dummer, a justice of the King's Bench, who was granted 1,200 acres for his wife and 1,200 acres for each of his seven children. By 1787, 3,200,000 acres had been granted to Tories in Upper Canada alone.

The three advance agents of the 500 Tory exiles did not remain, however, at Annapolis Royal. They made their way to Halifax, then set out to re-cross the peninsula and explore the fertile Annapolis Valley, where is found the setting of the lovely village of Grand Pré, the home of the Acadians, later made legendary by Longfellow's *Evangeline*. As has been pointed out, this poem "has elicited the interest and pity of the world," yet the plight of the Tories "remains an obscure incident. But the number of those who fled to Nova Scotia and the valley of the St. John's River in 1782 and 1783 was far greater than of those [Acadians] who were deported by the British in 1755; their sorrow at leaving their native land and their hardships in a strange country were also severe. Nor were the causes of these tragedies dissimilar, for in each case, the displaced persons were paying the penalty of loyalty to their king." [6] With the landing of the Loyalists, Nova Scotia became the setting for a kind of Acadia in reverse.

The agents' reports about Nova Scotia and what is now New Brunswick were glowing. They predicted for the region great business opportunities, such as sawmilling, fishing on a large scale, and the raising of cattle and poultry. Such a large number of applications for migration came into the office of Sir Guy Carleton in New York that he realized several voyages would be necessary to transport all the Tories. He gave orders that each migrating family should be provided with enough supplies from the royal warehouses to sustain them for a year, and that the provisions should include comfortable clothing, various medicines, farming tools, and arms and ammunition for hunting as well as protection. [7]

Buoyed by this generosity, on April 26, 1783, some 7,000 exiles set sail from New York in what was called the "spring fleet." Half of these went to the mouth of the St. John River and half to Shelburne, as we have seen. According to a diary kept by Mrs. Sarah Frost, who was on a vessel named *Two Sisters* headed for the St. John region, one convoy was made up of 14 vessels carrying 2,000 of the Loyalists, and was accompanied by a frigate of war. On board the *Two Sisters* were 250 passengers, seven families being crowded into Mrs. Frost's cabin. The people on board seemed cross and quarrelsome. Children were crying in discomfort, especially when frightened by a terrific hail storm with thunder and lightning.

After twelve days, the ships reached the St. John River, where they were becalmed for three days in a dense fog. An epidemic of measles caused the mothers more trouble and worry. But on Sunday morning, June 29, Mrs. Frost went ashore with her children and remarked, "It is, I think, the roughest land I ever saw." [8] Most of the settlers were housed in tents, a situation bearable until winter came. Many of the women were unaccustomed to such living, and this was made more serious by their having to care for their children, some of whom were quite young. Living in the tents with snow at times six feet and more in depth caused much suffering.

Governor John Parr and his associates were kept busy trying to provide shelter and other accommodations for the mob of "guests" who had recently descended upon them. Flour mills at Sackville were kept busy night and day to provide additions to government rations. Parr himself, a dedicated if sometimes misguided man, worked steadily and methodically, often, it was reported, for as many as 20 out of the 24 hours a day, in supervising the arrangements for subsistence. The greatest problem was how to house the newcomers. Every shed, outhouse, store and shelter in Halifax was crowded with people. Up at a fortress called the Citadel, thousands more were under canvas, as was the case at Point Pleasant and everywhere that tents could be pitched. Hundreds were sheltered in the churches of St. Paul and St. Matthew for months. Of course, many died from the hardships and unsanitary conditions analogous to such conditions.

Food—such as it was, mainly pork and flour—was furnished by the British government and was painfully slow in arriving. The Nova Scotia authorities strove hard to supplement this diet with fish, molasses and hard biscuit. Meal and molasses were felt to be sufficient to sustain the numerous Negroes who had been brought by the wealthier Tories. Governor Parr reported to England that although his merchants were helpful in the crisis, some of them took advantage of the occasion to extort as much as three pounds and ten shillings for a 100-weight of flour. But diversion was afforded by the Indians in a celebration at Point Pleasant of the Festival of Saint Aspinquid. Many whites also attended to watch the Indian dances and take part in consuming huge dishes of clam soup and the accompanying rum. All went merrily and well until a few rebel sympathizers in the crowd, doubtless buoyed into indiscretion by the refreshment, proposed a toast to the "new Yankee Republic in rum distributed among the people; so the festival closed in great confusion." [9]

On May 17, 1783, Governor Parr wrote to friends in England that Nova Scotia was increasing in population; some 8,000 "souls have already arrived from New York and those will soon be followed by many more." This was no understatement. Soon afterward, a minister reported that the Tories had brought measles and whooping cough with them, which with "a singularly sickly season have carried off great numbers." The Reverend Bailey stated that 1,500 persons had arrived at Annapolis by November, with the church being used to shelter them. He related that "nearly 400 of these miserable exiles have perished in a violent tempest" and he was persuaded "that disease, disappointment and poverty will by another spring finish the course of many more." Yet such conditions did not deter the Reverend Charles Inglis, former pastor of Trinity Church in New York City, from seeking refuge in Nova Scotia. He was described in London as "possessed of an independent private estate and of the best ecclesiastical preferment in North America, he little thought that he should be entirely stripped of the one and compelled to abandon the other . . . he sees not where he can go but, along with thousands of others equally distressed, to Nova Scotia." He did go.[10]

The immigrants to Nova Scotia consisted mainly of soldiers, farmers, merchants, artisans and those who had no vocation at all. But Halifax itself already had its well-to-do class and for a long time was a favorite station of the British army and navy. During the influx of the Tories, it was compared to Boston, Salem, Portsmouth and New York in its social life. The wealthier gentry went about in sedan chairs, this being a means much favored by the principal ladies of the town for arriving at balls. At the Great Pontiac, one of the wooden hotels where such balls were given, a creek ran nearby; on the occasion of dinner given here by the naval officers, ships' boats manned by white-clad sailors would row up with hot dishes for the guests. A favorite dish was said to have been porcupine.[11]

All through the summer, fall and winter of 1783, the ships plied back and forth between the United States and Nova Scotia. It seemed that the people of the new nation were determined to drive out all who had taken part against them in the Revolution. In June the "summer fleet" transported about 2,500 more exiles northward, a process repeated until, by the end of the year, Governor Parr estimated that 30,000 people had come in this manner to Nova Scotia. By January the combination of the influx and the winter's cold caused the governor to write to Lord North in alarm, wondering where he would find housing for them, fearful because he did not want to send them into the chill countryside. He described vividly the women and children who were still on board the ships in the harbors because there was no shelter available for them on the land.[12]

Not all of the newcomers were poor. A considerable percentage of them were from the wealthy and educated classes of the colonies and they viewed the prospects with a sense of foreboding. Those who had held official positions in the seceding colonies tried to obtain similar positions. The coming of these Loyalists infused into the life of the province a spirit of controversy and activity which was reflected in their political campaigns and in the debates and resolutions in the assemblies. The Loyalists made those already living in Nova Scotia more appreciative of their home situation. And the influx acted as a great stimulant to the opening up of the country, as new settlements sprang up suddenly along the coast as well as inland. But most were at first isolated from others because of the lack of roads and bridges between them.[13]

"I can't bear the idea," wrote one of the older exiles to General Clinton, "and it is distressing to me to think I should be drove with my wife in our old age and my two dear daughters to begin a settlement in a cold climate, and in the woods where we are to cut down the first tree. I can hardly expect to live to see the settlement so far advanced as to be in a tolerable comfortable way and then what a situation shall I leave my dear wife and children in." [14]

Such presentiment was not helped by a current pamphlet of the day which described the climate of Nova Scotia thus: "It has a winter of almost insufferable length and coldness . . . there are but a few inconsiderable spots fit to cultivate, and the land is covered with a spongy mass in place of grass. . . . Winter continues at least seven months of the year; the country is wrapped in the gloom of a perpetual fog; the mountains run down to the seacoast, and leave but here and there a spot to inhabit." Nor did such contemporary rhymes as the following add to the Nova Scotian enjoyment:

> *Of all the vile countries that ever were known*
> *In the frigid or torrid or temperate zone,*
> *From accounts I had there is not such another;*
> *It neither belongs to this world nor the other.*[15]

Even so, Ward Chipman wrote his friend Jonathan Sewall that in New York conditions were so violent against the Loyalists that the mob ruled there. "It would really astonish you to see," he added, "the numbers daily emigrating from hence to Nova Scotia. . . . I have determined to become as large a proprietor as my claims will warrant and look forward with pleasure I assure you to a settlement in Nova Scotia." And well he might. Chipman eventually became chief justice of the province. But before leaving New York, he watched the American troops come in under the leadership of General Henry Knox and take over the city from the British. Chipman paid his respects to the new occupants as follows: "A more shabby, ungentlemanlike crew I never saw." [16]

Edward Winslow found a somewhat better human scene in Halifax, according to his report to Chipman. The former stated that there was assembled an immense multitude, not of dissolute vagrants such as commonly made the first efforts to settle a new country, but educated gentlemen, formerly independent farmers, and reputable mechanics who by the fortunes of war had been deprived of their property. "They are as firmly attached to the British constitution as if they never had made a sacrifice," he added. "Here they stand with their wives and children looking up for protection. . . . To save these from distress, to soothe and comfort them by extending indulgencies which at the same time are essentially beneficial to the country at large, is truly a noble duty. By Heaven, we will be the envy of the American states." [17]

Just where did these American Tories come from?

Most of them were from New York, New Jersey and Pennsylvania, having assembled in New York City for their embarkation. Some came from New England and a considerable number from the Carolinas. Though the majority were English in origin, many were of Scotch and Irish ancestry and some from New York were of Dutch descent. As we have seen, about 2,000 Negroes came to Shelburne and Halifax. Of the 30,000 of all types who came, about 21,000 remained as permanent settlers, two-thirds of these being civilians, the rest ex-soldiers and their families. The population of Nova Scotia was doubled, the result being that the Tories were the largest single group, and they were to play an important part in the shaping of the populace and social structure of modern Canada. Those who did not go inland and secure land or who did not sail for England or the West Indies or return to the United States settled along the coast from Halifax to Canso. On the harbor called Antigonish, the Loyalist town of Dorchester arose. Disbanded soldiers took up land between Merigomish and Pictou. Between Amherst and Tatamagouche, the Loyalists' settlements blossomed at Wallace, at Pugwash, and inland at Westchester and Wentworth. From the Shubencadie River westward, disabled soldiers and North and South Carolina civilians staked out land. Some 800 had settled on Cape Breton by 1784.

A township was laid out on the shore of Country Harbor by exiles from North and South Carolina and was called Stormont. The settlement was progressing fairly well until winter came and supplies ran short; then privation set in. But word had been sent to Halifax and a ship with provisions was expected at any time. In their anxiety, the settlers established a constant watch on a high point commanding a view of the mouth of the harbor so that they would know the moment the ship arrived. Weary days dragged by and still no ship came, and finally the starving people began to die. When the vessel did arrive at last, some 40 graves marked the new burying ground of the settlement. And the elevated spot where the watch was maintained through the long and anxious time is still known as Point Despair.[18]

A large proportion of the immigrants were accustomed to a softer life back home and were ill adapted to the clearing of the forests, the endless labor of cultivating fields, building houses and other stern tasks of the pioneers. Often, even after their back-breaking labor in clearing the land, they found it too stony and barren to raise crops. But some of the Tories introduced new varieties of apples into the fertile Annapolis Valley and thus started the modern apple industry there. One of those who brought such trees with them was General Timothy Ruggles, a Harvard graduate from Boston who came to Nova Scotia at the age of 72 and began life anew on a forest farm. He had served with distinction in the French and Indian War under Sir William Johnson and later was chosen speaker of the Massachusetts House of Representatives. He was even elected president of the Stamp Act Congress which met in New York in 1765 and was highly praised by John Adams for his work. But as soon as Ruggles found out the real aims of the Congress, he left it and won the bitter condemnation of Adams. It has been said of this prominent Tory that "No man in Massachusetts was regarded as so inimical to the cause of rebellion as General Ruggles, whose known and recognized ability, great energy and unflinching courage made him an object of fear as well as dislike." Such sentiment was vividly shown by the rebels who, while the general was inside his Massachusetts home preparing to leave, closely cropped the mane and tail of his horse and painted its whole body. After land was granted to him in Nova Scotia, it was reported that even at his advanced age, General Ruggles went at the work of preparing it undismayed, a labor, one historian commented, "which few if any of the young men of today would voluntarily undertake." One reason advanced for his lasting good health was that he did not eat meat and drank no liquor, "small beer excepted." His three sons, Timothy, John and Richard Ruggles, followed him to Nova Scotia and settled there, but his four daughters who were married in the United States before the Revolution evidently remained there.[19]

Not all of the newcomers were so sturdy. The increase of population during the years immediately following the great influx of 1783 was partly offset by the number of those leaving the province. Sir Guy Carleton put his finger on one of the reasons for the exodus when he stated that it was important that Nova Scotia not allow intruders to break in and take up what lands they pleased so that the deserving Loyalists would not have enough left on which to settle. He had also heard, he said, that "the Republicans have great interest and influence in that province and that some of them are in offices of trust and confidence; these informations have greatly discouraged the Loyalists, who apprehend fresh distrubances may arise therefrom, and that the same persecuting spirit which has driven them into the woods of Nova Scotia, will not suffer them to remain there in peace and tranquility."

A memorial of 72 North Carolina Loyalists petitioned Lord Sydney, cabinet member in London, to help them go to the Bahama Islands, which they conceived to be the best place in the British empire to afford them the most promising advantages. They stated that several of them had gone to Nova Scotia with a view to settling there, but found it "altogether impossible in the present state of their finances, to clear the ground and raise the necessaries of life, in a climate to Southern constitutions so inhospitable and severe." [20]

Conditions may have seemed bad elsewhere, but often, for the wretched exiles, they were worse back home. For example, on May 19, 1783, the citizens of Worcester, Massachusetts, passed a resolution directed against Tories who would return: "That in the opinion of this town, it would be extremely dangerous to the peace, happiness, liberty and safety of these states to suffer those who, the moment the bloody banners were displayed, abandoned their native land, turned parricides and conspired to involve their country in tumult, ruin and blood to become the subjects of and reside in this Goverment; that it would not be only dangerous but inconsistent with justice, policy and our past laws, the public faith and the principles of a free and independent state, to admit them to ourselves or to have them forced upon us without our consent."

As time passed the fortunes of the Tories who fled to Nova Scotia rose and fell depending on who and where they were. Halifax, for example, has been described as resembling in late 1784 a town that had suffered the inroads of an invading army. On the shores were collections of old shacks, and along the beaches there were poignant remains of old tents and spruce wigwams where the chilled settlers had once huddled. Their one-time occupants had either returned to their first homes in the new nation to the south, embarked to England or the West Indies, or more likely had simply gone inland to become an integral part of the new Canada. Still there was silent evidence of the poverty and suffering of the great multitude which, in its passage, had made the town a resting place for a time. Some of them had held on and now were successful merchants. Enormous amounts of fish, lumber, rum and bread had been imported and sold to great advantage. [21]

On the seamy side, there were still those who tried to get something for nothing. In view of the free subsistence coming from England, many who were not Loyalists at all tried to qualify for aid. Edward Winslow told Brook Watson that "Every man who arrived in this country called himself a Loyalist and presumed he was entitled to the rations of provisions for himself and his family, and they applied for orders without an idea that any scrutiny could possibly be made either into their circumstances or character or supposing any conditions required on their part." A board was appointed to look into such chicanery, and by its exertions "many abuses were corrected and all the idle vagrants who had been loitering about the streets of the metropolis and were daily committing irregularities, were by being precluded from the bounty of provisions forced to take possession of their lands, and on producing certificates of their being actual settlers, they were restored to the enjoyment of their rations." Not all were so fortunate in this clean-up campaign. During 1785 alone, 20 "criminals" were hanged in Halifax, mostly for minor offenses and petty robbery. Three of these were Negro slaves who had come from New York with Loyalist families. One was put to death for the theft of a bag of potatoes. A printer summed up the situation in these words:

Like hounds who have quit their huntsman in the chase
They're now engaged in wild confusion's race:
Each takes his way in swift pursuit of game,
Or right or wrong, to them 'tis all the same.[22]

On the other hand, Colonel Thomas Dundas, one of the commissioners who were sent to inquire into the losses of the Loyalists, reported to Earl Cornwallis at about the same time, that he had visited all the different settlements in Nova Scotia and that they surpassed anything he could expect to have seen "in a climate which has seven winter months." "The new settlements made by the Loyalists are in a thriving way," he reported, "although rum and idle habits contracted during the war are much against them. They have experienced every possible injury from the old inhabitants of Nova Scotia, who are even more disaffected towards the British Government than any of the new states ever were."[23]

Some of them had experienced even greater injuries before they arrived in Canada. One of these was James Moody of New Jersey, who in 1786 came to Nova Scotia not only as a refugee from the Americans, but as one who had led, during the war, a sort of Robin Hood existence in behalf of the royal cause. At the beginning of the Revolution, he lived on a large and fertile farm, serenely content with his wife and three children. He did not even take part in politics, but evidently his sentiments were known, for he was shot at three times by Whigs while walking on his own grounds. Finally, he resolved to flee to the British side. Accompanied by 73 of his neighbors, he roamed the Jersey and Pennsylvania countryside for years, and the cry, "Moody is out!" became for the patriots one of terror, so fiercely did he take revenge against his foes. It was soon learned that he was adept at entering the enemy lines and obtaining information. In June of 1779, Moody and his men captured a Whig colonel, a lieutenant colonel, a major, two captains and several others of lower rank, and destroyed a considerable magazine of powder and arms. Assailed by a force twice the size of his, Moody routed them at bayonet point, killing their leader himself. He stayed close by the camp of Washington at times, and also spied on Generals Gates and Sullivan. Moody was on the point of capturing the Whig governor of New Jersey, William Livingston—who had a reputation for persecuting Loyalists—and probably would have succeeded had not one of Moody's men been captured and revealed the plan. Moody was himself captured by the troops of General Anthony Wayne and sent to West Point, where General Benedict Arnold treated him cruelly, putting him in a filthy dungeon and in chains. When Washington heard of this, he had Moody brought out though almost dead from the abuse. But the intrepid Tory soon escaped—and with some important dispatches of Washington's, which he gave to the British. A few of the documents dealt with the plans of Rochambeau and the American commander-in-chief. The spy became so expert at getting information that he attracted the attention of the highest commanders. Moody went through enough hair-raising experiences and narrow escapes for a dozen men. Once when the enemy was nearby, he stood upright in a stack of corn fodder for two days and nights without food or drink. At the end of the war, he was invited to England by Sir Henry Clinton to recuperate, but instead went to Nova Scotia, where he died in 1809 at the age of 65.[24]

Danger and tragedy dwelt not only within the colonies for those who disagreed with the rebels' struggle for liberty. Tragedy befell at least one family in a small Nova Scotian town. In the parish church there is a small brass tablet, a memorial to a beautiful woman, Catherine Ogden, daughter of Colonel Peter Ogden. He was an upright man, a staunch churchman and

Royalist, proud of his record, and a familiar figure around the community.

It was the fall of 1786, and there was celebration in the Ogden home in honor of the betrothal of his daughter to a British army officer. Yet all the town knew that Catherine was not happy, that she was tired after long weeks of pleading by her father to reject her rebel lover and become the wife of one loyal to the king. During the celebration, Catherine stood before the fireplace to watch the flames leap high among the logs, and to dream for a moment about Richard John Cottman, the New Englander from whom she had been separated, and who had been forbidden to come near her. Suddenly her dream became real, and he stood there beside her. Eager questions, hurried pleading, loving words poured out as music came faintly from the ballroom upstairs. The inner door opened and firelight gleamed on the scarlet coat and then uplifted sword of Colonel Ogden. There were bitter masculine words, and soon the young man lay wounded at her feet.

The rest of the story is set forth in a New England journal: "Richard John Cottman has died of wounds contracted while engaged in private enterprise and not in these New England states. He held a respectable and amiable character, and was distinguished for his activity and devotion to the Colonists' cause during the late War for Independence." [25]

[3]

HOME IS THE HUNTED

Fair lands, golden lands!
Lands of the ageless race!
With open arms and stretched out hands,
Received into your warm embrace,
And sheltered with a kindly grace,
Those noble, hardy pioneers—
The Loyalists of old.

THERE WAS A WELCOME SHELTER in New Brunswick for Tories
but it was a rough one. When the Loyalists landed there on
May 18, 1783, what is now the city of Saint John was a dense
forest, a shelter for wild beasts. Temporary tents and huts
hastily erected were the only homes for the exiles, and into
these bears sometimes intruded. But there was a great supply of
salmon, moose and other game, so the newcomers were not
hungry. Men had to be well fed and filled with stamina to face
with composure this wild and lonely shore where the brush had
to be cut before even tents of hurricane sails could be set up or
shacks built. Before the exiles was a jagged wilderness with some
remaining snow, and behind them the gray expanse of the Bay
of Fundy, cold with drifting icebergs and floes from the frigid
north.

    Women, children, and some of the men, although accus-
tomed by now to the rigors of adversity, could not restrain their
fear and feeling of loneliness. The grandmother of Sir Leonard
Tilley, statesman of later years, told him, "I climbed to the top
of Chipman's Hill and watched the sails disappear in the distance, and such a feeling of loneliness came over me that though
I had not shed a tear through all the war, I sat down on the
damp moss with my baby on my lap and cried bitterly." [1]

Before the close of the first year, Lot Number 405 in King Street, Saint John, next to one later to be occupied by Benedict Arnold, was sold by the grantee for two gallons of rum. It can more happily be reported, however, that half a century later, this same lot brought $10,000. Other parcels of land went for practically nothing. In an old Sunbury County record book, the following transactions are recorded: "On October 14, 1783, Samuel Sullivan, a soldier in the King's American Dragoons, executed a quit claim deed to his lot of 100 acres in the township of Prince William, for the sum of two pounds to William Chase; on the same date, Philip Service of the same corps sold his lot in the same township to Jonathan Miles for one guinea. On March 9, 1784, William Rusiers of the Royal Guides and Pioneers sold to Ensign Jonathan Brown his lot of 100 acres on the east side of the St. John River, for ten pounds."

A few years after this settlement, the famous "Old Coffee House," which was long used as a favorite meeting place of the Loyalists, was erected on King Street. Here they gathered year after year to discuss their affairs, both public and private, to tell of their losses, sufferings and expulsion from their native land, to amuse themselves, to read the news, to transact business and devise means of developing the rich resources of the colony.[2]

But most of those who had arrived did not intend to remain at the spot where they landed. They turned their anxious eyes up river. About the first thing they saw was a military fortification upon a hill at the entrance of the stream, named Fort Howe in honor of that ill-fated general who had abandoned Boston and later occupied New York and Philadelphia. Although the war was over, this symbol of British strength gave the refugees some feeling of security. Below the fort was a community known as Portland Point, composed of only a few families who were engaged in operating a trading post. As one historian has observed, "We may well believe that the arrival of the Loyalists produced great excitement among the people of the hamlet at Portland Point. For 20 years they had been accustomed to regard themselves as the lords of creation on the shores of the harbor of Saint John and they now found themselves swallowed up, as it were, in a single day in a vast, mixed multitude."[3]

As for the St. John River itself, it was navigable for about 100 miles of its lower course and in the rainy season for another 100. The government at Halifax had made haphazard grants of land along the river to settlers, the surveys of which were scarce.

As a consequence, squatters had occupied many of the best sites beside the stream and eked out a living by cutting timber, tilling the soil where it was fertile, and by fur trade and fishing. "Since no other available spot seemed to offer equal opportunities, in 1783 Saint John became like Shelburne an object of desire." And the city-to-be at the mouth of the river became a rude little settlement named Parrtown, in honor of the governor of Nova Scotia, with frame houses and log cabins scattered amid stumps which had appeared like large mushrooms after trees had been cut on the rocky spruce-clad peninsula. But clustered on this limited and uncomfortable spot, housed in the inconvenient and dreary dwellings, was a group of refugees who had been numbered among the gentry of the old colonies.[4]

With the spring fleet had arrived about 3,000 people; in the summer came 2,000 more; and along with autumn appeared some 3,000 additional souls to magnify the already growing problem of settlement. Most of the arrivals wished to go farther inland, but because of the primitive conditions and the delays by the government in clarifying land titles, they were delayed for months where they had landed. Many who erected permanent dwellings later found that they did not hold legal title to the land on which they had built. Many died of cold and hardship in the first winter, especially up the river at St. Anne's, where winter began with six inches of snow on November 2. Tents with spruce boughs furnished the only shelter, and heated boards were placed against the backs of sleeping children to keep them from freezing. Yet as two current historians proudly point out, "The Loyalist experiment succeeded. Just as the first British Empire in America had fallen, a second rose on its ruins. Symbolic of this was the appearance on the walls of the Trinity Church at Saint John of the Royal Coat of Arms. It had been removed from its former place in the Council Chamber of the old colony of Massachusetts at Boston." [5]

Edward Winslow agreed with these prospects, for in a letter to Ward Chipman during the midst of the preparations, he stated, "We cut yesterday with about 120 men more than a mile through a forest hitherto deemed impenetrable. When we emerged from it, there opened a prospect superior to anything in the world, I believe. A perfect view of the immense Bay of Fundy on one side, a very extensive view of the river St. John with the falls, grand lake and islands on the other—in front, the fort which is a beautiful object on a high hill, and all settle-

ments about the town with the ships, boats, etc. in the harbor—
'twas positively the most magnificent and romantic scene I have
ever beheld." [6]

In order for the Loyalists to enjoy such a view permanently, the British government made a large financial grant for
their assistance. From the supply of the chagrined residents of
Portland Point, every one of the exiles received 500 feet of
boards and a proportionate amount of shingles and bricks.
Within a year, Major Gilfred Studholme, commander of
Fort Howe, generously issued some 2,000,000 feet of boards,
1,500,000 shingles and 7,500 clapboards. By June of 1784, an
astonished visitor saw 1,500 frame and 400 log houses at Parrtown. A few hardy souls went on up the river to Kingston Creek
where the mothers were soon kept busy caring for their children
through an epidemic of measles. This problem was softened,
however, by the visit of some friendly Indians who brought
them some moose meat which was warmly welcomed. When lots
were drawn, land was set aside for church and school purposes.
Then the new occupants set to work with enthusiasm and by
common consent, clearing ground for their cabins and cutting
logs, which they had to carry some distance with their hands
because they did not have horses or oxen for the purpose. By
November, every man and his family were beneath their own
roof in the shelter of the thick forest, where they passed a comfortable winter.

The exiles who came in the fall were mostly disbanded
soldiers. Among them, now at partial strength, were some of the
most distinguished Tory units, such as the Queen's Rangers,
originally a Virginia outfit that had fought at Brandywine and
through the Southern campaigns until it surrendered with
Cornwallis at Yorktown. The King's American Regiment represented North Carolina. It had taken part in the storming of
forts Clinton and Montgomery as well as fighting at Norwalk
and in the crucial battle of King's Mountain. The New York Volunteers had been organized at Halifax in 1776 and had gone to
participate in the British sweep of Long Island. It had also
taken part in the battles at Savannah, Camden, and Eutaw
Springs. The Loyal American Regiment recruited by Colonel
Beverly Robinson had participated in similar campaigns. In addition, there were two battalions of De Lancey's Brigade which
had originally been raised for the defense of Long Island but
had later been sent south for service there. Largest of all the

units were the three battalions of the New Jersey Volunteers which had been recruited by Cortlandt Skinner, the last royal attorney general of New Jersey. As "Skinner's Cowboys" they had become renowned for their raids against the patriots. Other disbanded corps which settled in the St. John region were two battalions of the 60th British Regiment, the Prince of Wales American Regiment, the Pennsylvania Loyalists, the American Legion, the Royal Guides and Pioneers, the British Cavalry Legion and the Maryland Loyalists. The last-named had lost half its men when the transport ship *Martha,* on which they were sailing, struck a reef off the southwest coast of Nova Scotia and sank. This ship had sailed along with others from Sandy Hook in September and had on board 174 persons. Of these 99 perished and 75 were saved by fishing boats. Captain Patrick Kennedy, of the Maryland Loyalists, who comprised most of the passengers, stated that neglect on the part of the master of the ship played a large part in the disaster. According to Kennedy, the ship had left New York with a set of old sails and only a dozen men and boys as a crew. When the *Martha* reached Nova Scotian waters, night was coming on just as land was sighted. It was thought that the captain would anchor the ship until morning. Instead, according to this version, he allowed the vessel to continue. His meager crew were attempting to rig and erect a new main topsail to replace one which had been ripped apart by strong winds. The ship struck a ledge, and the mainsail fell and smashed the long boat. The captain then was said to have ordered that the jolly boat be launched, proclaiming loudly at the same time that he would be the last to leave the ship. But as this only remaining little boat was put over the side, he jumped into it, rowed to a nearby cutter and "inhumanly pushed off for the shore. The empty jolly boat was turned adrift in full view of the unhappy people on board, the master turning a deaf ear to the solicitations of Captain Kennedy, who begged him to pull in toward the stern, in order to discuss some means of saving the lives of the passengers." Lieutenant Michael Laffan of the Marylanders and three other officers and two soldiers managed to hang on to a piece of the wreckage for two days and nights. An officer and a soldier drowned. On the third day, the survivors drifted to an island where without food, fire, or clothing and only a little water which they "sipped from cavities in the rocks," they existed on a few raspberries and snails until rescued.[7]

Most of the men of the New Jersey Volunteers and the King's American Regiment made their way up the river to St. Anne's, where they were forced to spend a cruel winter. They had hardly begun to build their cabins when the harsh climate bore in upon them in the form of heavy snows. Often it was so cold that some of a family had to stay up all during the night to keep fires going so that all would not freeze. The women were unused to such cold but cared for their babies valiantly in canvas tents surrounded by deep snow. Supplies were slow to arrive, and at one time starvation faced them. So affected were the men that some of them, in utter despair, were said to have simply lain down in their snow-bound tents to die. Graves were dug with axes and shovels and in the wintry storms their loved ones laid them to rest without religious ceremony, for there were no ministers yet present. Their remains are in the Salamanca cemetery at Fredericton, formerly St. Anne's.

Such suffering was not lost on the sensitive Edward Winslow, who noted that the Loyalist soldiers had served throughout the war and now wanted only the land to which they were entitled, just a spot to call their own where they would not be further molested. Winslow and Colonel Stephen De Lancey had gone 130 miles up the river to plan for the orderly settlement of the discharged troops, had made sensible recommendations for the fair distribution of the land, and were incensed to note the confusion among the men as well as the lack of cooperation on the part of Governor Parr and his staff. To De Lancey, the situation appeared "almost incredible." [8]

Revealing details of the hardships experienced by the newcomers to New Brunswick are set forth in a narrative by Miss Hannah Ingraham, who was 11 years old when she and her family left their farm some 20 miles north of Albany, New York. There they had "a comfortable farm, plenty of cows and sheep," she recalled, but when the war began, her father, Benjamin Ingraham, joined the British army and the rebels took all their possessions except one heifer and four sheep. Her mother had to pay rent, she said, for her own farm. They did allow her four-year-old brother to keep his lamb, after he made an emotional request.

Hannah's father was in the British army for seven years. The rebels took her grandfather and put him on a prison ship, where he suffered a paralytic stroke and never recovered. The father returned home on September 13, 1783, and told his family they were to go to Nova Scotia. They killed the cow, and sold the beef; candles for their trip were made from the tallow. Their uncle threshed 20 bushels of wheat for them and the grandmother came and made bags for it, so they embarked with the wheat, a tub of butter, a tub of pickles and a supply of potatoes. They traveled down the Hudson River in a sloop and then boarded a transport ship, the *King George,* for Saint John. A bad storm greeted them in the Bay of Fundy but they made it ashore in a canoe. No deaths occurred aboard the vessel, but several babies were born. Ashore, they "had to live in tents," Hannah related; "the government gave them to us and rations too. It was just at the first snow, and the melting snow and rain would soak up into our beds as we lay. Mother got chilled and developed rheumatism and was never well afterwards."

Up the St. John River the family went in a schooner and in nine days arrived at St. Anne's. They lived in a tent while the father explored the neighborhood for a site on which to erect a house. At a leaf-covered spot where he found a spring of fresh water, Benjamin Ingraham decided to build. One morning when they awoke in the tent, Hannah recalled, "we found the snow lying deep on the ground all round us and when father came wading through it he told us the house was ready and not to stop to light a fire and not to mind the weather, but follow his tracks through the trees, for the trees were so many we soon lost sight of him going up the hill. It was snowing fast and Oh, so cold!" At the "house" they found "no floor laid, no windows, no chimney, no door, but we had a roof at least. A good fire was blazing and mother had a big loaf of bread and she boiled a kettle of water and put a good piece of butter in a pewter bowl. We toasted the bread and all sat around the bowl and ate our breakfast that morning, and mother said, 'Thank God we are no longer in dread of having shots fired through our house. This is the sweetest meal I have tasted for many a day.' " [9]

Such a scarcity of food and building materials, added to the inequality of land grants allotted, caused a growing sentiment against Governor Parr and the government of Nova Scotia. He sent the provincial chief justice, Bryan Finucane, to try to smooth matters out, but the task was found to be a formidable one. It should be explained that Governor Parr had been under a severe handicap in his administration. The opposition of the North-Fox ministry in England to Lord Shelburne, who had appointed Parr, threatened the position of the provincial governor and gave "aid and comfort" to his enemies. Not only had the disorderly circumstances of the Loyalist settlements exposed him to sharp criticism, but the people seemed to expect him to comply with every request they made. And it was not until 30,000 of the exiles were on Nova Scotian shores that Parr received detailed instructions for dealing with the emergency. His surveyor-general had only 23 deputies in his office, and nine of these were unauthorized, so it is not difficult to understand the confusion and inequity in the thousands of grants all over the large, wild territory. Finally, in desperation, Parr threatened to make no grants of land at all and he reported to Lord North that his task was the greatest that any governor had ever had. So when the North-Fox coalition fell in Britain, and Pitt came to office, the St. John Loyalists interpreted this as disastrous to their cause. This was the situation when Chief Justice Finucane arrived, along with his brother, Andrew, who was known as "the toady." The Finucane visit served mainly to intensify the local squabbles. The principal material result was the selection by the chief justice of a rich grant of land for himself, that being 500 acres of easily available standing timber several miles above St. Anne's, comprising the whole of Sugar Island, an appropriate name indeed for such a great personal prize.[10]

Although general developments both politically and economically were leading toward a climax in the St. John settlements, the people themselves adjusted remarkably well to the harsh surroundings. As early as July of 1783, Edward Winslow had expressed himself as gratified at the situation and behavior of some of the disbanded veterans. "I never saw more cheerfulness and good humor than appear among the men," he wrote. "They are encamped on one of the pleasantest spots I ever beheld and they are enjoying a great variety of . . . partridges, salmon, bass, trout, pigeon, etc." Yet he also noted some "vices generated in camps" from a "a promiscuous rabble with continual acts of licentiousness." [11]

The coming of warmer weather as the year 1784 passed appeared to harbinger a more pleasant land for these Loyalists. The settlers got together and built their houses, using logs with roofs of bark bound over with small poles. Chimneys and fireplaces were made of stone laid in yellow clay. The windows had four small panes of glass. Logically, the first house finished was that of the community doctor. All the cooking was done at the open fireplace since there were at first no stoves. Before the fire, meat was roasted and stews and soups were prepared in large iron pots which hung from a crane. Delicious bread was cooked in a Dutch oven or bake kettle set on the hearth, the top covered with hot coals and ashes, the same lying underneath the oven. Wild game such as moose and caribou was available at times, but pigeons and fish were more abundant. Meal was made from home-grown Indian corn, and beans as well as potatoes were raised among the stumps in small clearings. What tea could be imported cost two dollars a pound, so native herbs were often used as substitutes. At St. Anne's there were no horses for some years, the only domestic animal during the first year being a black and white cat which became a favorite pet, until "some hungry, evil-minded strangers from the United States, roasted and ate the cat, to the great sorrow and indignation of the community." The kitchen often comprised dining room, living room, and sometimes the bedroom. In winter the family sat around the fire until bedtime, then heated logs or hot water bottles which they placed in the cold beds to make them warmer. Women made and wore homespun clothes; the men wore leather breeches during the week and hopefully had one broadcloth suit for Sundays which lasted them usually about 20 years. Clothing of dead men was valued and sold as part of their estate, then was worn again.[12]

Into this scene of burgeoning domestic life in the spring of 1784 came Stephen Jarvis of Connecticut, a Tory whose own home affairs had been marked by violent disruption. He and his family landed at Saint John in June and then proceeded up the river to Fredericton. Even this primitive land must have been a welcome sight to the weary exile after his hectic experiences during the Revolution. Soon after the battle of Bunker Hill, young Jarvis of Danbury, Connecticut, was willingly drafted into the patriot militia which was to garrison New York City. He served for ten days on historic Governor's Island in the harbor, then decided that he wanted to board a British ship. Not succeeding in this, he returned to his home and apologized to his father, a Tory.

"I was wrong," said the son, "in espousing a cause so repugnant to your feelings—and now contrary to my opinions also."

At this time, three Tories escaped from the infamous Simsbury Mines in Connecticut and joined the British army. With them went Jarvis, but there were several interruptions before he accomplished his purpose. Hearing that some rebel soldiers were in the vicinity of Norwalk, Jarvis hid in a house on January 1, 1777. When patriot searchers approached, he sprang onto a horse and dashed away, hiding again in another house; then he joined his father, who gave him some money and clothes and helped him on his way. Walking and running, Jarvis waded through icy streams and, traveling mostly at night, arrived at Stamford, where he "was laid low by smallpox." When he had recovered, he bade his father goodbye and made his way to Long Island by crossing over the Sound in "a canoe loaded with potatoes and two or three calves." In New York, he was told that units of the British army had gone to Danbury, where they had mistakenly killed his father. The report of his father's death proved to be untrue, but Jarvis knew no better. "This melancholy news determined me for a military life," the younger Jarvis said. The British obliged his decision by giving him a sergeantcy in the army. He was then sent to Kingsbridge to join an ill-equipped regiment.

"I stated the danger we were of being fired on as rebels in our country clothes," he wrote. "The captain hemmed and hawed. I said 'Sir, you command a company in the British Army and you are not fit to command an English wagon.' If he or myself had known anything of military duty, I must have been shot, agreeably to the articles of war."

The company marched to lower New York City, boarded a ship and landed at Amboy. They were encamped at Strawberry Hill and served at Brandywine, Pound Ridge, Norfolk, Charleston, Ninety-Six, Monks Corner, South Carolina, and at St. Augustine. Jarvis, who became a lieutenant, complained of the food, singling out especially the "oat meal biscuit full of maggots."

When the war ended, Jarvis returned to visit his father and family, reaching Danbury on May 21, 1783, to the great joy, he recalled, "of my aged parents and the rest of my family. Their meeting with me can better be imagined than described. I had been absent for seven years without having the least communication with my home. And here I met the lady to whom I was engaged and to whom I was the next day married." That lady was Miss Amelia Glover, who apparently had waited faithfully for him through all the anxious years. But even this marital affair was to be marred by disturbances which belied the idea that the martial conflict was over. A public wedding was planned until Jarvis was notified by a sympathetic American that militiamen were coming after him. His father urged him to leave, but he refused. He then embraced his bride-to-be and asked her and the family to leave. They refused. Jarvis bolted the door and said, "I'll dispatch as many of them as my two pistols and sword will assist me in doing." Meantime, his father and brother went to see officials of the town who were their friends.

A mob arrived and clamored at the door. Jarvis went downstairs and talked with some of them. A few knew him and shook hands, some condemned him as "a damned Tory. Others charged me with cutting out prisoners' tongues," he said. This scene lasted for some time. Then he was told he must not be seen within 30 miles of Danbury by sundown. He refused to go, declaring that he was determined to marry Amelia. "I now warn you against injuring a hair on her head," Jarvis cried. ". . . I am now in your power and you may destroy me, but not unrevenged, if not by myself, my friends in New York will avenge my death an hundred-fold on your near and dear friends." Such revenge was currently common among both Tories and patriots in the United States.

By this time, the commanding officer of the American troops had arrived and, at the request of the elder Jarvis, stationed a squad of dragoons at the house to protect the threatened couple. Feeling that he must act fast, the younger Jarvis sent for a minister and he and Amelia were married in the home that evening. But in the night, the local sheriff appeared, burst into the bedroom of the newlyweds, and tried to arrest Jarvis. The groom was so incensed at this invasion of privacy that he threatened to blow the sheriff's brains out. So frightened was the latter that in leaving the room, he stumbled and fell all the way down the stairs. In the morning, however, a posse was found surrounding the house; whereupon, Jarvis arose, bade them a sarcastic "Good morning," and then threw them down a dollar and suggested that they spend it in drinking to the bride's health. "Their countenances now began to brighten," Jarvis observed, "and when they sent for a bottle of bitters they said I must drink their health first. But how to get the bottle up to me was a question. However, by tying together pocket handkerchiefs, the difficulty was got over and I received the bottle with a glass in a bucket. Nothing would do but the bride must make her appearance at the window, also, which she at last did, and touched her lips to the glass as we drank their health, and then conveyed the bottle in the same way to them; and before they had emptied the bottle, they swore I was a damned honest fellow, I had married the finest woman in the country, that my conduct had deserved her and that they would protect me with their lives."

Jarvis resolved to go right to the top of the American command to assure his safe conduct until he could leave the United States. So he went to New York City, and proceeded to the headquarters of General George Washington, where he met some officer who he thought was Alexander Hamilton; but this was incorrect, for Hamilton had left the army almost two years previous. Jarvis wrote, however, that he did succeed in seeing Washington and "asked him for a passport to go into the country. He received me very civilly but declined complying with my request, as his command had ceased and civil government was again in operation; but at the same time said there was no difficulty, that I was perfectly safe under the Treaty of Peace to proceed and transact my business, reporting myself to the authority of the place to which I was bound." This was a significant statement from Washington, a far cry from his remark early in the war in which he urged Tories to commit suicide. It appears from this statement that he was willing, now that the war was over, for even their military officers to circulate in the new nation, certainly a contrasting attitude to that of many of his American contemporaries.

Jarvis went back to Connecticut and joined his wife in Reading at his brother's house. After an absence of four months from her, he found her "as women wish to be who love their lord." The rest of the winter of 1783-84, Jarvis and his wife spent pleasantly in Connecticut, during which time he visited his uncle, the Right Reverend Abraham Jarvis, later the second Bishop of Connecticut. But again threatened by a mob in the spring, the Tory officer took his wife and moved to Newtown where she gave birth to their first baby, a daughter, Eliza. Then they made their way to Norwalk and prepared to leave the country, but not before he made several trips at night back and forth to Danbury to see his relatives and friends. On one of these trips, Jarvis spotted one of the mob who had tormented him and revenged himself. "With my good hunting whip, I lashed him every step to his door," he recorded with satisfaction.

From Cold Spring, Long Island, Jarvis and his family embarked on a ship called the *Sholdrum* and arrived at Saint John in 15 days. He had in his pocket "half a guinea only with one year's half pay to draw for." They made their home at Fredericton, at first in a rented house in which Mrs. Jarvis became very ill from the dampness. But she recovered by the summer and his principal troubles seemed to be with visitors. "All my old brother officers appeared to be interested in my welfare," he wrote, "drank my wine, feasted upon my hospitality, and then either left the country or died without paying their debts; so that at the end of the year I found myself a loser to the amount of about 200 pounds."

Yet, Stephen Jarvis prospered in his new country, being only 27 years of age when he arrived. He eventually became a colonel and adjutant general of militia and later "Gentleman Usher of the Black Rod" in the Canadian House of Parliament. He moved to Kingston, Ontario, and lived to be 84 years of age.[13]

At the time of the arrival of the Jarvis family, a proposal had been made to separate the region from that of eastern Nova Scotia. The ubiquitous Edward Winslow suggested it in July; he believed multitudes would come and that from the very nature of the situation a separate government would be necessary. The distance of Parrtown from Halifax made it difficult to transact business with the government, and as has been shown, the Halifax officials were not in wholehearted sympathy with the new settlers along the St. John. The fact that a new government would provide new offices for the lately arrived Loyalists was not lost sight of by the latter, who, in any case, resented irascible Governor John Parr. Had he been more astute and experienced, there might have been no division of Nova Scotia. But the exiles to the west quite naturally relayed their sentiments to their friends in London and by the time the plan was suggested, it was already a familiar and rather acceptable one in England. The British too saw an advantage and learned a lesson —that of keeping colonies small and divided.

At first it had been proposed to name the new province New Ireland, making it the third in a trinity which included New England and New Scotland (Nova Scotia). But just at this time, Ireland, taking a leaf from the American Declaration of Independence, made its own such unpopular declaration. It was decided to call the colony New Brunswick, after the German home of the then-ruling British dynasty. The governorship was first offered to General Henry Fox, who had been in command at Halifax in 1783, and then to General Thomas Musgrave, a former colonel who, during the battle of Germantown in the American Revolution, had successfully held out with his men against repeated attacks by the artillery of Henry Knox. Both men declined. The first governorship of New Brunswick was eventually accepted by Colonel Thomas Carleton, a brother of Sir Guy Carleton, who liked the job so well he held on to it for 33 years. One historian has stated that Colonel Carleton was a normal type of the rather stilted British officer of the time, with a chilly manner and little tact or capacity to unbend. He was an ardent patriot, a sincere member of the Church of England, a friend of well-guarded education for the upper classes and a generous contributor to what he thought to be good causes. He had, however, a rather wooden mind, was suspicious of democracy, was indolent, and firm in the conviction that office brought privileges as well as duty. Carleton was fond of growing vegetables in his large garden at the new capital, Fredericton. It was believed that he moved the seat of government there from Saint John because he liked the company of his old army cronies, now gentlemen farmers, who lived up river better than he did the merchants and traders of Saint John. The reason he gave was that the latter place was more open to attack from the sea. As a consolation, Saint John was incorporated, the first such city in Canada.[14]

The secretary of the province of New Brunswick was the Reverend Jonathan Odell, grandson of the first president of what is now Princeton University. The witty and poetic Tory counterpart of the Whig poet Philip Freneau, Odell had been secretary to Sir Guy Carleton in New York. His son, W. F. Odell, succeeded him as secretary of New Brunswick, the two between them holding the office for some 65 years. Back in the States, Jonathan Odell had paid his respects to the rebel organization with the following lines:

> *We will, we must—though mighty Laurens frown,*
> *Or Hancock with his rabble hunt us down;*
> *Champions of virtue, we'll alike disdain*
> *The guards of Washington, the lies of Paine,*
> *And greatly bear without one anxious throb,*
> *The wrath of Congress, or its lords, the mob.*[15]

The chief justice was George Duncan Ludlow, former Supreme Court justice of New York, the other judges being retired officers who had engaged in the war. The position of attorney general had been offered to Sampson S. Blowers of Halifax, but he declined and became instead attorney general of Nova Scotia. The New Brunswick post went to his friend and fellow Harvard graduate, Jonathan Bliss, formerly of Massachusetts. Ward Chipman was named solicitor general and his friend and correspondent, Edward Winslow, was made a member of the council. It was an aristocratic Loyalist line-up.

The new governor arrived at what was still Parrtown on November 21, 1784, and was greeted with enthusiasm by the residents, who described themselves as oppressed and insulted Loyalists who had once been free and hoped to be again. The charter of the city was drawn up by Ward Chipman and it was at his suggestion that it was called Saint John. The name of Parrtown now seemed obsolete and Governor Parr himself had admitted that the name had been the product of his wife's vanity. In the first election, for members of the assembly, in October of 1785, the right to vote was extended to all males of 21 years of age who had lived in the province three months. The contest went off very smoothly except in the city of Saint John. There the inhabitants had split into two groups known as the Upper Cove and Lower Cove. The former represented the aristocratic element and might have been called the "Upper Crust," while the other was made up of lower class persons. The class feeling had been increasing ever since 55 of the former New Yorkers had tried to obtain, as a reward for their war service and social standing, huge grants of land in Nova Scotia, as contrasted to the small lots meted out in Saint John itself. Added to this strained situation, rum was so plentiful and cheap that a number of the disbanded soldiers reorganized themselves as rioters. Governor Carleton had to call out troops to put the rioters down. When the assembly did meet in early 1786, it gathered behind closed doors and the people did not know what was going on inside.

The American Tories of the higher social and economic classes were in a minority, just as they had been in the colonies. Among the lower class, there were those who knew how to climb: for example, one William Newton, who had been the valet of Major George Hanger of the British Legion. After arriving in Nova Scotia, Newton began courting a wealthy widow, named Munroe, telling her that he was "particularly connected with the honorable Major Hanger," that his circumstances were rather affluent, that he had served in a money-making department and that he had left a considerable property behind him. Not being sure of this story, the widow applied to Edward Winslow, who, with his usual ebullient humor, blithely assured her that indeed Mr. Newton had been connected very closely with the Honorable Major Hanger, and that "he had left a large property behind him." So the nuptials were immediately celebrated with great pomp. Newton, the ex-valet, therewith came into possession of an excellent house handsomely furnished, good stables and the most delightfully situated farms in the community.[16]

Regarding the class distinctions, a recent historian has concluded that the idea of Massachusetts settlers in New Brunswick being first family-Harvard people is mainly a myth; "most of the individuals were hustling for their daily bread." [17] Nonetheless, the hopes of the Loyalist leaders were high and they seemed to feel that they could make one of the finest communities in the world along the St. John River. Like the founders of Shelburne, they expected much trade with the West Indies, where other Tories had fled. They had fish and timber and fertile soil; what they mainly needed was patience. Although the work of settling the new region progressed, many of the high hopes were never realized. Actually there were few opportunities for "gentlemen" there. Hard toil was the answer. On the northern and eastern shores, the English, Scots and Irish mingled with the Acadian families who worked with the soil and sea. About 15,000 persons were added to New Brunswick by the Tory exodus, including 1,000 who eventually left. Sir Brook Watson, who later was commissary general of the British forces in New York and eventually lord mayor of London, acted for years as the London agent for New Brunswick.

If New England sent its nobility to the budding province, then old England sent over its "ignobility" in the person of Benedict Arnold. Although he was and is known in America as an arch traitor, it must be recalled that to many of those on the other side in the war, he was held in higher if mixed repute. Arnold is still a controversial figure, and any new light thrown upon his character by his activities subsequent to the conflict may be helpful in getting to the final verdict about him.

Benedict Arnold has well been called a figure of fascination for biographers. Whether he is painted as a scheming scoundrel of the deepest hue who venally sold out his country for a mess of

British pottage, or whether simply as a mixed-up man whose
motives were darkly shadowed by the clash between events and
his personal interests, one thing is clear: he had a madly moti-
vated and "vaulting ambition which o'er-leaped itself." For it
was in this province of New Brunswick that Arnold spent six
years after his service as a military leader and his change to the
British side.

Arnold had fled to England after the Revolution, and there
was received at court by King George III. But his anticipated
pleasant sojourn in that country turned into an often bitter
experience. He found that no one loved a turncoat—who may
turn again—and even some of his old American Tory friends
who saw him in London turned away at the sight of him.
Arnold had made claims for thousands of pounds to compensate
for his personal losses in America. Then eventually he realized
that his claims were exorbitant and asked that they be with-
drawn; he had already been paid a certain amount and his wife
was to receive a pension. Even though he thought these rewards
were "not a full compensation for the loss of my real estate, for
risks run and services rendered, yet I have upon duly considering the great expense which I shall probably incur by remaining in London to prosecute a further claim, the loss of time and
difficulty attending it, thought proper to withdraw my claim for
any further compensation." [18]

But if Benedict Arnold withdrew any such claims, it was
not for altruistic reasons. He had in mind a new venture, in
keeping with his enterprising, volatile nature. He bought and
equipped a brig and gave it the impressive name of *Lord Mid-
dleton*. In this he planned to journey to New Brunswick and
establish a business, so he spent the summer of 1785 readying
the ship with as typical zeal as if he were going to war again. For
he had been extremely restless in England, a land too sedate and
stable for his tempestuous nature. Although two of his young
children had died in the two years preceding, he still had two
sons and a daughter besides his spirited wife, Peggy, who had
been a Tory before he married her. He left his family in London and sailed in October; after a voyage of five weeks, he
arrived at Halifax on November 19. His sudden arrival there
surprised some of the citizens. Attorney General Blowers, for
example, wrote to Ward Chipman in New Brunswick, "Will
you believe! General Arnold is here from England in a brig of

his own, as he says, reconnoitering the country. He is bound for your city, which he will of course prefer to Halifax, and settle with you. Give you joy of the acquisition." [19]

This was just ten years after Arnold had led his company of patriot troops to Boston in 1775, where he was commissioned a colonel under Washington. Later he was to win and lose battles for the Americans and was wounded twice in the same leg, as symbolized by the only material patriot tribute to him, a statue —if such it can be called—of Arnold's boot on the battlefield of Saratoga, where he distinguished himself along with Daniel Morgan. This was not the first time Arnold had been in Canada. Soon after his arrival at Boston, he was sent by Washington to lead the renowned expedition to Quebec. Although Morgan did most of the leading, Arnold had received major credit and was wounded when he took over command after the death of the young general, Richard Montgomery. Morgan again stepped in, and heroically led the remaining troops until they were overwhelmed.

The reputation of Arnold had sunk so low by the time of his new venture to Canada that Lieutenant Hugh Gordon at Halifax wrote to Edward Winslow and predicted that Arnold would be right at home with Samuel Hake, who had been a storekeeper at Fort Howe and was then under charges of embezzlement. But high or low, Benedict Arnold was not an ordinary man. With characteristic individuality, he arrived off the coast of St. John with only the captain and the pilot he had hired. Here again Arnold's judgment seemed to have been plagued by the gods of misfortune, for upon entering the harbor from the Bay of Fundy, the pilot of the ship, stupidly ignoring the course of the other vessels in the harbor, headed for the Marsh River behind the town. As a result, the brig ran upon the flats, "bilged" and was for a time presumed lost. Arnold, "confined to his bed by the gout, was fit to be tied." He roared and ranted in high dudgeon. He reminded the pilot that the winds were exactly right for entering the harbor and accused him of making the serious blunder on purpose. "There is no doubt," wrote Jonathan Sewall to his son, "but the whole thing was an infamous, preconcerted piece of villainy, done with an intention of injuring the credit of the harbor and to deter other vessels from coming round, by malevolent conclusions to be drawn from the loss of this brig; and that the captain was himself privy to it. This is General Arnold's account of the transaction and he has no doubt remaining of the pilot and captain's villainy, nor has any other person of discernment." [20]

Arnold wisely purchased a lot on Main Street in the Lower Cove section of Saint John and there built a general store and warehouse. He took in as a partner Munson Hayt, who had been a Tory and had served as a lieutenant and quartermaster in the Prince of Wales's American Volunteers. It is believed that Arnold had previously known him in New York. Other purchases made by Arnold were property fronting on the St. John River; a house and lot on Broad Street for which he paid 63 pounds; two lots in Carleton which cost two pounds; a farm on what is now Westmoreland Road and also property in Guys Ward, and on Prince William, Queen and Germain Streets in Saint John. From the surveyor Anthony Egbert and his wife, Mary, Arnold purchased land on Smyth Street. Apparently well-heeled with money or credit, Arnold branched out to Fredericton, where, in the spring of 1786, he negotiated for a house and lot on Waterloo Row. He was able to resume his cordial acquaintance with former soldiers of the British army now living in Fredericton, among them Andrew Phair, the postmaster, and Dr. William Stairs. Despite his ownership of property, there appears to be no substantiating evidence that Arnold ever lived long in Fredericton. When he was there, it was probably only on matters of business.

Benedict Arnold must have lived in rather pretentious circumstances in Saint John. Some of his household effects which were sold after he left New Brunswick indicated a high scale of living, of the kind which he had always enjoyed or coveted, and which has been given as one of the factors inducing him to leave the patriot cause. If he did not realize these material dreams in England, then to some extent he did enjoy them in Canada. For a time he occupied a house on King and Canterbury Streets in Saint John. This had been built by a resident named James Porteous; it was later converted into stores and an assembly room, then becoming the well-known Exchange Coffee House.

As to his business dealings, he plunged into them with typical impetuosity. Arnold purchased from Tristam Hill a half-interest in his sloop, *Nancy*, which was formerly the *Munson*. Two years later, Arnold hired Thomas Hanford to be master of the schooner *George* which operated to and from the West Indies. An indication of the estimated worth of Hanford may be judged by the fact that he was paid three pounds a month, this figure to be raised at a later time. The former general signed an agreement with others for fire protection of his property, the subscribers promising to bring in fire engines and dig public wells. Arnold paid ten pounds for this service. Later, this act was to assume more than passing significance. How the press of the community reacted to the activities of their notorious new businessman may be judged from an item which appeared in the local *Gazette* on June 6, 1786:

> "On Thursday last came through the falls of the City, now moored, a new and noble ship belonging to Brigadier General Benedict Arnold, upwards of 300 tons, of white oak, the *Lord Sheffield,* to be commanded by Captain Alex Cameron. The General's laudable efforts to promote the interests of this infant colony have, during his short residence, been very productive to its commercial advantage and as such deserve the praise of every well wisher to its prosperity."

So there was praise in journalistic quarters, at least, for Arnold. But not much from the Tory from whom he bought the *Lord Sheffield,* Nehemiah Beckwith at Maugerville. The vessel was purchased while still on the stocks. Later, Arnold, by insisting on some expensive changes in the design and structure of the ship, caused Beckwith to lose a considerable sum of money. This won him "the eternal enmity of Beckwith and resulted in financial disaster from which, however, the shipbuilder later recovered." In August, a notice appeared stating that the *Lord Sheffield* would sail on the 20th of the month for Campobello, an island of New Brunswick near Eastport, Maine, en route to and returning from Jamaica, and that extra accommodations for passengers were available.[21]

Soon after the arrival of his new ship, Arnold left Hayt in charge of his business in Saint John and sailed for the West Indies aboard the vessel. And during this period there seemingly occurred an episode in his many-hued career which has been common to military men long absent from home. Arnold apparently had an affair with some woman which resulted in the birth of an illegitimate son. Just when and where this happened has never been discovered. Had the affair taken place in New Brunswick it would seem likely that some people would have found out about it, and that those who did not like Arnold might naturally have revealed more details.

Whoever she was has remained a secret. And Arnold must have had his mind as well as body preoccupied, for he neglected to write his wife, Peggy, for such a long time that she wrote to her father in distress, expressing wonder at what had happened to this "best of husbands," as she fondly expressed it.[22] Arnold mentioned in his will that the boy, named John Sage, was "about 14 years of age." Since the will was made in 1800, the year of his birth would have been 1786. The youth was then living in Canada and his father left to him 1,200 acres of land, an annual sum for his education, and another sum to be paid to him when he reached the age of 21.

From the West Indies, Arnold made his way to England. Whether remorse had anything to do with it or not, he brought his wife and children, still in England, to New Brunswick. Here Peggy soon made friends, especially with Mrs. Ward Chipman and Mrs. Jonathan Bliss. Unlike her husband, who managed to make himself unpopular to some extent wherever he went, Mrs. Arnold, with her engaging and vivacious manner as well as her rare beauty, was popular everywhere. Apparently she held nothing against her busband. Whether this was entirely from personal devotion, or whether she was conscious of playing a leading part in shaping his eventful life from the time she met him in Philadelphia, is difficult to determine. There is no doubt that she was, regardless of his indiscretions, the brightest light in his often dark life; and Peggy returned this feeling with a true dedication.

The general now forcibly applied himself to his business. He established trading stations at Saint John, Campobello Island and at Fredericton. But soon more rough spots appeared, for his trading ventures were not so profitable as he had anticipated. Some of those with whom he did business borrowed money from him and did not repay, or if they did, it was done slowly. Others used his name as security for debts without his knowledge. The sharp competition and high insurance rates for his shipping also cut into his profits. This would have been bad enough, but his old undesirable traits began to reappear. Among these were a quick temper, irritability and arrogance. So he grew unpopular and fell to fussing with his business associates, often ending up in court over matters which should have been settled informally. For example, Arnold early placed Harris Hatch and Garret Clopper under bond for breach of covenant. On the other hand, Elias Hardy had Arnold served with a summons to answer John Hervey on charges of trespass. Arnold sued Edward Winslow for 63 pounds on a promissory note.[23]

Perhaps regretting the events of the past few months, Benedict Arnold sailed for England in 1788 with a cargo. Peggy, of course, was not happy about this new absence of her husband. She actually wanted to visit Philadelphia, but the birth of a son, George, in September of 1787 and the trip of her husband caused a delay. While he was in England, Arnold, on the advice of friends, insured his warehouse on Lower Cove for 1,000 pounds, the stock for 4,000 pounds, and the stock in his King Street store for 1,000 pounds. When he returned from England, he found that on July 11, fire had destroyed the warehouse and its contents, and that his son, Henry, who had been sleeping there, had barely escaped from the blaze. Arnold of course asked for damages. But rumors flew about that he had set the fire himself, this blame attributed to a man who had been a traitor to both king and Congress. Another rumor claimed that he had left instructions to his son to burn down the property which was "over-insured." The insurance underwriters attempted to evade payment of Arnold's claims, but eventually they had to compensate for the damages, although rumors still persisted—with good reason. For example, in the claim for compensation of Jonathan Ketchum of Norwalk, Connecticut, Ketchum stated that when the town was burned by the British army, his house and all his furnishings were destroyed by fire, with not even a bed remaining. The strain and exposure on Ketchum were such that he came down with a fever so that he could not work and support his family and they were "left naked and destitute of almost every necessary of life." His son, Samuel Ketchum, testified that earlier, "General Arnold who then commanded the Rebels, ordered him and a few more Tories to be shut up in a house and burnt." [24]

A year after the burning of Arnold's Saint John property, he fell out with his partner, Munson Hayt, and of course this dispute ended up in court. In the *Gazette* of October 27, 1789, there appeared this notice:

> "The co-partnership of Arnold, Hayt and Company being dissolved by mutual consent, all persons being indebted to said firm are requested to settle accounts with Munson Hayt."

The latter asserted in the suit that Arnold and his family had robbed him of 700 pounds, that he (Hayt) had accused

Arnold of burning his own store, and that it was not in his power to blacken Arnold's character for it already was as black as it could be. Arnold characteristically brought a suit for slander, retaining Ward Chipman and Jonathan Bliss as counsel. Hayt's attorney was Elias Hardy. Stephen Sewall wrote his brother, Jonathan, that the general had 30 witnesses and that Chipman had told him that this was "one of the most hellish plots that ever was laid for the destruction of a man," meaning Arnold.

In the trial, Hayt discovered that although Arnold had little regard for any other man's character, he was a fighter who would not stand for defamation of his own. Arnold produced promissory notes which showed that Hayt owed him almost 2,000 pounds, and stated that Hayt had promised to pay them, but despite several such assurances, had not done so. Instead, Arnold claimed, Hayt had tried to deceive and defraud him, and, as to the second charge, the fact that Arnold was in England at the time of the fire made it impossible for him to have set it, although his son's presence in the building at the time, plus the coincidental taking out of insurance policies by Arnold, did seem to constitute suspicious circumstances. The verdict in the case was in favor of Arnold, but instead of the $5,000 for which he had sued, the judge awarded him only twenty shillings.

Trial or not, Peggy Arnold did get to go to Philadelphia. Mrs. Elizabeth Sewall wrote to her son, Jonathan, "Mrs. Arnold goes sometime in October to New York with an intention to pass the winter in Philadelphia. . . . The ladies from this circumstance at Saint Johns will not be quite so sociable as Mrs. Arnold, willing to help, a little sociability which between you and I makes life less irksome and enables us to encounter much better, with the infirmities of our nature, the meeting with our friends now and then." In a later letter, Mrs. Sewall said that Mrs. Arnold was not sure of going to Philadelphia and this "seems to be a matter of satisfaction to the ladies." [25] Peggy had written her father, the once prominent Edward Shippen, that she would be very happy to see him and her mother again, but that she felt her pleasure would be mixed with pain because when she left them it would probably be forever. This premonition proved to be all too true. Peggy told her sister, Betsy, that she regretted leaving the general alone—and well she might, judging from his activities during the last such separation—but added that he had urged her to go and so she would. Even so, it was the fall of 1789 before Peggy actually set out for Philadelphia by way of New York. Her ship was at one stage reported to have been lost, but this was untrue and she arrived in her old home in early December. The new United States had just come into being under its constitution and the capital was in New York City. Within a year, it was to move to Philadelphia where Tories were largely a memory and the name of Benedict Arnold was anathema. Some of Peggy's old friends were still friendly to her, but others were cold and disdainful. In the spring of 1790, she returned to Saint John, glad she had seen her family but sad in the knowledge that a wall of tragedy had arisen inexorably between herself and them.

Circumstances now combined to make Peggy's forebodings seem even more perspicacious. Her husband began to think of leaving New Brunswick and returning to England, and his wife was with him in these thoughts. There was discouragement about the collection of Arnold's debts, for not only was it difficult to collect from business associates, but, too, Peggy's brother had borrowed 750 pounds from him which he was unable to pay. Arnold was in favor of letting this debt go, with the hope that it someday might be paid to his family. The proud Edward Shippen, however, intervened and promised that, if necessary, he would make good the debt of his son.

The year was 1791 and the people of Saint John appeared to detest Benedict Arnold more and more. Though he had won the slander suit, many still thought him guilty and doubtless wanted to feel this way about him. His harsh collecting of debts also worked against him. But even in the face of such antagonism, Arnold retained his haughtiness. The mutual hatred culminated in the march of a mob to his home, where they burned him in effigy in front of his own door. A label on the effigy stated "Traitor." It was with difficulty that the mob was restrained from entering and seizing Arnold himself.

Announcing the departure of the Arnolds, an advertisement of an auction appeared in the *Gazette* of September 22, 1791. At their residence would be offered for sale next day "A quantity of furniture comprising excellent feather beds, mahogany four-poster bedsteads with furniture, a set of elegant cabriole chairs covered with blue damask, sofas and curtains to match; card, tea and other tables, looking-glasses, a secretary desk and bookcase, fire-screens, girandoles, lustres, an easy and sedan chair with a great variety of other furniture. Likewise, an elegant set of Wedgewood gilt ware, two tea table sets of Nankeen china, a variey of glassware, a terrestrial globe, a double wheel-jack and a great quantity of kitchen furniture. Also a lady's elegant saddle and bridle."

The ending of the year saw the exit of the Arnolds from New Brunswick. Peggy left with a feeling of relief; her husband was still angry and was suffering from the gout as they reached London in early 1792. They were never to see their native America again. Arnold informed Jonathan Bliss that they had had "a rough and disagreeable voyage home, but our reception has been very pleasant . . . I cannot help viewing your city as a shipwreck from which I have escaped." [26] But from the prison within himself, Benedict Arnold would never escape. He was to live for nine years more and Peggy would survive him by three years. The *Gazette* in Saint John which once filled its columns with news about the traitor gave the news of his death in England in one sentence. He was gone and virtually forgotten.[27]

Other less noted but more respected American Tories are not forgotten, if prominent resting places mean anything. In the center of the city of Saint John, on what is probably its most valuable piece of real estate, is the old burying ground of many of the original Loyalists. Some graves have epitaphs, but others appear to have been unmarked. A local description of them is set forth in rhyme:

Successive generations here lay down
Rich, poor and old and young have equal room.
He who to children left wealth of renown
And he who hapless died remote from home
For whom nor wife nor child e'er came to weep;
But flowers bloom fair in summer air,
O'er the unmarked graves where friendless strangers sleep.

Not all of those who are buried here were unknown in their day. One of them is Judge James Putnam, former attorney general of Massachusetts, and later a supreme court judge in New Brunswick. John Adams studied law in his Boston office and held him to be an able and eminent barrister. He died at 64 in 1789. The judge had built a three-story building in Saint John, and after he died it was sold to Ezekiel Barlow. Unusual terms were included in the sale. The price was 2,000 Mexican silver dollars, to be counted before Ward Chipman, the lawyer.

Barlow complied and, to the amusement of the public, obtained
a wheelbarrow in which to convey the heavy and bulky load up
Chipman Hill to the office. For the transaction, two trips of the
wheelbarrow were necessary.

In the same vault with the body of Judge Putnam is that of
Jonathan Sewall, also a former attorney general of Massachusetts, a Harvard graduate and friend of John Adams. Sewall had
once attempted to dissuade Adams from embracing the patriot
cause. It was on one of their friendly walks that Adams said to
Sewall, "The die is cast; I have now passed the Rubicon; sink or
swim, live or die, survive or perish with my country is my un-
alterable determination."

Many of the lesser known Loyalists are memorialized in
verse on the now-crumbling stones in the old cemetery. One of
these is Ann Peel, wife of Humphrey Peel, "who departed this
life, January 10, 1815, in the 39th year of her age":

> *Now I am dead and in my grave*
> *And all my bones be rotten,*
> *These lines you see, remember me,*
> *When I am quite forgotten.*

As time has passed, the evidence of Loyalist occupation of
New Brunswick naturally lessens but there are still vivid re-
minders. Across the arm of the harbor at Saint John is a grim
stone structure called the Martello Tower, erected by the
Loyalists in 1812 to defend the port from United States attack.
Here ships dock at wharves built over the site where the Loyalist refugees once landed. A rock with a bronze tablet marks the
spot. Up the river, Fredericton is the home ground for the
United Empire Loyalists, whose ancestors were the American
refugees.

[4]

FROM ISLAND TO MAINLAND

Like a jewel in its setting, underneath the azure sky,
Mid the Bay of Funday waters, 'Quoddy tides run swiftly by.
Here lies Campobello Island, with its beauty and its charm,
And with salt tanged breezes blowing, over meadow, field and farm.
.... John L. Newman

LOYALISTS IN ENGLAND DURING THE REVOLUTION were quite aware of the plight of their fellow countrymen in America and made various proposals to help them. Conspicuous among these was the plan to establish a permanent Loyalist settlement in New England, as set forth by William Knox, Under Secretary for American affairs in the colonial office in London. Knox, a Tory expatriate from Georgia, was a leading pamphleteer in support of Parliamentary authority in America, and had gone to England as agent for Georgia, in 1761, where he gained the confidence of King George III and Lord North, as well as that of Lord George Germain.

William Knox's plan was to establish a refugee settlement for American Tories on the Maine coast. This, he believed, would be a useful outer defense for Nova Scotia and would also provide the beginning of a new province where the increasing stream of exiles could find a haven. Shortly after the British defeat at Saratoga, Knox found an eager ally in a Loyalist from Massachusetts, John Nutting, a carpenter who owned land in the Penobscot area. So "with a fine mixture of self-interest and loyalty," Nutting suggested the site for the settlement.[1] Knox's enthusiasm won over both Lord North and Germain to the settlement of an area still under British control, so on September 2, 1778, Germain ordered General Clinton to erect a settlement at the mouth of the Penobscot River.[2]

Thomas Hutchinson was to be governor of the new province and Daniel Leonard chief justice, though it is not believed either was enthusiastic about the rather uncertain prospects. Complications set in almost immediately in the instructions and transportation so that the detachment of Nutting and 650 soldiers did not land until June of the next year. Under command of Brigadier General Francis McLean, the troops began to lay out a fort, but news of their activities had reached the rebels in Massachusetts, a body of whom sailed in 37 ships from Boston and attacked the royal force. McLean was able, however, to hold off the amateurish assault until he was relieved by a British fleet under Sir George Collier, whose powerful guns proceeded to blow every one of the rebel vessels out of the water. The 3,000 Massachusetts troops were compelled to scurry homeward through the wild countryside.[3]

The new fortress now attracted many Tories, especially those from Maine and Massachusetts. It soon became overcrowded and a village of sturdy cottages as well as wharves and stores sprang up around it. Germain, with typical unreality, had fond hopes for the Penobscot province and told Clinton that it would be a "cheap method of disposing of these loyalists." But actually, comparatively few Tories were able to prosper there, for they feared to venture very far away from the protecting shadow of the fort, and little land was taken up. An attempt was made to improve the situation by extending the southern boundary from the Penobscot to the Kennebec River. But the refugees from New England who Germain had felt would take advantage of the opportunity did not appear in substantial numbers, and as a consequence, the ambitious plan held more vain hopes than it did ultimate success, despite the excellence of its military bastion, which never surrendered. "Rarely," says one historian, "has a more ignominious military operation been made by Americans. Had it been successful, it would not have been worth the effort it cost. Its object had no natural significance; it was an eccentric operation. Bad in conception, bad in preparation, bad in execution, it naturally ended in disaster and disgrace."[4]

When the war was over, the new state of Massachusetts which had contributed so much to the Revolution was able to obtain by the diplomacy of John Adams what she had not secured by military efforts: Penobscot was surrendered by the British and its 150 families with the garrison removed northward to Passamaquoddy Bay, where they were joined by Loyalists from New York and elsewhere. Not surrendered was Campobello Island, off the coast of New Brunswick, called by the French, Port aux Coquilles. The island site, formerly the summer home of Franklin D. Roosevelt, is now jointly operated as the Roosevelt Memorial Park by the governments of Canada and the United States.[5]

On another and larger island to the north, the Tories settled in greater numbers, but their reception was hardly more fruitful. About 600 of them fled to Prince Edward Island, which in 1783 was owned by a number of large landed proprietors. When the proprietors learned that the British government was settling Loyalists in Nova Scotia, they presented a petition to Lord North offering refuge to those who wished to settle nearby. A proclamation was therefore issued which promised lands to settlers on Prince Edward Island on similar terms to those granted in Nova Scotia and Quebec. As a consequence, encouraged Loyalists from New York and Shelburne responded, until by the end of 1784 about one-fifth of the population of the island was composed of newly arrived exiles.

But they found great difficulty in securing the grants of land which they had been promised. To be sure, they took up residence on the lands, cleared them, erected buildings and planted orchards, but often then were told that their titles were not good and so they were forced to move. Apparently the motive of the owners was to compel the new settlers to become tenants instead of freeholders. Even such a respected person as Colonel Edmund Fanning, the Loyalist lieutenant governor, was said to be involved in this reprehensible scheme, and the legal complications troubled the claimants for many years afterward.[6]

More fortunate were those Tories who headed for Quebec, for there they found real acceptance and a better organized system of government. Even in June of 1774, exiles from the American Revolution were flocking into this northern province, and by 1776 large numbers of Tories from the Mohawk Valley were going to Quebec. It was then that the earliest of the Loyalist regiments were formed in Canada. But it was not until the defeat of General Burgoyne at Saratoga in 1778 that the largest body of Tories set out for Quebec. It is said that even before the formal surrender, or convention, as it was called, a considerable number of Burgoyne's Tories, preferring the risks of flight to the terms of the surrender, struck out through the woods for the Canadian north. Alexander White of Tryon County, New York, tried to escape but only succeeded in falling into the hands of the rebels. He was taken to Albany and held in prison there for twelve months before he could obtain his release. He then went to New York City where he stayed four years more, finally securing passage to Quebec in the summer of 1783, five years after he had first started out for that province.[7]

General Frederick Haldimand, able governor of Quebec, hastened to provide for the proper receiving of the Loyalists. He established a place for them at Machiche, near Three Rivers, and placed them under the supervision of a protégé named Conrad Gugy. Nearby militiamen were ordered to build barracks for the refugees, and provisions were obtained from Three Rivers' merchants. By late autumn of 1778 there were here and at other Canadian locations some 1,000 exiled civilians, besides the soldiers, who numbered about 3,000.

After the signing of the treaty of peace in Paris, there was a hurried exodus of Tories to Quebec. These included some Negroes who had been fighting under the New York Tory, Sir John Johnson. Officers of the government in Canada were stationed at Chambly, Montreal, Sorel, Machiche, and Quebec as well as St. John and elsewhere, to dole out supplies to the incomers. By the winter of 1783–84, there were an estimated 7,000 Loyalists in the province of Quebec. Many of them had fought in such units as Johnson's Regiment, Jessup's Corps and Butler's Rangers. The majority were simple farmers from the frontier regions of New York, Pennsylvania and Vermont, with little property and less education, as evidenced by the fact that many of them signed their new oaths of allegiance with a cross. The group seemed to contain no outstanding leaders like those of Nova Scotia and New Brunswick. Nonetheless, they could and did serve to garrison the posts along the Canadian rivers, to strengthen and enlarge the fortifications of the region, to help defend the country from invasion, and to carry on scouting and secret service to the south until peace was certain.

The more help that these newly arrived exiles received, however, the more they seemed to expect. Some of them asked that their farms be stocked and that the government be changed. There were stories that Gugy at Machiche was cruel and unfair to the refugees, but he explained that the fuss was caused by a few discontented persons. Finally it was decided that those who arrived after 1784 would not receive provisions and that those who would not work would not eat; but General Haldimand was too generous-hearted to be very literal about such regulations. Adding to his problems was the discovery that smallpox had broken out among the early arrivals. He sent a physician at once to Sorel with instructions to take every precaution to prevent the spread of the disease. He also sent Abraham Cuyler, former mayor of Albany, then inspector of Loyalists in the province, to see that the Sorel refugees were properly taken care of. The smallpox victims were hospitalized, others were vaccinated and an epidemic forestalled.[8]

It would take more than disease to stop the Tory influx. The paternal Sir Frederick Haldimand offered them a wide choice of places in which to settle. The place which attracted most at this time was Cataraqui, now Kingston, east of the Bay of Quinte. Acting upon instructions from England, Haldimand sent Major Samuel Holland and a staff of assistants in the autumn of 1783 to survey the townships around the Bay of Quinte. This they carried out so hurriedly that difficulty with titles to the land arose later on. The townships were sub-divided into lots of 200 acres each.

Meanwhile, in New York City, Sir Guy Carleton was anxiously endeavoring to find places for the Loyalists fleeing to the threatened city and was relieved to learn that Cataraqui was available. According to a descendant, a harness maker in the city, Michael Grass, a Tory who had fled from his farm above the city inside the British lines, was called in by Carleton and asked if it were true that he had once been a prisoner of the French at Fort Frontenac in the Seven Years War. Grass replied that he had. Carleton inquired if Frontenac was a place where people could live.

"From what I saw of it, I think it a fine country," Grass replied, "and if people were settled there, I think they would do very well."

"Oh, Mr. Grass, I am delighted to hear you say so," Carleton reportedly said, "for we don't know what to do with the poor Loyalists. The city is full of them and we cannot send them all to Nova Scotia. Would you be willing, Mr. Grass, to take charge of such as would be willing to go with you to Frontenac? If so, I can furnish you a conveyance by ship to Quebec, and rations for you all until such time as you may have means to provide for yourselves."

Grass asked for three days in which to make up his mind. At the end of that time, he accepted. Notices were then posted about New York City asking those who wished to go, to join Grass, who was designated a captain.[9]

Ships were then found and the company of refugees sailed from New York under the command of Captain Grass. The fleet made its way past Nova Scotia, New Brunswick, and up the St. Lawrence River to Sorel at the mouth of the Richelieu where it arrived on October 17, 1783. If prior information about the climate had been more precise, the party probably would have remained at Quebec or Montreal until spring. But as it was, they landed somewhat precipitately with not a single place of shelter in sight. Some of the exiles had tents made of linen but these were no match for the fast-approaching winter. "The gravity of their position drove them to immediate action and every hand that could wield an axe or handle a saw was put in requisition and very soon there arose on the banks of the river, as if by the magic of an enchanter's wand, a village composed of rude and unsightly huts and shanties, which if any one of them had come upon a few months before, they would have taken as a settlement of some semi-civilized tribe but a remove above the Indians, and in these hastily improvised kennels, inferior to the cow sheds they had left behind, they were to pass a long dreary winter." [10]

There were five shiploads of these shivering people, an estimated 3,000 or more, composed of aged men and women, married couples with their children, some of which were infants, and young people most of whom had been in good circumstances in the States. As the winter came on in earnest, "every crevice was carefully filled with moss and clay to keep out the North wind," but even with the best they could do, their situation was miserable. "They were huddled together in these wretched holes like pigs, shivering day after day through weary months with cold and suffering with frost bites, wanting the most common utensils, but that did not matter much for they had little to cook. Their larder was mostly limited to hard tack." [11]

The spring of 1784 was especially welcome to these temporary sojourners. They were of one thought: speedy departure. In the middle of May the Tories set out again. Navigating the St. Lawrence was still slow and it was July before they reached Cataraqui. Years later, Michael Grass related his first impression of the site that is now Kingston: "Scarce the vestige of a human habitation could be found in the whole extent of the Bay of Quinte. Not a settler had dared to penetrate the vast forests that skirted its shores. Even on this spot now governed with stately edifices, were to be seen only the bark-thatched wigwam of the savage, or the newly erected tent of the hardy Loyalist." [12]

The desolate picture soon changed, and with the visit of Governor Haldimand, instructions were given regarding the distribution of land. It was felt that because of his leadership, Captain Grass should have the first choice. His selection was the land on which Kingston now stands. The second choice was given to Sir John Johnson, who chose Ernestown; third to Major Robert Rogers, Fredericksburg; the fourth to Captain Peter Van Alstine, Adolphustown; and the fifth to Captain Archibald McDonnell, who received the site of Marysburg. Grass was pleased by the favor shown him and remarked that he had "gained for persecuted principles a sanctuary, and for myself and followers, a home." [13]

Perhaps it was a home, but it was rather bare. Governor Haldimand was concerned about the need for food supplies. He sent to Montreal for turnip seed, a crop which could be planted and harvested at this late date, and gave each man a handful. Turnips served as an important and welcome part of the diet, for these ex-soldiers knew little about farming and could well utilize all the help they could get. Joseph Hadfield noted in his diary that "In seeing these soldiers become farmers, it revived the recollection of the Roman Age when they converted their swords into pruning hooks. Here it is astonishing how soon men's dispositions may be changed. No one would suppose that these had borne arms for eight or ten years, and many much longer. They seem to be very happy in general and all very thankful to the British nation for its generous support in the grants of lands, utensils of husbandry and provisions. They have declared to me that they shall ever consider themselves bound by gratitude to take arms whenever Great Britain shall require their assistance in this part of the Western World. These principles they instill into their children and the recollection of what they have suffered from the States will make this the barrier between them." [14]

The early settlers of Kingston received from the government, besides seed, provisions to last three years, consisting mainly of flour, pork, beef and a little butter and salt, distributed in a profligate manner. They were furnished axes, hoes and spades, a plow and one cow for each two families, a whip and cross-cut saw for each four families. Boats and portable mills were provided at convenient points for common use, and even church bells were given by the government. With the cows came oxen, and these sturdy animals pulled the slow carts, or "jumpers," as the rude sleighs that slid along the mud were called.

First in the order of their work came the felling of trees and the building of log cabins. In keeping with age-old custom, the newcomers combined forces, each helping the other. The cabins were of the usual primitive type, the furniture handmade; the first mattresses in the crude, hard beds were formed from the abundant supplies of green pine boughs, which afforded aroma if not much comfort. Even with this progress, however, there were still many settlers in need. Major Robert Mathews, aide to Governor Haldimand, wrote to Sir John Johnson "that the settlers at Cataraqui are in great disorder, not having yet got upon their land, many of them unprovided with a blanket to cover them, scarce any turnip seed and neither axes or hoes for half of them." [15]

The land for planting seed was discovered to be good in some places, not so in others. Just west of Cataraqui, the ground was found to be stony on the lake shore but good about a mile back. Seven miles west, the land was especially fertile; to the east it was lacking in favorable quality; but around the Bay of Quinte, the soil was generally good and well timbered. Fish abounded in the nearby waters. But often among the settlers not only was the skill lacking to put the natural advantages to good use, but there were complaints of injustice. The very generosity of the government led some of the Loyalists to fall into the habit of dependence, and when urged to go to work, they were resentful that, after their sacrifices in the war, they had to learn to shift for themselves. Some complained that measles and "chin coughs" had bothered them, to which Major Mathews wryly replied that this should have diminished rather than increased the consumption of provisions. He wrote that "with respect to the deserters, there are so many of the Loyalists who have old attachments to the colonies, that it would be in vain to attempt their going off. When it can be decently done, the best way is to wink at it. For the Province is well quit of those who do not remain out of choice." [16]

It was no wonder that many of the Loyalists felt like leaving. Many had "established homes in the American wilderness and now found themselves faced with the task of repeating the process in a new land under very similar conditions. Thus the Loyalist settlements . . . despite the special circumstances under which they were made, were in a sense really a part of that great frontier movement which has resulted in the settlement of the United States and Canada, a movement which saw the western fringes of society always moving on to new frontiers farther west." Thus it was that the face of this important part of Canada was changed. Along the lakes and rivers for some 500 miles, there were carved out breaks in the forest monotony which became dotted by the brown roofs of settlers' houses, with stumps marking the scanty fields around them. Soon villages appeared and devout people built churches of wood. It was not long before Kingston became a fortified city which echoed the tone of distant garrisons in England.[17]

While Kingston may have been fortified against military attack, it was not so well equipped in regard to famine. In the year 1788, the crops failed and there followed what became known as "the hungry year." Despite the resources of fish and wild game and fruit, legend says that some of the settlers died of starvation. Cows were sold for a barrel of flour or a few bushels of potatoes. One old couple was saved from starving only by eating the pigeons which they were able to knock from their roost. The wilder animals which roamed the thick forests would have been more available had the settlers been better supplied with weapons for hunting them. As it was, the bears and wolves became a menace, howling dismally on the cold winter nights, and carrying off precious salted provisions. A single mink could destroy in one night all the fowls of a farm, and pigs fell victim to voracious bears. A law was passed offering a premium for the heads of wolves and bears, and according to one account, years later when the wolves were growing scarce a Kingston man bred them privately in order to obtain the bounty.[18]

During the famine, people dug wild, tuberous roots and ate them, some to ill effects. Early buds of brass wood were gathered and boiled with weeds for food. "Gaunt men crept about with poles, striving to knock down the wild pigeons, or they angled all day with awkward home-made hooks for a chub or perch to keep their families from starving. In one settlement, a beef bone was passed from house to house, that each household might boil it a little while and so get a flavor in their unsalted bran soup." Jacob Lindley, who saw the suffering, told of the condition of the family of Jeremiah Moore. It had an allowance of one spoonful of meal per day for each person; strawberry leaves, beech leaves, and dried flax seed were ground in a coffee mill and then eaten. A son carried his little sister two miles on his back so she could eat a breakfast, while he had no food until dinner time. The children leaped for joy at one robin being caught, from which a whole pot of broth was made, while mustard greens, potato tops and sassafras roots were added for relish.[19]

The summer of 1789 brought brighter times, and by 1791, most of the settlers were in good condition. There was ample communication and the transportation was becoming adequate. Mrs. John Graves Simcoe, wife of the lieutenant governor, observed the neatness of the farms settled by exiles from the Mohawk Valley and saw on them wheat that she considered to be finer than any she had seen in England.

> *But long and arduous were their labors ere*
> *The rugged fields produced enough for all,*
> *For thousands came ere hundreds could be fed;*
> *The scanty harvests gleaned to their last ear*
> *Sufficed not yet, men hungered for their bread*
> *Before it grew, yet cheerful bore the hard*
> *Coarse fare and russet garb of pioneers.*[20]

The stream of American immigrants continued and new settlements were added. As we have already seen, some of them, under Sir John Johnson, Major Robert Rogers, and other leaders, had joined the large group under Captain Michael Grass and settled Cataraqui or what is now Kingston, Ontario. The main routes taken by the Loyalists on their flights from New York were seven in number. Usually their way led up the Hudson River some 175 miles from New York City to Albany, and then from Fort Stanwix, now Rome, they used the Mohawk River and Wood Creek for several miles. Then the exiles took a ten-mile portage to Oneida Lake, and went along the Oswego River to Lake Ontario. The second route was by way of the Hudson, across the Mohegan Mountains and down the Moose and Black Rivers to Sackett's Harbor. At times, the Oswegatchie River was used to La Presentation, now Ogdensburg. Another route ran up the Hudson, across lakes George and Champlain, then down the Richelieu or Sorel River to Montreal or west on the St. Lawrence to Cornwall. Still others made their way up the Hudson and over the mountains to the Racket River, thence to the St. Lawrence, or overland westward from Lake Champlain, then up the southern shore of Lake Ontario to Niagara. The chief way to the west was a water route which led up the Hudson, along the Mohawk, West Canada Creek and Black River to Sackett's Harbor, on up Lake Ontario to the Niagara River and its portage, and from there by Lake Erie to Long Point or Detroit. A number of the travelers crossed Lake Erie from New York and Pennsylvania, but the usual route to Lower Canada was across western New York. The last way was to travel up the Atlantic coast by ship to the Maritime provinces, or up the St. Lawrence River to Quebec.[21]

Ranking next in size to the Cataraqui settlements was that at Niagara. Prior to the Revolution, Chief Joseph Brant of the Mohawk Indians lived with a body of his men near the British fort at Niagara. John Butler and his son, Walter, leaders of the notorious Tory rangers, made Fort Niagara their rendezvous, and here also gathered large numbers of Indians and Tories, from which expeditions large and small were made up to go out and ravage the upper parts of New York and Pennsylvania. At Niagara plans were made for the fearful massacre at Wyoming Valley in Pennsylvania as well as that upon Cherry Valley in upper New York State. Reputable survivors of these bloody events denied that the Butler men committed the cruel ravages with which they were charged. The Indians undoubtedly killed widely, according to their tribal customs.[22]

By 1776 five Tory women and 36 children in a starving condition had arrived at Fort Niagara. They were soon joined by hundreds of others who were either driven from home or came by choice to escape persecution. They huddled together in tents or huts of brushwood under the walls of the fort and were fed by the commissaries in the absence of the able-bodied men, most of whom, under Sir John Johnson and Colonel John Butler, were off fighting the patriots. This fort was to be a refuge for Tories all during the long war and for thirteen years afterward. The Americans did not take possession of it until 1796.[23]

The exiles who took advantage of this fort had left the new nation to the south both from fear and from lack of hope of being restored to their former homes. Colonel Allan MacLean wrote in 1783, "Colonel Butler says that none of his people will ever think of going to attend courts of law in the colonies, where they could not expect the shadow of justice . . . that they would rather go to Japan than go among the Americans, where they could never live in peace." By the next year, Butler's group showed a strength of 469 men, 111 women and 257 children. The regiment was disbanded in June of 1784, it being understood among them that they would take up their residence on lands assigned them in the immediate Niagara vicinity. Butler himself was regarded as the mainstay of the settlement. He served as judge of the district court and deputy superintendent of the Indians until his death in 1796, the year that the fort was taken over by the Americans.[24]

While this settlement was going on, a Tory named Robert Land came northward and assumed squatter's rights over property near Burlington Bay at the head of Lake Ontario. About him there is a remarkable story. Land, an ancestor of Charles Lindbergh, first lived at Cocheton, New Jersey, on the banks of the Delaware River, a successful farmer with half-grown children and what seemed to be a bright future. But the Revolution changed that. This family had no sympathy with the American rebels. The Lands were Tories, as were their neighbors, the Kane family, who lived on a farm just across the Delaware River, next to the Mordens, a Quaker family. Apparently Robert Land made no secret of his sentiments, for he was suspected of Loyalist leanings long before the war broke out. His eldest son, John, was thrown into prison and remained there throughout the war. The rest of the family were insulted, boycotted, annoyed and abused by their patriot neighbors. Meantime, Land joined the Tory forces, and his family was hard put to make a living.[25]

By the autumn of 1778, events began to reach a climax. The oats and corn were ripe, there was some hay in the barn and a few golden pumpkins spotted the nearby fields. But rumors flew that raiders were to come; it was no wonder that young Kate Land was frightened the night she heard a noise at the foot of her bed. Sitting up, she saw, by the moonlight coming through the window, a gleaming Indian spear. At first, the girl thought it was some practical joke and banteringly said, "Go away." But it was no joke. A strange voice which sounded Indian asked her to get up quickly and go to the white man's house across the river. "He want you bad," it concluded. Kate hastily dressed and went outside. No one was there. The brave girl then ran to the river, jumped into a canoe and paddled across. There were no lights at the Kane farmhouse. Entering the doorway, she stumbled over a body, felt down—it was Mr. Kane, their Loyalist friend. Then she found other bodies lying in pools of blood. The whole family had been murdered.

Kate, horrified, rushed home, and as she neared the house, she heard from a clump of bushes the same voice which had spoken to her outside her bedroom.

"Your house burn! Get children out!"

She quickly warned her mother and family, and as quietly as they could, they slipped out and into a nearby wood where they huddled together. Soon they heard voices, saw shadowy figures of Indians and white men, and watched their house go up in flames. The barn soon followed and even the grain in the fields was burned. At times the marauders came near to where the family was hiding, but failed to find them. For several days, Mrs. Land and her children hid in the woods. From what they had seen, they were convinced that the "Indians" who had fired their homestead were actually patriot neighbors disguised and seeking vengeance. Finally, hungry and exhausted, the mother and children made their way to New York City, where they remained until it was evacuated by the British. Along with other Tories, they then went to New Brunswick.

Shortly after the destruction of the farm buildings, Robert Land passed through the section, carrying dispatches for the Tories. He found only ashes on his farm and no trace of his family, so he assumed that they were dead, as he heard the Kanes were. Brokenhearted, he regretfully decided to leave the scene of his home forever. The Mordens asked him to stay, but he refused. They did stay and were also killed, even though they were peaceful Quakers. The rebel raiders pursued Land too and shot and wounded him badly, then followed his trail of blood. Convinced he was dead, the rebels so reported him, and his family in New York heard the dreadful news. The hardy father, however, dressed his wounds with herbs, and traveling only by night, made his way to Niagara and safety. There on the Canadian side of the river, he settled in 1778. He received a grant of 200 acres of land.

Within the sound of the great falls, Robert Land went to work, but thoughts of his family haunted him. Land finally

Disembarking at the site of the present city of Saint John, New Brunswick, the refugee Tories set to work at once to build new homes in this wild but inviting land. (*From a print of the painting by J. D. Kelly, in the Public Archives of Canada.*)

Shelburne, Nova Scotia, from the harbor, a century after the town was founded by Tory refugees. It blossomed into a small city of 10,000, then virtually disappeared. (*Reproduced from the Collections of the Library of Congress.*)

Captain Gideon White
(1754–1833), one of
the leaders of the
American Tory settlers
of Shelburne.

Above: After the land
was surveyed, the
Tories drew lots for
it, as shown in this
lithograph by J. E.
Laughlin. Sometimes
the more prominent
ones obtained large
sections. (*From a print
in the Public Archives
of Canada.*)

Encampment of the Loyalists at Johnston, an early Canadian settlement on the banks of the St. Lawrence River. (*From a watercolor by J. Peachey in the Public Archives of Canada.*)

This crude and comical fire engine was presented to the Tories of Shelburne by King George III. Though simple, it was useful and appreciated.

One of the houses built by the Shelburne Tories which remained standing and in use for many years. (*Both pictures reproduced from the Collections of the Library of Congress.*)

Loyalists on their way to Upper
Canada by land. Most of these
made their circuitous way through
New York State until they
reached the land still under
control of Great Britain.
(*From the C. W. Jeffreys Imperial
Oil Collection.*)

The log cabin built in Canada
near Niagara (*above*) by
Colonel Robert Land (*right*),
Tory ancestor of the American
hero Charles Lindbergh. Colonel
Land, who passed through much
danger escaping from the
colonies, found a happy ending
in Canada. (*Courtesy of the
University of Toronto Press.*)

managed to exchange his grant of land for a similar one on Lake Ontario, 40 miles away. Here in 1780, the poor Loyalist began to clear his land, and to some extent his mind, and gradually he adjusted to the strangeness of the place.

In the meantime, his eldest son John had been released from prison. He returned to the old home place in New Jersey and was allowed to live and work on it. The mother and younger children were still in New Brunswick, but not doing very well, even after seven years of residence. Like other residents of this new province, they had heard stories of the mild climate and fertile land of Upper Canada, so they decided to make their way to Niagara. They took a detour by way of New Jersey, and saw John, who now was living contentedly on the family farm. He was asked to go with them, but declined. All of the Lands were still under the impression that the father was dead. So it was as if a kind fate drew them slowly westward and to the region near the great falls. There they lived, the sons supporting the mother and sister by hunting, trapping and now and then doing work for the older settlers.

One day a wandering trader stopped by the Lands' and remarked that it seemed a coincidence that a man by the same name lived down at the end of the lake. Young Robert decided to go visit the man, thinking perhaps he might be some distant relative. The rest of the family decided to accompany him.

Down beside his cabin, the elder Robert Land was sitting outside smoking his pipe after finishing dinner. He heard a sound in the edge of the clearing and looked up. There were his wife and his family, quite grown up but still recognizable. They saw him, and it was, in a sense, like the dead greeting the dead.

In 1791, Robert Land planted a weeping willow beside his cabin to commemorate the remarkable event. The cabin was enlarged and the family settled there. By the time the willow overhung the house, the Land men held an area of a thousand acres. In time, the settlement around the cabin grew until it was called Hamilton. When the War of 1812 came, all of the Land sons, except John, fought against the United States.

In 1812, when England and the new United States were again at war, an incident which exemplifies the pioneer spirit of the Niagara Loyalists is said to have occurred. The battle of Queenston Heights was the second serious reverse of the Americans in the War of 1812, and arose out of an attempt to invade Canada across the Niagara River. According to Captain James Fitz-Gibbon of the Glengarry Light Infantry, a Mrs. Laura Secord, wife of James Secord, a Queenston Loyalist soldier, helped by her heroism to win an important victory against the advancing Americans at Beaver Dam. This story, which has fascinated Canadians ever since, tells how she had saved the life of her husband in the earlier Queenston conflict. There, Mrs. Secord said, "cannon balls were flying around me in all directions." After the battle, she found that not only was her husband wounded but their house had been plundered and other property destroyed. Two American officers forced their way into her house and remained there for some time. She overheard one of them talking about plans for a surprise attack on FitzGibbon at Beaver Dam. "That position once captured," one said, "Upper Canada is ours."

Laura Secord decided to do something with this valuable information. Since her husband was unable to go, she determined to seek out Captain FitzGibbon and tell him what she had learned. Bidding goodbye to her husband and five children, Laura, 38 years of age, "left early in the morning, walked nineteen miles in the month of June over a rough and difficult part of the country" until she came to the vicinity of Beaver Dam, not far from the present city of St. Catharines. The weather was very hot for this time of year and after a rainy season the streams were swollen and the ground like a marsh. "By this time, daylight had left me," she recalled. "Here I found all the Indians encamped; by moonlight the scene was terrifying. . . . Upon advance to the Indians, they all rose and with some yells said, 'Woman,' which made me tremble. I cannot express the awful feeling it gave me, but I did not lose my presence of mind." She went up to one of the chiefs and told him she had great news for the Canadian commander; that he must let her by or he and all of his Indians would be destroyed. After some hesitation, they let her pass through the camp, and some accompanied her to FitzGibbon. Laura then told him of the plans she had heard of the imminent American attack, and he took advantage of the 30 hours before it to lay his own plans to meet the assault. Early on the morning of June 24, the advancing Americans were discovered by Indian scouts. By 9 a.m. the invaders were attacked in their rear by 400 Caughnawaga and

Mohawk redskins. After three hours of firing at shadows in the surrounding woods, the Americans were ready to surrender but were afraid to trust themselves to the mercy of the savages. Then Captain FitzGibbon appeared with his men and the surrender was made to them. And despite the skepticism of some historians, the victory is largely credited to the courage of Laura Secord, who returned safely to her home.[26]

Not all the newcomers were so heroic, however, nor had they been so in their earlier homes in America. Some did not take any active part in behalf of the British during the Revolution but came to Canada mostly to "falsely profess an attachment to the British monarch and curse the government of the Union, for the mere purpose of thus wheedling themselves into the possession of lands." As a result, the executive council of Upper Canada ordered in 1816 that no petitions for land from sons and daughters of United Empire Loyalists would be received unless accompanied by an official certificate that the parent maintained his loyalty during the War of 1812 and was under no suspicion of aiding the enemy. "Loyalists had no monopoly on loyalty, for many later American immigrants also opposed the American invasion." Official reports stated that early Canadian settlers would make malignant representations against an angel; that some of them would not carry the chain to mark out their own lands without exorbitant pay from the government; that there was trickery in disposing of their lands and seeking further compensation; that there were land speculators and jobbers; that there were clamors, jealousies and grasping greed.[27]

Southward on the coast of Lake Erie some of the early Loyalist settlers at Long Point were of a different sort. One of these was Colonel Samuel Ryerse, whose daughter, Mrs. Amelia Harris, has left a charming narrative about life in that region. Her father had served with the loyal New Jersey Volunteers throughout the French and Indian War. Upon announcement of the Declaration of Independence, he went to New Brunswick and there married. After the Revolution, Ryerse returned to New York but found that rancorous bitterness existed against British subjects. Added to this, their four children died within eight weeks in New York. The mother later gave birth to four more, three of whom also died, leaving only Amelia. At the invitation of Governor Simcoe, Ryerse went to Canada, taking his family with him. The hardships they encountered at first were like those of a neighbor, who worked from dawn to dark, then walked three miles to fish for family food. A grandson of Amelia, John Harris, claimed that his grandfather was the first settler at Long Point. Describing the clothing of the people at that time, the younger Harris related that in the absence of regular attire the men used skins of animals. In mild weather, the girls wore a buckskin slip. A 15-year-old girl named Sally Sprague wore such a dress and, noticing that washing of clothes was done by boiling them in soap and water, one day took advantage of the absence of her parents to wash her only garment, the leather slip. The action of the heat and the soap on the leather was not what Sally expected. When she took it out of the big pot, it was a shrunken, slippery mess which she could not wear. In desperation, the slip-less girl fled into the "potato hole" under the floor, where she was later found by her embarrassed but amused parents.[28]

In a more serious vein was an occurrence which took place in the Lunenberg district of Upper Canada. A Tory named Thomas Golden reported to Governor Simcoe that on January 5, 1792, he was in Price Hunwell's barn, sitting on an upper mow of wheat, when he overheard Hunwell and a friend, Cromwell Thirty from the United States, enter the barn. Apparently they were unaware of Golden's presence, for Thirty asked Hunwell if he felt he could raise some dependable men in the area. The latter replied,

"Yes, by God, I can raise a hundred men who can be depended on, for the people are as much divided here as they were in the colonies."

Plans were then made by the two to raise the men and "burn the garrison at Oswegatchie, slip through the woods next spring, take possession of the hills above the garrison and then command all the country." When Hunwell learned later that Golden had overheard the conversation, he offered him a yoke of oxen not to tell, but Golden refused. Hunwell then admitted that he had been a soldier in the American Continental army and that his object was to open a line of communication between Fort Oswegatchie and Fort Stanwix for the purpose of an invasion of Canada, this being an intermediate time before the British had given up the western posts in the United States and while agitation for resumption of the Revolution was still going on. As a result of the testimony given to Governor Simcoe by Golden, both Hunwell and Thirty were jailed and their neighbors forced to take oaths of loyalty to Canada.[29]

With firm loyalty to the Crown, Joel Stone came to Cornwall, a town above Montreal, a few years before the foregoing episode. He was a native of Guilford, Connecticut, and was a merchant there when the Revolution broke out. He observed that his "once happy country was involved in all the dreadful horrors of an unnatural war and filling the pleasant land with desolation and blood." Yet amidst it all he was resolved, he said, "rather to forego all I could call my property in the world than flinch from my duty as a subject to the best of sovereigns; sooner to perish in the general calamity than abet in the least degree the enemies of the British Constitution." Leaving at night, he made his way to New York and there offered his services to the British. This offer was accepted in 1777 and Stone was active on Long Island, but was seized while asleep by "a company of whale-boat men" and carried to Fairfield, Connecticut, where he was imprisoned on charges of high treason. Told he was to be hanged, Stone managed to escape back to Long Island, where he was made a lieutenant in the provincial militia, being soon after promoted to captain. In 1780, he married Miss Leah Moore there, the officiating minister being Reverend Charles Inglis, rector of Trinity Church. At the close of the war, Stone went to London, leaving his wife with Mrs. William Smith, whose husband was going to Canada and later became a chief justice there.[30]

Joel Stone arrived at Cornwall in 1787 and purchased some land. For a time he was associated with Daniel Jones, a fellow Tory from Glens Falls, New York. His brother, David Jones, had been engaged to Jane McRea, the beautiful girl who was cruelly murdered by Indians on July 25, 1777, near Fort Edward, New York, while she was on her way to meet her fiance, who was with General John Burgoyne's forces advancing to the scene of the battle of Saratoga.

Joel Stone's wife died in 1792, and five years later he became interested in the widow of Abraham Dayton, who lived at Leeds near Kingston. The letters which passed between them tell of an appealing if unusual romance. Stone told of being tired of being a widower and said he was now determined to marry, "provided I can find a person whose age, character, inclinations, etc., promise to add happiness to both. You are the person I have fixed my hopes upon." Abigail Dayton replied that she had about decided to remain single, "for the world appears to be in a great tumult. . . . I lost a tender companion which I do not forget. There is no one who knows the loss of a kind friend but those that experience it. Therefore, if you think it proper to form any further acquaintance on the subject by the lines I have wrote to you, act your own pleasure."

Joel Stone's pleasure was to pursue the courtship. But he assured her that he did not wish to stand in the way, provided she should have a good offer from another. "I only trust in your good sense," he added. She had the good sense to marry him not long afterward, and they lived a happy and fruitful life for years to come.[31]

Among the American Tories, such romance was sometimes gained but often lost. Writing from the lovely Mohawk Valley, Mrs. John Cameron, a Scottish-American settler, told her friend, Mrs. Kenneth Macpherson of The Manse, Blair Athol, Perthshire, Scotland, how hard it was to depart from her picturesque home in America. "At last we are preparing to leave forever this land of my birth," she wrote. "The long, weary years of war, followed by the peace years, that have been to us worse than the time of fighting, are over." This was in May of 1785. "Our lands are confiscated and it is hard to raise money at forced sales," Mrs. Cameron continued. "We expect the journey to be long and hard and cannot tell how many weeks we will be on the road. We have four horses and John has made our big wagon as comfortable as he can. Through the forests we must trust to Indian guides. Many of Scotch origin will form the band of travellers. The children little realize the days of hardship before them and long to start off. I love friendship and neighborly kindness and am so glad that there will be no more taunting among the elders, no more bickering among the children. Bitter feelings are gone forever. Patriot or rebel we are what we see is right to each of us; conscience may make cowards. When I leave this beautiful Mohawk Valley and the lands I had hoped we would always hold, I shall hear no more the words, 'Tory and Parricide.' " Mrs. Cameron added revealingly that they hoped to found in Canada "a new Glengarry," then went on to say, "Our grandparents little thought when they sought this new land, after the risings of Prince Charlie, that a flitting would be our fate, but we must follow the old flag wherever it takes us. It is again 'The March of the Cameron Men' and wives and children must tread the hard road." [32]

Not all of the Loyalists went to places now Canadian. At first it was the intention of Governor Haldimand to found a large settlement at Detroit, but the difficulties of communication with that distant post probably proved to be insurmountable. Some of Butler's Rangers did settle there, and in 1783 the commanding officer at Detroit reported the arrival of two Loyalists named Girty and McCarty who had come to see what inducements might be offered by the British to them and others of their kind. But apparently few ever came, for in 1784, Jehu Hay, the British lieutenant governor of Detroit, reported only one Loyalist there.[33]

More settled on the site of what is now Columbus, Ohio, in a kind of reverse-refugee movement. All that part of the city of Columbus which lies east of the Scioto River and 5th Avenue on the north and Steelton on the south, some four and one-half miles, is on what is known as the "Refugee Tract" which was set apart by the United States Government for the benefit of "refugees from Canada and Nova Scotia." Odd as it may appear in view of the foregoing discussion, not all of the people who lived in Canada at the time were in favor of Britain in the American Revolution. Prominent among those in sympathy with the colonies was Colonel Edward Livingston of Montreal, a native of New York and member of the prominent Livingston family there, who had gone northward to practice law. When an American expedition under General Richard Montgomery invaded Canada in 1775, Colonel Livingston hurriedly gathered together about 300 patriots in Canada and joined Montgomery below Montreal. The fact that Montgomery, a young Irish-born professional soldier who had gone over to the American side, had married a Livingston doubtless added to the eagerness of the colonel to join his relative. The Canadian "patriots" under Livingston are said to have aided Montgomery greatly in capturning Montreal and St. John; then they went on with him to Quebec, where, in the assault on the city, Montgomery was killed and Benedict Arnold took over command. Arnold was wounded, and Daniel Morgan succeeded him in making a strong stand with the remaining Americans, but was overwhelmed at the last.

After the Quebec defeat, Colonel Livingston withdrew to New York, where he served for the remainder of the war in Washington's army. He was especially familiar with the upstate New York region and a price was put on his head by the British when they noted how effectively he was opposing the Johnson and Butler Tory forces. He was never captured, however. As a reward for his wartime services, Livingston and other refugees from Canada were given grants of land in the "Refugee Tract" on which the city of Columbus now stands. But it was not until

1789 that Congress took definite action to provide Ohio land for those in Canada who had supported the patriot side during the war. Three years later, an act was passed dividing townships into sections containing 320 acres each. The entire grant was 136,000 acres, but only about 50 claims were made, totaling 45,280 acres, by Colonel Livingston and his associates. The land was then wilderness, unsurveyed and uninhabited, and required a long and difficult journey for most claimants. Too, almost 20 years had elapsed since the war, and many who could have claimed this land had already obtained homes elsewhere or were too advanced in years to be able to take advantage of it. Some has died, but grants were issued to their heirs. Other grantees did not desire to enter the wilderness and sold their land to speculators or enterprising young men who wished to try their fortunes in the west. Finally, in 1816, all the Ohio grants which had not been claimed under the act were sold as public lands.[34]

As stated earlier, the English government had taken steps to aid its refugee Loyalists soon after the peace treaty in 1783, when the coalition government of Lord North and Charles James Fox appointed a royal commission to inquire into the losses and service of all who had suffered in America as a result of attachment to Britain. The long inquiry did not end until 1790, and members of the commission visited New York and Canada in their thorough search. In all, the commissioners examined about 5,000 claims, and in the end they granted 3,112,455 pounds in addition to the lands and positions given out. Merged into one country in 1867, the provinces of Nova Scotia, New Brunswick, and Prince Edward Island united with Ontario and Quebec to form the Dominion of Canada, still loyal to the Crown.

> *The world shall bless their heritage*
> *Fair Canada, who found in thee,*
> *Through struggles clearing forest lands*
> *Earth's happiest home of loyalty.*[35]

In modern Canada, ex-soldiers with Loyalist ancestry are fond of talking about theories of maneuver which might have won the American Revolution for the British. UEL (United Empire Loyalist) members wear the monogram of George III and like to put the initials UE after their names. They open meetings by singing "God Save the King" before the Union Jack.

[5]

IN ENGLAND

Better it were to quit the shore
And go beyond the sea, sir,
In Britain they will love us more
Than here we e'er can be, sir.

THIS RHYME WHICH APPEARED in the *Pennsylvania Packet* on
November 20, 1781, may have been written with the best of
intentions, but it proved to be far from true. England was officially the mother country for Tories as well as most other Americans; her maternal relationship, however, turned out to be
parchment deep. For of all the Tory exiles, those who went to
England were probably the most unhappy.

The deep irony of this situation is brought out in the
words of a report by an American Congressional committee to
Silas Deane, the diplomatic agent. "Tories are now of various
kinds and various principles. Some are so from real attachment
to Britain, some from interested views, many, very many, from
fear of the British force; some because they are dissatisfied with
the general measures of Congress; more because they disapprove
of the men in power and the measures in their respective
states." [1] Only a few months before this was written, the first
contingent of American Tories had embarked with General Sir
William Howe in the British ships which evacuated Boston and
took them to Canada and England. Here they were to test the
"real attachment" and to find it sorely wanting in both directions. Those who went on to the British Isles were generally the
more affluent who could afford to do so. They were significant
beyond their numbers, being former colonial judges, clergymen, customs collectors and a few royal governors. These were
joined by fellow Loyalists from the Middle colonies and the

South, until it was estimated that in 1776, there were almost 3,000 of them in England.[2]

Prominent among these exiles was Governor Thomas Hutchinson of Massachusetts; his kinsman, Judge Peter Oliver; Thomas Flucker, Provincial Secretary of Massachusetts and the father-in-law of Henry Knox; Judge Jonathan Sewall, the brother-in-law of John Hancock; and Sir Egerton Leigh of South Carolina, son-in-law of Henry Laurens, president of the Continental Congress. Other Tories of similar stature included the brother-in-law of Gouverneur Morris, Isaac Wilkins; Judge Samuel Curwen and Colonel Richard Saltonstall of Massachusetts. Myles Cooper, president of King's College, now Columbia University, fled to England early in the war. John Tabor Kempe, Judge Thomas Jones (who wrote a history of New York from the Tory viewpoint), William Aztell, Andrew Elliot, Samuel Quincy, Abraham C. Cuyler, and Peter Van Schaack, all of high standing, also left for the motherland, as did military officers Oliver De Lancey, John Harris Cruger and Archibald Hamilton. Some of these individuals were too old or infirm to take an active part in the war.

While some of these had hoped, like Hutchinson, to play a part in the political life of England and perhaps influence the colonial situation, most saw England as simply a refuge. Peter Oliver visited the Tower of London and noticed that the lions which were kept in the moat had lost their ferociousness. "If the omnipotent American Congress were caged in the same manner," he said wishfully, "would their diabolical ferocity subside?"[3]

Such remarks by the exiles must be considered in the light of the loneliness which they felt. Although they were loyal to the Crown, they were not at home in this strange land. They had been uprooted from their homes and had made a hurried and worried departure. For most of them, London was an uncomfortable place with damp and friendless streets. Those without sufficient means—and this was the majority—stayed in plain lodgings, without any definite occupation, pining away for all they had left behind and eating their souls out in painful solitude. In this strange city, they felt more American than ever, yet of the America they had left, they were not a part.[4]

Added to the loneliness of being a stranger in England was the distance of many of the refugees from their families whom they had left in America. Judge Sewall declared that he would rather see his two sons than to know what the future held for himself. His rough treatment by the patriots left him embittered until the end of his life, and although he longed to see his old home, he admired the freedom of speech of England, where "my chimney sweep can condemn the conduct of the King's Ministers, members of Parliament and even of the King himself." Sewall was convinced that no good would ever come to him and his fellow Tories in the former colonies. He wrote to a friend, "As to Massachusetts Bay, I wish it well, but I wish never to see it again till I return at the millennium. The harsh conduct of my countrymen has given me a dose I shall never get over— God mend them and bless them—but let me never be cursed with a residence among them again." [5]

Sewall was impressed with the great display of wealth in London and he bemoaned the fact that even with 500 pounds a year, this would be but a drop in the bucket of expenses. He found the city to be friendless and godless and decided it was no place for a man who had been used to small and simple Boston. Bred in the comparatively Puritan atmosphere of New England, the Massachusetts Tories were appalled at the immorality evident in the big city. They complained of corruption, debauchery, luxury, pride and riches, and felt that the place was lost beyond recall. The size of the city and its millions of people overwhelmed the newcomers. Once, Nelly Boucher, wife of Jonathan, asked him to wait with her until a crowd had passed. He explained to her that the crowd was the same as usual and would just keep passing.

Samuel Curwen left his wife in America, and perhaps with good reason, for he later said he did not wish to see her again or ever to be buried near her for fear of having to see her first on the Resurrection morning. Curwen found that there were so many New Englanders already in London that it seemed a great deal like Boston. Certain taverns, such as the Jerusalem Tavern, St. Clemens Coffee House, and the New England Coffee House on Threadneedle Street, had become favorite meeting places for the American Tories. Curwen joined the New England Club, which met for dinner weekly at the Adelphi Tavern on the Strand, and had tea with John Singleton Copley, the expatriate painter who had left Boston in 1775; and he also met Benjamin West, the artist, whom he admired very much. Curwen left a long journal of his life in England, some typical excerpts from which follow:

March 13, 1776	Heard "The Messiah" at Covent Gardens
14	Surveyed the New River at Spafields
19	Attended lecture at Salter's Hall
April 1	At Governor Hutchinson's
4	At our New England Club dinner. 25 members present
May 14	Viewed pictures in exhibition room at the Strand
15	Visited Pinchbeck's to view stained glass
June 10	My finances visibly lessening. Wish I could remove from this expensive country.
19	To the British Museum accompanied by Mr. Danforth
July 14	Worshipped at All Hallows, the officiating priest being Mr. Peters, refugee from Hebron, Connecticut.
15	Visited Stonehenge
December 31	My little bark is in imminent danger of being stranded unless the wind shifts quickly. In plain English, my purse is nearly empty.
Sept. 14, 1777	In afternoon attended once more John Wesley, having the heavens for his canopy.
October 21	Went coursing with two greyhounds. A ramble of 15 miles over hedge and fence.
December 18, 1778	The situation of the American Loyalists, I confess, is enough to have provoked Job's wife, if not Job himself; but still we must be men, philosophers and Christians.
March 23, 1781	Today got a sight of that extraordinary person, Lord North. Heard Burke speak.
June 28	Saw more Bostonians at the New England Coffee House.[6]

While Curwen kept fairly busy, many of the Loyalists were not so resourceful. Some almost became obsessed by a fear of dying and being buried in England. A former Boston boardinghouse keeper, Andrew Jolly, on his deathbed, stated that when the war was over, he hoped his remains would be taken to America for interment. Charles Paxton, a one-time customs commissioner, offered 100 guineas to be buried beside his parents in Boston. In order to console Paxton—although he, too, fervently wished to be buried in America—Governor Hutchinson said that if he had a bad leg or tooth, he would not care what became of them and so would not be concerned with his other bones.[7]

Despair led to desperation and personal rancor among the Tories. Lloyd Dulany of Maryland, a former friend of George Washington, went to England. There he was slandered by the Reverend Bennet Allen, a former rector of a Maryland church, who charged that part of the Dulany family remained in America to prevent their property from being confiscated, while other members sought refuge in England in order to save their large possessions, no matter which side won. Upon learning of this charge, Dulany challenged Allen to a duel. It took place in Hyde Park in London and Dulany received a wound from which he later died.

Besides those who took such a positive stand, there were many persons in America who were either undecided regarding the merits of the Revolution or who changed their minds at some point. The career of the Reverend Jacob Duché of Philadelphia illustrates the latter situation. He had been an eloquent preacher and was the brother-in-law of Francis Hopkinson, a signer of the Declaration of Independence and America's first musical composer of note. Duché was elected chaplain of the Continental Congress and once invoked a blessing on the American states in a sermon which moved John Adams. When General William Howe entered Philadelphia with his troops, Duché suddenly changed his view, offered prayers for King George and wrote Washington urging him to convince Congress to abandon the war, abrogate the Declaration of Independence, as the head of the army, negotiate for peace, and, finally, resign his command. Washington turned the letter over to Congress, and as a result, the Reverend Duché was banished and his property confiscated. He went to England, where he became chaplain of an orphan asylum in London and continued to deliver sermons so eloquent that Mrs. John Adams went to hear them while she was there.[8]

Conversations among the exiles, especially those in which comparisons between England and America were made, were a staple of daily life. Often these loyal but displaced colonists joined with the rebels in denouncing the narrow outlook of the English. The Loyalists found that the common run of people whom they met were often ignorant and apathetic toward national questions of importance. Peggy Hutchinson, daughter of the former governor, told of a family dispute over which was better, old or New England. She and her father favored the latter, he noting that it was not propitious to be a good Christian in England. Such an attitude on the part of Hutchinson is not easy to understand. When he arrived in England, he was received personally by the king, and often afterward visited at court where he was treated with great kindness by both King George and Queen Charlotte. A baronetcy was offered him but he declined it because of insufficient means to support the title, his property in America having been confiscated. But he was given a pension of 500 pounds a year, not so great a sum when divided among the 25 members of his sons' and daughters' families who were dependent upon him. In daily contact with Hutchinson were Loyalist exiles, once men of wealth and position, now discredited, disheartened and in danger of starvation. Thomas Hutchinson himself died in 1780, a broken and pitiable man who had longed to return to America but instead was buried at Croydon near London. John Singleton Copley was also buried in the Hutchinson family tomb at Croydon.

In the breaking up of families, there is the poignant example of Samuel Quincy of Massachusetts, a friend and addressor of Governor Hutchinson, who left his wife behind when he fled the colonies for England and then spent years in pitiful efforts to unite with her again. Born in what is now Quincy, a town named after his family, Samuel Quincy was a brother of Josiah Quincy, who with John Adams made the courageous defense of Captain Thomas Preston, commander of the British troops at the Boston Massacre. A Harvard graduate, Samuel had become solicitor general of Massachusetts, and it was his duty to prosecute Preston while his brother defended him, the attorneys on this occasion reversing their political positions, since Josiah later became an ardent patriot while Samuel remained a staunch Tory. Their father, Josiah Quincy, Sr., was also a patriot and was saddened by the stand of his son who chose to remain loyal to the Crown.

By May of 1775, Samuel Quincy had decided to leave his native land where his views were becoming increasingly unpopular. His sister, Mrs. H. Lincoln, urged him to change his mind. "Let it not be told in America," she told him, "and let it not be published in Great Britain that a brother . . . fled from his country—the wife of his youth—the children of his affection —and from his aged sire, already bowed down with the loss of two sons." But Quincy had made up his mind. He wrote Henry Hill, the brother of his wife, "I am going, my dear friend, to quit the habitation where I have been so long encircled with the dearest connections. I am going to hazard the unstable element and for a while to change the scene—whether it will be prosperous or adverse is not for me to determine. I pray God to sustain my integrity and preserve me from temptation." [9]

By July 25, Quincy was in London. He informed Hill that "everything is peace here; I wish it may soon return to my dear, dear country." But he did not like the way the colonial cause was being treated in England, observing that every proposal made to advance their cause and redress their grievances was spurned unless attended by concessions. He believed that the people of England were united in their attachment to the king. To them, the "political subordination of the colonies" was a sacred tenet, and even the yeomen, merchants and manufacturers who had previously been advocates for America were beginning to murmur against them and to say in substance that while the colonies were reasonable in their demands and had real burdens, the English were willing to support them, but now could not "venture to assist American *independence,* lest we lay a foundation for the destruction of both countries." Quincy felt that the consequences of the recent battle of Bunker Hill eventually would be disastrous for the Americans, and added that he viewed the "dangerous and doubtful struggle with fear and trembling; I lament it with the most cordial affection for my native country, and feel sensibly for my friends. But I am aware it is my duty patiently to submit the event as it may be governed by the all-wise counsels of that Being 'who ruleth in the heavens and is the God of armies.' " [10]

As the months passed, Quincy began to lament the separation from his wife, Sophia. He wrote her that it had become almost too burdensome to bear. "But I see many faces I have been used to," he wrote. "America seems to be transplanted to London. St. James Park wears an appearance not unlike the Exchange in Boston." After repeating that he was very lonely without her and his children, he commented upon her previous remark that his countrymen would not take his life if he returned. He said that he had never considered difference of opinion to be a capital offense, adding that nonetheless he was not afraid to return, had never been, was willing to die if necessary but thought he had done nothing to deserve death. Then Quincy deplored the fact that although it had been almost two years since he had left, he had heard nothing of his father or family at Braintree. "God bless you all," he said at the ending of his letter. "Live happy, and think I am as much so as my long absence from you will permit." [11]

It appears that at about this time, Quincy received word that his property in Massachusetts had been taken over by others, thus adding to his "depredations." But his main concern was still the separation from his wife and family. She had apparently considered going to join him, for he told her in late 1777, "If things should not wear a more promising aspect at the opening of next year, by all means summon resolution to cross the ocean. Mrs. Hutchinson tells me this is your greatest dread. Believe me, you will find it infinitely less terrifying and dangerous than imagination suggests. Nor is the ocean more tumultuous than the times. The recompense which awaits you shall be the careful attention of friendship and the embrace of a faithful partner." He assured her he meant to return to America when he could if there was a chance for him to make a living there, but at the same time he did not rule out the possibility of accepting a position in England if one should offer itself.

Meanwhile Quincy occupied his time in commendable attachment to the political affairs of London. He went to Parliament and heard what he considered many fine speeches on both sides of the colonial question. "But it were to be wished," he astutely observed, "that great men were more activated by principle and less by motives of interest and the pride of resentment." He visited the House of Lords on one occasion and "saw the great Lord Chatham come down to the house tottering on his feeble limbs to give his voice and advice on the present critical and dangerous exigence of the state." Chatham listened to a fiery speech by the Duke of Richmond, then suddenly fainted, and was carried out "pale and speechless." It was soon after this that Chatham died.

One reason Quincy did not wish to return to America was a mixture of pride and a dread of loss of stature. He remarked that he would like to return but could not until he was convinced that he would be as well thought of as he deserved to be. "I am too proud to live despised where I was once respected," he said, "an object, instead of a child of favor, a beggar, where I have always been a Gentleman." The unhappy exile heard that his family were now in straitened circumstances and expressed his concern about it. He explained that when he left the colonies, he had no expectations of being absent more than a few months, "little thinking operations of such magnitude would have followed in so quick a succession. I left it from principle," he declared, "and with a view of emolument. If I have been mistaken, it is my misfortune, not my fault." [12]

But if Quincy blamed the patriots in his native land, he still longed for a reconciliation between them and England, as well as between him and his family. Like other exiles of high standing, he gave much thought and effort to the problems which separated the mother country and its colonies. He hoped fervently for "a reunion of the two countries whose interests," he wrote with perspicacity, "in my opinion, can never be divided. I have lived to see the beginning and thus far the progress of this cruel convulsion; my prayer is that I may live to see the end of it. It has produced effects wonderful and illustrious; in some of which we may discern and admire the great hand of Providence; in others the havoc of corrupt passions and ambition. Devastation and death are inseparable attendants in the train of war." He pointed out to his wife that there are many things in this world which people are obliged and enabled to encounter and said that such trials brought out the best lesson of philosophy and religion—resignation.

This was evidently the attitude which Samuel Quincy adopted, lonely and unhappy in a strange land. But he had interesting company at least part of the time. He wrote to Sophia about the Jonathan Sewalls, who lived with him in London until their little daughter died. Then they moved to Bristol. Copley lived just across the street from Quincy. Thomas Flucker and his family lived at Brompton, about a mile away.

Such distinguished company, however, could not remove

the pain of absence and separation. When Quincy learned that Massachusetts had passed an act prohibiting the return of those who had left it since April 19, 1775, the date of the battles of Lexington and Concord, and had "joined the enemy," he wrote to Sophia that he was not sure what was meant by "joining the enemy. The love of one's country," he continued, "and solicitude for its welfare, are natural and laudable affections; to lose its good opinion is at once unhappy and attended with many ill consequences; how much more unfortunate to be forever excluded from it without offence." Thus his conscience was clear, but it must not have been comforted by the message from his friend John Amory in Boston that he had supplied Sophia with 65 pounds to help out financially. In return, Quincy commented that she had given "many kisses, for which he will not ask my pardon, but he has my forgiveness. At the same time, he has excited my envy." [13]

The Massachusetts act of banishment, the passing of time and the painfulness of his separation pressed upon Quincy and drove him to decision. He obviously cared for his wife and family, but his mind seems to have been occupied most with the problem of what he should do in regard to a career. He considered returning to America and entering one of the Southern colonies, but the climate there, the lack of friends, the uncertainty of being able to establish a business, and the form of government which he might have to live under, turned him away from that prospect. "But to stay longer in England," he cried, "absent from my friends and family, with a bare subsistence, inactive, without prospects and useless to myself and the world, was death to me!" From this depth of desperate anguish, the exile burst into poetry:

> *Remote, unfriendly, melancholies grow,*
> *Where mountains rise and rude waters flow.*
> *Where'er I go, whatever realms I see,*
> *My heart untravelled, fondly turns to thee.*
> *Still to Sophia turns, with ceaseless pain*
> *And drags with each remove a lengthened chain.*[14]

Samuel Quincy decided to go to the West Indies. There he had relatives and friends and felt that this situation would make the islands less of a strange place. He confirmed that the Massachusetts act of proscription shut the door against him to his own country. Through friends he obtained the position of Comptroller of the Customs of the Port of Parham in Antigua, an important and euphonious-sounding assignment. When settled, he wrote Sophia, he hoped to send for her. "I grow old too fast to think of waiting longer for the moving of the waters," he continued, still in poetic vein, "and have therefore cast my bread upon them, thus in hopes that at last, after many days, I may find it."

He sent his father his affectionate regards, although apparently he had never heard from the parent-turned-patriot. Quincy also asked to be remembered to his mother and his children and gave instructions for disposal of his property. He seemed to feel a finality in this important step he was taking, especially since it did not lead him home. Recalling that it had now been four years since he had left Boston, Quincy noted that he had been racked by misfortunes and feelings of distress for his family and friends but admitted that despite this, a good providence had blessed him with health and that kind friends had comforted him. "If I have not been in affluence, I have been above want," he stated, "and happy in the esteem of numbers in this kingdom to whom I was altogether a stranger." He philosophized that "old friendships are indeed valuable and the loss of them to be regretted, but new ones have also their pleasure." [15]

Unfortunately a fleet bound for the West Indies had already sailed from England, so Quincy boarded a cutter in pursuit on June 16, 1779. This proved to be a futile move, for the chase became a "Crusoe voyage"; the ship ran out of provisions and the voyager found himself hungry for three days, also "without drink, without beds and without success." Quincy had to return to England and wait six months until the next fleet set out, but this was one of 100-sail, and he had what he termed a "beautiful" voyage to Barbados, which was reached in eight weeks. This island he found "desolated by excess of cultivation, blast worms, ants and droughts." He arrived at Antigua on February 24, where he set himself up in his new position and also served as a barrister. Quincy found that his reputation as one of the attorneys in the Captain Preston case in Boston had preceded him and helped him to obtain legal business. But he had to live in a house which he described as "not so handsome as what was once my barn." However, he won a case against the governor general and this so enhanced his reputation he was able to increase greatly his fees. In a letter to his wife, he "summoned" her to the West Indies but warned that she would find "no fine fresh butter, no changes of poultry, no wild geese, pheasant or duck, but good pork, beef, fish and fruit." Apparently there were predatory men on Antigua, for Quincy warned Sophia, perhaps with tongue in cheek, that she might feel "the rude talons of an ungentle tar or rapacious Buccaneer." He told her that not only did he have affection for her but frankly admitted that he needed her and his family for the purpose of prestige! [16]

By the middle of 1781, Sophia still had not joined her husband. He reminded her that they had now been separated six years and urged her to come, but again pointed out the hardships to be encountered. Evidently she took his warnings seriously or did not wish sufficiently to risk the journey, for she did not go. Doubtless the political differences of herself and family as well as that of the other Quincys also influenced her to stay. At any rate, she died in November of 1782 in Massachusetts, without ever seeing Samuel again. As he wrote her brother, his attitude was sorrowful but resigned. This was the climax to his bitter misfortunes. "To die is the lot of humanity," he observed. . . . "If the events of life were under our control, it is probable we should endeavor to govern them to the purpose of our views. In that case I should soon be in the society of my nearest friends; it would be immaterial to me in what part of the world, for I have long since learned that happiness is not confined to any particular spot: diffused equally through the immense space of air and earth, the animal parts of creation, whether rational or brute, possess it in every region; and most likely were we permitted to carve for ouselves, our fortunes would still be more chequered than they are." [17]

So readjusted to life was Samuel Quincy that he married again, this time the widow of Abraham Chadwell of Antigua. The second wife evidently was quite attached to him and he seems to have had a rather happy and successful second career in this chosen island of the British West Indies. In 1789, the year that the United States Constitution went into effect, Quincy interestingly delivered a damning indictment of the new document. "I am exceedingly sorry to hear of the distracted political situation," he stated. "A constitution founded on mere republican principles has always appeared to me a many-sided monster, and tho ever applauded by a Franklin, a Price and a Priestley, that in the end it must become a suicide. Mankind do not in experience appear formed for that finer system, which in theory by the nice adjustment of its parts promises permanency and repose. The passions, prejudices and interests of some will always be in opposition to others, especially if they are in place. This, it may be said, is the case in all governments, but I think less so in a monarchy than under a republican code. The people at large feel an overbalance of power in their own favor; they will naturally endeavor to ease themselves of all expenses which are not lucrative to them, and retrench the gains of others, whether the reward of merit or genius, or the wages of a hireling."

Within three weeks after writing the foregoing, Samuel Quincy became ill and set sail for England in order to try to restore his health. His wife accompanied him but the effort was unsuccessful, for he died within sight of the English coast. He was buried at Bristol. His widow was so upset that she immediately re-embarked for the West Indies, but found it a tempestuous voyage. Reportedly, the violence of the storms and the grief for her late husband were too much for her, and she died on the homeward passage.

Thus the life of this prominent Tory ended, away from his former home, on August 9, 1789, at the age of 55. His philosophy of life was evidently sincere and is expressed in some of his last words to a relative in Massachusetts. "Keep alive the cause of truth, of reason, of virtue and of liberty, if I may be permitted to use that name, who have by some injuriously been thought in a conspiracy against it. This is the path of duty and will be the source of blessing." [18]

Whether England seemed a blessing or curse depended often on the fortunes of the Loyalists. Had the affluent ones been able to transfer their American wealth overseas, doubtless their view of the older country would have been more generous. Sensitive and hurt, fearful of the future, they naturally looked with concern upon their new associates. Some of the Americans found the English friendly and well-bred, others thought them to be cold and heartless. Few if any of the exiles really felt at home.

Most of them were too proud to receive gifts without being uncomfortable in regard to reciprocating, and this lack of ease was conveyed to their hosts as well. It was one thing to be a visitor but quite another matter to appear as a displaced sort of invader come to stay. The Loyalists were amazed at the brutal prize fights, the rowdy scenes at English elections, and especially at loud boasts and threats against Americans, who were generally thought to inhabit a place where convicts had been dumped. Even the loyal Americans were often mistaken for rebels or spies. They in turn became critical and resentful of the sharp-spoken residents. Such asperity was heightened by the necessity of most of the newcomers to spend many months shivering over a meager fire or no heat at all, whereas back in America most of them had enjoyed huge blazing hearths with plenty of oak and walnut logs to enhance the cheerfulness. Ward Chipman had already observed that England was the worst place in the world to be without money.

While London was too large for them, the countryside, especially in winter, was too bleak. Seeking moderate-priced and medium-sized places, the restless Loyalists searched for English counterparts of their hospitable American towns and usually never found them. The dialects of parts of England and Scotland were hard for them to understand, as were the sometimes coarse and forbidding features of many of the local people. The class system also appeared unjust to the Americans and they could not understand the attention paid to the various ranks of royalty. For example, in New England it was perfectly respectable for educated men to be engaged in trade, but in old England, the upper classes looked down upon such former colonial merchants as Samuel Curwen. When Curwen explained that he had also been a judge of the admiralty court, his social stature grew.

Bristol was a favorite place with many Loyalists, probably because it reminded them of their homes. By the time the Revolution was underway, Bristol was the second city in England, with 5,000 parliamentary electors. It had long been the chief port for colonial trade. A handbill dated October 4, 1774, advertises the fact that its merchants, some of whom held mortgages on colonial plantations, wished to be represented by a man who knew commerce and had the right position on America.

WANTED IMMEDIATELY

one other candidate

to represent

this fallen city in Parliament

He must be a wild, dissipated, uncultivated American, without abilities, application, connection, interest or qualification: He must also be debauched, debilitated, vain and insincere: He is not required to be either an historian, grammarian or an orator; if he can on any public meeting repeatedly exclaim *My Good God Gentlemen!* He will be sure to meet with encouragement and support on this important occasion, even from those who on any other, have insulted, abused and rejected him as undeserving any confidence, connection or regard.

CIVIS

Jonathan Sewall was particularly fond of Bristol and remarked that he intended to remain there "till the restoration of peace and perhaps till the restoration of all things." [19]

All too much of the property of the Tories in America was never restored. Probably none felt this loss more acutely than the wealthy Philipse family of New York, the manor house of which still graces the suburban city of Yonkers on the Hudson just above New York City. For over a century, from 1672 to 1778, the family, headed first by Frederick Philipse, held title to the vast property. During that period, the family was among the leading ones of the colony, exercising an important influence in its history. The home was located on the colony's first great highway and was a conspicuous landmark, sheltering many of the great figures of the period. The Philipse Manor also consisted of surrounding farms, mills, tenants' residences, and a church, and was populated by slaves, cattle, horses and swine. Between the eastern side of the house and the old Post Road, there stretched a velvety lawn with garden terraces and chestnut trees. On either side were laid out formal gardens and ornate grounds dotted with spreading trees, rare shrubs and beautiful flowers. Among these wound graveled walkways bordered with boxwood. To the west of the huge house, the green yard sloped to the river, with here and there a fine tree interspersing the area under which deer were wont to graze in peaceful foraging. The windows of the manor house looked out upon grand views in all four directions. Inside the structure, the walls were wainscotted and the ceilings adorned with arabesque work in relief. The main entrance halls were eleven feet wide and had broad staircases in proportion, with mahogany hand rails and balusters, giving an air of grandeur which impressed all who entered.[20]

So did Philipse Manor come down to Frederick, who was called the Second Lord of the Manor (a territorial title), in the middle of the eighteenth century. Among the visitors to see the pretty daughters of the head of the house was a young man named Beverly Robinson who had come to New York from Virginia. Robinson paid court to Susannah, eldest of the daughters, and they were married in 1750. He took her to live in his new home which was just across the Hudson from West Point. Robinson was opposed to the oppressive measures of the British ministry in regard to the colonies, but he was also opposed to separation from the mother country. Against the advice of friends who wished to see him at more peaceful pursuits, he entered the British military service and raised a regiment in New York which became known as the Loyal American Regiment, a euphonious if misleading title. He became colonel of the outfit, and his son, Beverly Robinson, Jr., lieutenant colonel.

In the story of Benedict Arnold's treason, the name of the elder Beverly Robinson occurs again and again, and it is believed that Arnold approached him on the subject before deciding to go over to the British side. It was Robinson who accompanied Major John André to Dobbs Ferry to meet Arnold, but this meeting failed to take place because of an accident. After the trial and conviction of André by an American court-martial, Robinson was part of the delegation sent to General Washington by Sir Henry Clinton to plead for the life of the young and well-liked spy. Washington had known Robinson before the war, had borrowed money from him, and had called on his sister-in-law before she married. But such relationships carried no weight with the stern commander of the American forces. After the war, Robinson and his family went to England, where he was awarded 17,000 pounds as payment for his wife's part of the Philipse estate. They lived unhappily in retirement abroad and he died in England at the age of 70, Susannah outliving him by 30 years, dying at the age of 94 in 1822.

Another attractive member of the Philipse family was

Mary, considered one of the most beautiful and accomplished young women in New York at that time. She is said to have been the inspiration for "Frances" in *The Spy* by James Fenimore Cooper. According to Jared Sparks and others, Miss Philipse, at age 26, had among her admirers George Washington, then a colonel in the Virginia militia visiting in New York. The future President met Mary Philipse at the home of Beverly Robinson. The fact that she owned some 51,000 acres of land doubtless did not detract from her attractiveness to the practical Washington. He lingered a few days but left before any understanding was reached, although it is felt that there was some thought on their part of a match. Washington returned to Virginia and learned within a few months that she was married to Captain Roger Morris, who, like Washington, had once served under General Edward Braddock. Washington Irving commented about Washington: "That he was an open admirer of Miss Philipse is an historical fact; that he sought her hand but was refused is traditional but not very probable." [21]

In a conversation with a descendant of Mrs. Morris, Lorenzo Sabine said that he was told, "Her fate, how different had she married Washington." He replied instantly, "You mistake, sir. My aunt Morris had immense influence over everybody; and had she become the wife of the Leader in the Rebellion, which cost our family millions, *he* would not have been a Traitor; *she* would have prevented that, be assured, sir." In similar vein regarding Philipse Manor, Sabine speculated, "Had the old families continued their rule; had the 13 colonies continued dependent; had the resources of the American continent been developed only as the mother country permitted; had population, wealth, the facilities for transportation, manufactures and commerce increased only as in colonial possessions they ever have, and still do—how much would . . . additional years of colonial vassalage have added to the value of the Manor?" [22]

What value was to be added to the manor was mainly sentimental, for the fortunes of war and confiscation sealed its fate. But in the meantime, Mary Philipse became the bride of one who opposed the new order. Her wedding to Roger Morris took place in a brilliant ceremony within the manor hall and was one of the major social events of the province. Though the weather was mild, the sleighing was good and the feast a delight. Their honeymoon was a short one because Captain Morris was soon to become involved in the French and Indian War. In the meantime, during the years from 1758 to 1775, he divided his time between public affairs and the management of his own and his wife's large properties, and these years were the happiest in the lives of the handsome and wealthy couple.

At the outbreak of the Revolution, Morris became a colonel in the British service and went to England within a month after the battles of Lexington and Concord, after placing Mary and their children in the care of relatives. From London he wrote her with the same feelings of regret and loneliness that other Tories expressed in similar conditions: "God Almighty grant that some fortunate circumstance will bring about a suspension of hostilities. As to myself, I breathe only. Pleasure can I have none until I am back with you. How much I miss you! Your repeated remarks of tender love and esteem so daily occur to my mind that I am totally unhinged. Only imagine that I who, as you well know, never thought myself so happy anywhere as under my own roof, have now no home and am a wanderer from day to day." Later Colonel Morris added, "My chief wish is to spend the remainder of my days with you, whose prudency is my great comfort and whose kindness in sharing with patience and resignation these misfortunes which we have not brought upon ourselves is never failing." [23]

After her husband went to England, Mrs. Morris spent part of the time with her sister-in-law at the manor hall. During this time, the American forces were nearby, and in an official letter to Mrs. Philipse, General Washington took occasion to pen a postscript, "I beg the favor of having my compliments presented to Mrs. Morris," showing that he still remembered the belle of his younger and happier days. In December of 1777, Colonel Morris returned to New York from England and was appointed inspector of claims of refugees. But at the end of the war, his property having been confiscated, he and his wife went to England and settled in Yorkshire near General Oliver De Lancey, another American Tory who had also fled from the wrath of the patriots. Colonel Morris died in 1794 at the age of 67, the same as that of his old friend George Washington when he passed on five years later. But his wife, Mary, lived to be 95 and died in 1825. Both were buried in England.

The Morris family lived a much easier life in England than most Tories, if a London newspaper of the time is to be believed. "The Loyalists in this country," a letter to the paper stated, "are most shamefully and traitorously abandoned. Our fears at present surpass all description. Never was there upon the face of the earth a set of wretches in a more deplorable situation. Deprived of all the hope of future comfort or safety, either for themselves or their unhappy wives and children, many have lost their senses and now are in a state of perfect madness. Some have put a period to their miserable existence by drowning, shooting and hanging themselves, leaving their unfortunate wives and helpless infants destitute of bread to support them." [24]

Nor was the prime minister of Great Britain without knowledge of these conditions. At about this same time, May 19, 1783, Samuel Curwen entered in his *Journal*, "Informed that the refugees', or as they affect to denominate themselves, loyalists', petition to Parliament is presented and supported by Lord North and all in administration, that all who have pensions may receive them by their agents, go where they will, even if they shall return to either of the United States."

"Such is the *lenity* of this land of *tyranny*," wrote Jonathan Sewall to Ward Chipman in a similar if ironic vein about England, "that enemies or rebels have free ingress, egress and regress." Then he continued, "You know the Israelites hankered after the leeks and onions of Egypt, their native land—so do we Americans after the nuts, cranberries and apples of America. Could you next autumn, send me two or three barrels of Newton pippins, large and round, a few of our American walnuts, commonly called shagbarks, and a few cranberries?" Then in a fatalistic turn, he commented, "Let wars and rebellion continue, let my little all go, let me be banished from my native country which heaven knows I dearly love, give me my life till my dear boys are upon their own legs, and take it heaven when you please." [25]

Sewall may have been willing to give up during his exile, but not before he delivered himself of some fiery comment to Chipman about the new government in America. "Republican governments are too vigilant and too despotic to leave a possibility of being overturned by their own subjects," he observed. "The mass of people can never disturb the mildest government without able leaders to direct their fury, the mere effect of instinct and passion. These, when put in motion by ambitious politicians, form that Leviathan whose strength is irresistible, but the demagogues who raised the tempest can at all times,

'*ride in the whirlwind and direct the storm*' at their pleasure—
and when their ends are obtained, can bridle, saddle, load, whip
and spur this mighty beast, the Vulgar, with as much ease and as
effectively as if they were a herd of jackasses—aye, and more
easily too, for I verily believe four or five thousand jackasses
would kick and bray with more obstinate resolution and in
short make a more noble resistance to the curb and whip than a
herd of men consisting of the same or any given number, and I
would sooner undertake to subject to my sovereign will, a herd
of the latter than of the former. . . . Look back, Chip, to the
beginning of the American Troubles and trace them down to
independence and say whether you don't see clearly the mark of
the Beast, Jackass, on the forehead of every American below a
committeeman." [26]

At least, Sewall was apparently in good health even though
his mind was obviously disturbed by American events. Other
Loyalists were not so fortunate, some of them becoming ill on
the ships which took them abroad. For example, the commander of a transport vessel, William Falconer, reported ten
Tories on his ship as dangerously ill with "gail fevers," which
was probably typhus, while three others had died from it. His
record shows three to have been ill with diarrhea, and there
were thirteen infected with venereal diseases, seventeen con-
valescents and eight sick children.[27]

Physical ailments were not among the points of complaint
most frequently mentioned by the exiles. At first, the more
prominent, such as Thomas Hutchinson, felt like joining the
English establishment and becoming an active part of it. After
all, he had had an interview with the king and with Lord North
as well as other ministers, had been given an honorary degree by
Oxford University and in general had been lionized almost like
a visiting head of state. He even admitted that he had been
tempted to forget that he was an American and was urged to
forget about that faraway place and embrace old England as his
new home. But the newness wore off, less attention was paid
to him in the hurly-burly of the war efforts, and within himself
the able and loyal public servant felt an increased longing for
his home. By the time he had stayed in England for more than a
year, Hutchinson had no illusions about the place and realized
that he and his fellow Tories were not needed or even much
desired. "I had rather live at Milton than at Kew," he wrote in
his homesickness. "My thoughts day and night are upon New

England which is in my heart in as strong characters as Calais was upon Queen Mary's." [28]

Nor was it as easy to live and get around. Samuel Curwen complained that it took him three weeks to secure permission to see the British Museum. Of course Curwen traveled more than the average exile and was a keen observer who wrote down many of his impressions. The indignities he had suffered from the patriots in America still rankled in his mind, and he at first wanted the British to win because he believed that the future of the young nation hinged on whether or not unprincipled men there were restrained from breaking the laws of "justice, truth and religion." Curwen hated the mob. But as he moved about England, he found that many of the local people sympathized with the colonies. Some of them were avowed friends of America, and once he had supper at a roadside inn with some fellow travelers and passed the evening with them, "talking treason and justifying American independence." [29]

So Curwen remained more American than English, and almost a patriot in his leanings toward his former friends. Such tendencies were somewhat salved, however, when he arrived at the Treasury in London and, accompanied by Samuel Sewall, was given a hundred pounds and was informed that he would receive a like amount each year while the troubles in America continued. This he needed, for his pockets were nearly empty, a situation likely to alter completely the viewpoint of a less sensitive man. With the surrender of General John Burgoyne to the Americans at Saratoga in late 1777, Curwen was convinced that the colonists would settle for nothing less than independence. Had his English counterparts been as perspicacious, historians might have a different story to tell about the Revolution. After the war was over and John Adams arrived in London as representative of the new government, Curwen and others felt disturbed at his presence because of the harsh remarks he had previously made regarding the Tories. But they were relieved to learn that the sometimes irascible Adams had kindness in his heart, as well as statesmanship in his head, for he let it be known that he had buried his old animosity with the war, something of course not so hard to do when one was on the winning side.

Curwen was anxious to return home, and as soon as he was assured by friends in Massachusetts that he would be safe from harm, he made arrangements to leave his interim home and the hundred pounds a year which went with it. He particularly regretted leaving his old friend Sewall, for this meant that they would probably never see each other again in this world. "God only knows," wrote Sewall, "what kind of one the next one will be, whether more or less dirty." Curwen also paid a last call on Copley and visited the Tower of London, from the top of which he could see the new American flag flying from ships in the Thames. But back in Massachusetts, he found that home was not so appealing as it had been. The rich friends he had known had fallen into poverty and men of lowly origin had taken their places. Curwen believed that the unfortunate Tories were hunted down mainly from greed for plunder. To the patriots, he was the lawless one.[30]

Treated but little better in England were those who had not only upheld the royal cause in America but who had served in a military capacity as well. Joshua Loring, a Bostonian who became commissary of prisoners under General Sir William Howe, was a case in point. As a young merchant, he had courted and married Miss Elizabeth Lloyd, "a very handsome woman but very gay and reckless. A British officer said that she lost 300 guineas at cards at a single setting." Upon the evacuation of Boston, Loring accompanied the British troops to Nova Scotia and then to New York, where he received his appointment as commissary. But Howe was personally more interested in Mrs. Loring than he was in her husband, and apparently she returned the sentiment. As the Tory historian Judge Thomas Jones expressed it, Loring "was commissioned to the office, with a guinea a day and rations of all kinds, for himself and family. In this appointment there was reciprocity. Joshua had a handsome wife. The general, Sir William, was fond of her. Joshua made no objections. He fingered the cash, the general enjoyed madam." [31]

Later when Howe was dallying in Philadelphia instead of fighting the shivering and starving American troops, Francis Hopkinson wrote a song about him which swept the colonies. In it, the most popular stanza was,

> Sir William, he, as snug as flea
> Lay all this time a-snoring;
> Nor dreamed of harm, as he lay warm
> In bed with Mrs. Loring.[32]

Judge Jones credited Mrs. Loring as being the one "who, as Cleopatra of old lost Mark Antony the world, so did this illustrious courtesan lose Sir William Howe the honor, the laurels and the glory, of putting an end to one of the most obstinate rebellions that ever existed." [33]

In England in 1783, Joshua Loring wrote to his friend Edward Winslow, suggesting that Winslow contact his own friends there, including General Howe, for help in his struggles as a Tory. Loring also remarked that he himself had little prospect of getting half pay and that his only hope was for some compensation to be made to the Loyalists by the British government.

That Howe did not end the rebellion, the American Tories in England realized all too well, especially in their dwindling finances. Ward Chipman summed up the situation when he told Edward Winslow, "Of all the countries in the world, this is the worst to be in without a great deal of money, and even then has not half the rational social enjoyments and pleasures that our country affords, or rather of an American society such as we have been used to." Years later, Benjamin Marston emphasized the sentiment to Winslow, stating, "Americans used to call this country home, but it has become a very cold home to us in general. The original connections and attachments are long since worn out and dissolved." [34]

There were other connections with England than political. A considerable number of American students continued to go to England until prevented by hostilities, in order to obtain the kind of education they desired. Businessmen also went there for commercial purposes and some stayed just for this reason, preferring established order to martial activities such as were going on in the colonies. Thomas Hutchinson mentioned four young men who had come over in 1775 to avoid the conflict. Others went for various reasons. Mary Rothery of Norfolk, Virginia, went to England in 1774 because, she said, "of the storm which she saw coming on, her town being divided in sentiment and many refusing to suffer tea to be drunk in their houses." When she applied for compensation, the commissioners considered her claim vague and doubtful. She admitted that she had not been driven away, but could have remained safely. Upon further investigation, it was learned that her father had made himself unpopular because of his stand on inoculation, and she had come to England because her friends were there.[35]

A more prominent figure, but with ulterior interests also, was Paul Wentworth of New Hampshire, related to the governors there by that name. Wentworth was so attracted to England that he went there ten years before the Revolution and became a familiar person in commercial and financial circles in Paris as well as London, where he speculated in stocks for high stakes. Wentworth was quite a man of the world, having a mistress in Paris and mixing with such philosophers as the Abbé Raynal. He did not entirely sever his American connections and, during the early stages of the contest, showed some sympathy for the colonial cause. He served as agent for New Hampshire and assisted Dr. Edward Bancroft—who appeared to serve as a double-spy—in the preparation of a tract on American liberty. Wentworth claimed that he was offered several posts by the Continental Congress but refused out of loyalty to Great Britain. But though he professed some allegiance to the colonies, the fact that he received a salary of 500 pounds a year from England would seem to deny this. He himself eventually became a spy on the Continent, of a rather indeterminate nature.[36]

Another active Tory who became a spy for the British was Christopher Sower, who spent some time in England, then made his way to New Brunswick, where he became the king's printer and a worthy citizen of that new province. Born in Germantown, Pennsylvania, he had just reached 21 when the war broke out. Young Sower inherited from his father the publication of the *Germantown Gazette* as well as Quaker views in regard to war. Apparently his work brought him into contact with Benjamin Franklin, Joseph Galloway and the Muhlenbergs.

Sower refused to enter the Revolutionary army but did contribute a modest sum for the cause of patriot recruitment. But when he refused to take an active military part, he was fined four pounds and his desk was seized and sold to cover the fine. Meantime, Sower was publishing in his newspaper "what was favorable to the government and took care to avoid publication which might inflame." He did print the resolutions of the Continental Congress and regarded them as "so extraordinary that they must open the eyes of the people." But on December 16, 1776, the local Committee of Safety refused to allow Sower to publish any more, so he and his wife fled to the British camp at Philadelphia during the battle of Germantown. In the numerous skirmishes which followed this rather indecisive battle, the Tory forces sent parties against the rebels encamped to the north of Germantown. Sower was acting as a guide on one such raid of December 5, 1777, when he found that he was near

Fleet Street in London at the time the Tory exiles lived there in the late 18th and early 19th centuries. The exiles were hard put to find occupation, money and even sustenance. (*From the collections of the New York Public Library.*)

Governor Thomas Hutchinson of Massachusetts, probably the most eminent Tory, who went to England,
where he spent his last years longing for his native
America. (*From a portrait by another Tory, John
Singleton Copley.*)

Samuel Quincy, prominent Tory who fled to England and then to Antigua. *(From a portrait by John Singleton Copley in the Museum of fine Arts, Boston. Used by the kind permission of Miss Grace W. Treadwell, the owner.)*

Peter Van Schaack, a New Yorker who was slow in deciding, but finally cast in his lot with the Tory side of the war. He spent several years in exile in England, then returned to the United States and was welcomed there.

Samuel Curwen, an admiralty judge of Boston and one of the most bitter of the Tories in his denunciation of the new American nation, as his journal shows. He spent a number of years in London before returning home.

The little community of New Plymouth on Green Turtle Cay in the Bahamas, founded by Tories whose descendants still live there, resembles a toy town.

An aerial view of Spanish Wells in the Bahamas, showing this peaceful little community which was founded by American Tory exiles. Its residents, descendants of the Tories, lead a quiet and almost idyllic existence. (*Bahamas photographs by courtesy of the ministry of Tourism.*)

A Tory house still standing in Bermuda which was built by John Green, who went from his home in Philadelphia to live on the island. He espoused the cause of the king. (*Photograph from Bermuda News Bureau.*)

his old home, so he stopped to obtain some personal papers. Spotted by a former boyhood acquaintance, Captain Nicholas Coleman of the patriot forces, Sower was promptly arrested "almost under the eyes of Sir William Howe, the commander." The young editor was brought before General Washington and interrogated personally by him, one account stating that the American commander-in-chief remarked dryly during the process, "Well, Mr. Sower, now we will give you some sour sauce." [37]

Sower was exchanged, however, within six weeks for George Lusk, a gunpowder manufacturer whom the Americans considered valuable to their cause. Sower and his wife then went to New York City for the purpose of taking over a book and stationery store, but this had to be abandoned because of his work for the British army. For the next four years, he recalled, he "served as a guide, a German printer and translator, and from time to time procured intelligence for three successive commander-in-chiefs, Sir William Howe, Sir Henry Clinton and some for Sir Guy Carleton." [38]

According to the reports of Clinton, Sower worked mainly as an undercover agent in the German-populated parts of Pennsylvania, where he found some of the leaders loyal to Britain. He also laid plans for espionage which helped in the campaigns of Colonel John Butler against the patriots in New York and Pennsylvania. Apparently Sower was responsible to Major John André, who did not seem to place the confidence in Sower which the latter hoped for, especially in regard to the optimistic reports which he made to André about the loyalty of many of the people to the king. If the American spy was too sanguine, André was too impractical to take advantage of what was realistic in the reports he received. This trait was to show up later in the capture of André, who had failed to heed the warnings of his superiors about being caught as a spy.

In a report from New York to André on May 1, 1780, Sower said that "Every person from New Jersey, Pennsylvania and other provinces who has lately come to this city, gives us a horrid description of the distress and oppression amongst them, and I flatter myself to be well informed that Mr. Washington's Continental army now at and near Morristown did on Monday last, when they were received by their chief and the French ambassador, not exceed 3,000 effective men." This was probably a correct estimate, and if the British had taken advantage of the low state of the American army at this and other times, the results of the war might well have been a different story. But even if André did not pay too much attention to Sower, the latter was deeply grieved when André was executed. Sower was reportedly quite emotional and given to impulses. When later he saw a group of miserable prisoners from Washington's army at the docks in New York before the British evacuation, he did a noble thing. For among them he recognized none other than Captain Nicholas Coleman, who had arrested him at Germantown. Instead of rejoicing at the sight, Sower in a wave of generosity had Coleman released into his custody, took him to his own house, gave him new clothes and treated him with all the kindness of a friend until arrangements were made for him to be exchanged as a prisoner.

When Lord Cornwallis was caught at Yorktown and surrendered his forces, Sower saw immediately that as far as serious fighting was concerned, the war was over. So he switched his activity from trying to help win a military victory to trying to save the peace for the Tories by means of diplomatic moderation. In some way, he hoped, the colonies' ties with England could still be maintained. Sower was an ardent admirer and friend of the eminent Tory leader in Philadelphia, Joseph Galloway, and tried hard to help him make some headway against the radical patriot viewpoint, but to little avail. When Galloway left for England after being harried and threatened, Sower became a prominent spokesman in America for the moderates. In fact, he went to England himself in 1781, having to borrow twelve guineas to pay for his passage. There he got in touch with Galloway but found that the time for compromise had now passed. Nevertheless, he prepared, probably with the help of the able Galloway, a plan for dealing with the colonies which he is said to have presented personally to King George III. At this stage of hindsight, the document seems remarkable for its reasonable logic. Among other things it advocated that Parliament repeal every act binding on the colonies and that a general and generous grant be given to them, somewhat similar to that of Ireland, independent of Parliament and irrevocable, but the king to retain his authority over America as he did Great Britain and Ireland. Then, Sower believed, the colonies would be convinced of the good intentions of Great Britain to make them happy, and wish to return to the maternal fold. The fears of the colonists would cease and their "recollections of

former happiness will operate against the power of Congress."
He was convinced that the voice of the current rulers in America was not that of the people at large. "These are the sentiments of one who has seen the rise and progress of the calamities
in this country and who wishes the peace and welfare of both
Great Britain and the colonies (whose happiness is inseparable), and who is fully of the opinion that such a procedure
would have the desired effect. . . . Something real must be done
to support the people at large," Sower correctly prophesied, "by
removing every jealous idea from their breasts." [39]

Though the proposition was logical it was not feasible, and
its author returned to New York late in 1782 on the same ship
as Sir Guy Carleton. Sower hoped to assist the royal cause in
New York but found that the situation was hopelessly against
him. All he could do was to wait for the British to withdraw
from America. The next year, he and his wife and small
daughter—his son had died shortly after being born in New
York—left with other Tories including Brook Watson for
London. Sower and Watson were close friends and Christopher's second son, born in London, was named Brook Watson
Sower, after the lord mayor-to-be. The Sowers took over a
book and stationery shop at 24 Charles Street. But he again
became engaged in other activity, this time lobbying for Revolutionary War loss compensation. Especially did he work on his
own application, gathering written support from prominent
men such as Generals Howe and Clinton and Lord Rawdon.
The result was a pension of 40 pounds a year, the decision
stating that "This man appears to have behaved extremely well
and to have shown great zeal in the cause of Great Britain." A
year later, Sower and his family moved to New Brunswick in
Canada, where he not only became postmaster of Saint John but
was, like Benjamin Franklin in America, a printer at the same
time, and at long last did operate successfully a book and
stationery store.

Successful as a lawyer was Peter Van Schaack of New York,
a reluctant Tory who was highly esteemed by the leaders of
both sides, and who did not decide to remain loyal to the
Crown until he had done extraordinary soul searching. Up
until 1775, he was an adherent to the patriot cause in a luke-
warm way. Then when his friends such as John Jay and
Gouverneur Morris threw their considerable energies into wartime service, Van Schaack unhurriedly retired to his farm at

Kinderhook and isolated himself with his books and conscience in an effort to resolve the question of his allegiance. He particularly studied Locke, Montesquieu and Grotius, and then formulated his conceptions of the American Revolution. His studied conclusion was that Great Britain was not so villainous as she had been locally painted. He failed to see any dire plot to enslave the colonists. In fact, he had favored their cause until the Continental Congress had turned its course toward independence from Britain. This Van Schaack could not in good conscience support, and he concluded that every man should decide such questions for himself. But no such philosophical dalliance was in the minds of the patriot leaders: a man was either for them or against them. And no matter how honest Peter Van Schaack appeared to be, he must take the oath of allegiance to the new American nation or be banished. He chose the latter.[40]

Van Schaack was summoned to Albany in 1776 and charged with failing to show his attachment to the patriot cause by taking the oath of allegiance. He was "banished" but was allowed to remain in the country until 1778, and he sailed for England on October 16. Meantime, his wife, who had been in the last stages of consumption, was not even allowed to go to New York City from Kinderhook for medical treatment, or even to see a renowned English doctor who had been captured at the battle of Saratoga. Again Van Schaack was asked to swear allegiance to the new government, and again he refused. His sentence to permanent exile was signed by one of his former law students, Leonard Gansevoort. It was a hard verdict, especially under the circumstances, because by this time, Van Schaack had lost his wife, six children, his father, his father-in-law, his law business and the sight of one eye. He feared total blindness.[41]

"Torn from the nearest and dearest of all human connections," he wrote, "by the visitation of Almighty God and by means of the public troubles of my country, I am now going into the wide world, without friends, without fortune, with the sad remembrance of past happiness and the gloomy prospect of future adversity, having no other compass to direct me than my own frail understanding and no other consolation than that consciousness of my own integrity, which, as far as relates to the immediate cause of my now leaving my country, I possess in the fullest measure." He explained to Gouverneur Morris: "Could the American contest have been decided without blood, I should have been happy. While the appeal lay to reason, I reasoned; when it was made to the sword, I thought it my duty to join in the general issue." While it is not quite clear just what Van Schaack meant by "the general issue," he apparently had in mind that he could no longer stay out of the contest, and so left it.[42]

The exile landed at Cork and went from there to London. He remained in England seven years, and while there observed and recorded his impressions and experiences in an exceptionally candid and interesting way. In August of 1779, for example, Van Schaack visited Westminster Abbey and happened to see General and Mrs. Benedict Arnold there also. "They passed to the cenotaph of Major André," he noted, "where they stood and conversed together. What a spectacle! The traitor Arnold in Westminster Abbey, at the tomb of André, deliberately perusing the monumental inscription which will transmit to future eyes the tale of his own infamy." Instead of greeting his fellow Tories, Peter Van Schaack turned away from them in disgust.

True to his prediction, the exile suffered from lack of money while he was in England, so he petitioned the government for a small sum for his support, stating that he had lost his property and was not at the time practicing his profession of the law. He was eventually allowed 60 pounds a year, which was considered enough for the living expenses of a single man in his circumstances in England. That his loneliness intensified his interest in women as well as other things is evident in the observation he made during the early part of his London sojourn. "It is said that the three instances wherein England is distinguished from other nations," he penned, "are their women, their gardens and their inns. The last indeed are at a degree of excellence not to be exceeded; the second consist of serpentine walls, shaded and bordered with shrubs, trees and flowers, disposed in the greatest imaginable variety. The women of this country are indeed beautiful and healthy, not generally tall, and full chested, numbers pitted with the smallpox. They seem generally of a pleasurable turn and I fancy more disposed to spend a fortune than to save one. That of intrigue is a very prevailing spirit among them. Music is more an object of their attention and business than the domestic duties. The number of places of dissipation and pleasure are inconceivable, especially about London. Sundays are days of riot, excursion and dissipation." [43]

But even in such circumstances Van Schaack remained. He was there when peace was made. And there were compensations for his loneliness, for his distaste. In his leisure time, he had attended the debates in Parliament on American affairs "when the walls of St. Stephens resounded the thundering bursts of eloquence from the lips of the indefatigable Charles James Fox and the labored and philosophical argumentations of the gigantic Burke. . . . He had visited England's famed public schools and universities of learning. He had personally attended the courts of Westminster Hall and there witnessed the displays of bright luminaries of the law and eloquence and had heard the law expounded from the lips of the great Lord Mansfield. He had seen many characters distinguished in literature, arts and science, in politics and in the church. He had heard Mrs. Siddons on the stage and had enjoyed the society of Hannah More. He had been in the company of the literary colossus, Samuel Johnson." [44]

But as he wrote his son, Peter Van Schaack was longing for his home. He observed that vast numbers of English people avowed the cause of the colonies and believed that most of them loved the Americans, even though the ties were dissolved. When John Jay arrived in Paris as one of the commissioners to negotiate peace in the summer of 1782, Van Schaack wrote him as an old friend, but was extremely careful not to ask any favor. Jay replied as a friend and said generously that "No man can serve two masters; either Britain was right and America wrong; or America was right and Britain wrong. . . . No man is to be blamed for preferring the one which his reason recommended as the most just and virtuous." Jay then reminded Van Schaack that although the two had differed in their conscience, yet this had never kept John Jay from being the friend of Peter Van Schaack. To his credit as a gentleman, the latter had not even let Jay know that he was in straitened financial circumstances, so it was especially touching when Jay wrote that, "Whenever as a private friend, it may be in my power to do good, tell me. While I have a loaf, you and your children may freely partake of it. If your circumstances are easy, I rejoice; if not, let me take off their rougher edges." [45]

It is not clear whether or not Van Schaack received material aid from Jay but certainly there was moral support and needed solace. The exiled Tory told his friend that he still felt himself to be an American, and declared that if he could return, he would be as good a subject of the new government as he had been of the old one. "My heart warms whenever our country (I must call it my country) is the subject, and in my separation from it, I have dragged at each remove a lengthening chain." So anxious was he to return that Van Schaack even rejoiced at American independence, although he did admit that the joy was mingled with pain at the sufferings of those who had sacrificed their lives and fortunes for the cause in which they sincerely believed. In an intimate admission to Jay, he revealed that his remaining eye was worse and he feared for his sight.[46]

Jay and Van Schaack met in London on October 14, 1783, a little over a month after the Peace of Paris was signed. They greeted each other "with the cordiality of old friends who had long been absent, without the least retrospect to the cause of their absence," a reunion of two real gentlemen. Again Van Schaack was careful not to burden his already hard-worked friend with personal problems, though one can readily sense how fervently the exile longed for help and home. And happily he had in his possession a recent letter from Gouverneur Morris assuring him that "the rage against Loyalists will soon give place to more favorable sentiment. Time will be my judge." Morris was right. Jay also told his old friend that he felt conditions would soon be ripe in America for the return of Van Schaack.

But more was required than personal sentiment to enable Van Schaack to return. It had to be official. So it was with great relief and happiness that he received in November of 1784 communications from both John Jay and Governor George Clinton of New York informing him that he definitely would be permitted to come to America. Van Schaack set sail and arrived in New York on July 20, 1785. Jay himself went aboard the ship and escorted him ashore, taking him to see Governor Clinton and other public officials who gave him a warm welcome. The exile was to take up his life anew and live it actively and honorably for an additional 47 years, dying quietly at his beloved Kinderhook at the age of 85, a grateful prodigal long since come home.[47]

[6]

RECOMPENSE

Plots, true or false, are necessary things,
To raise up Commonwealth and ruin Kings.

ALTHOUGH DRYDEN WAS NOT THUS POETIZING about the American Tories, he might have been as far as their claims for compensation were concerned. Of all the results of the Revolution, this problem was perhaps the most complicated, at least for those directly affected. If they could not win the war, the Tories reasoned, surely they could benefit from the peace to the extent of being rewarded for their loyalty and services. But again this posed the question of who were the real Loyalists.

Most of those who had fled the country felt that their exile would be only temporary and that it would just be a matter of time until Britain won. They had reason to feel this way. But with the news of the defeat of Burgoyne, they could see the end, and only then did they begin to realize the inexorable nature of their unfortunate situation. Even so, they hoped that the coming of peace would be accompanied by merciful measures to them and a full appreciation on the part of England of their role in the conflict. In fact, such sentiment was encouraged by the treaty of 1783 itself, which stated that provisions regarding the Loyalists should be carried out "not only with justice and equity, but with that spirit of conciliation which on the return of the blessings of peace, should universally prevail."

Suitable action did not match the sentiment. Article 5 of the treaty stated that "Congress shall earnestly recommend" to the state legislatures that they "provide for the restitution of all estates, rights and properties which have been confiscated" and which belonged to real British subjects. Also the Loyalists were to be permitted to go to any part of the thirteen United States and remain there for twelve months, unmolested in their endeavors to obtain such restitution. Article 6 stated that there should be no future confiscations or collection of damages and that those confined should be released and not prosecuted.

On its face, this seemed a humane document. But alas for the Loyalists, most of the states ignored the recommendations and even after the war patriots continued to confiscate Loyalist lands without being punished by the courts. Those who dared to come for a year to recoup their losses, received in many cases, instead, tar and feathers and worse. So Britain used this lack of compliance with the treaty as an excuse for retaining the Western forts and for pursuing the fur trade which centered around them. As an example of what the states did in connection with the peace treaty, in New Jersey sales of forfeited Loyalist property were made to the highest bidder for several years after 1783. Included in the estates were those of Oliver De Lancey, Benjamin Thompson, Andrew Lambert, Cortlandt Skinner, Philip Kearney and John Leonard. In Georgia, the estates of Sir James Wright and John Graham were advertised for sale after the peace treaty. Pennsylvania did likewise in the case of Andrew Allen. In New York, the sheriff of Westchester County called on "a great number of Loyalists who had been indicted of high treason against the state, to appear and traverse the indictments," and declared that if they did not, their estates would be adjudged forfeited.[1]

Some of the Tories could hardly appear unless they were willing to risk their lives. One, Phillip Henry, a former South Carolina plantation owner who had fled to Dublin, Ireland, petitioned the British ministry for financial restitution, stating bitterly that he had had to sacrifice for his king, "while many in England have annually enjoyed the bounty of royal liberality, who were not only without property in America, but were destitute of spirit to support the British legislature."[2]

As far as Parliament was concerned, the peace treaty did not go through without heated discussion of the clause relating to the Loyalists. Astute members were not unaware of the probable consequences. Even in the House of Lords, where it was not supposed that there was much acuteness in such perception, a lively set-to took place. "It was contrary to natural justice and humanity," declared Lord Carlisle, "to sacrifice to the cruel and inveterate malice of their enemies, men who had persevered in the midst of the greatest perils and dangers in their loyalty to Britain; men who had left their families, given up their fortunes and risked their lives in the service of Government." Lord Walsingham joined in with, "Their claim upon us was self-evident; they had been invited to join us by their own acts; it was a Parliamentary War, and therefore it was incumbent on the legislature to protect them." As far as Lord Stormont was concerned, he commented that "These were men whom Britain was bound in justice and honor, gratitude and affection, and every tie, to provide for and protect; yet alas for England as well as them, they were made a part of the price of peace." Lord Sackville remarked that the abandonment of the Loyalists "was a thing of so atrocious a kind, that if it had not already been painted in all its horrid colors, I should have attempted the ungracious task, but never should have been able to describe the cruelty."

In reply to these charges, Lord Shelburne, who had been a key person in the making of the treaty, said, "If better terms could be had, think you, my Lords, that I would not have embraced them? . . . If it were possible to put aside the bitter cup the adversities of the country presented to me, you know I would have done it; but you called for peace; I had but the alternative either to 'accept the terms,' said Congress, 'of our recommendation to the states, in favor of the colonists, or continue the war.' "

Over in the House of Commons, Lord North, the man held most responsible for the adversities, spoke with a heavy heart. "I cannot but lament the fate of those unhappy men," he said, in reference to the Loyalists, "who I conceive were in general objects of our gratitude and affection. Men who had sacrificed all the dearest possessions of the human heart." [3]

A further complaint by the British was to the effect that the American states had most unjustly confiscated the property of the American Loyalists who were British subjects, and deprived them of the means of paying their debts to the American citizens. The British government, on the contrary, although it felt justified under the laws of retaliation, had not confiscated the property of American citizens, whether they were in England or America, nor had in any respect hindered them from paying their debts to the British merchants. It was further pointed out that Britain had from the first encouraged the Loyalists to resist the American rebels, with the view that after a time, normal conditions would return and debts and credits would be honored. But when, after the war, American courts were opened, many of the debtors who had been solvent at the peace were found to have become insolvent later and their debts were therefore forever lost to their British creditors. This loss was also due to the failure or reluctance of the American courts to handle Loyalist claims.[4]

As has already been shown, England attempted to establish another western part of her empire, by providing a substitute for the lost colonies in Canada. But while this territory later developed into an important dominion, during the time of the hardships of the Loyalists following the Revolution it was of little help financially; in fact it was a drain. It did not even replace as food-producing units and an arm of the industrial fabric the part which the American colonies had played. The new Canadian colonies were too poor, too lacking in resources and too isolated to take the place of those which had gone.[5]

As for the American Tories, it seemed to them after the initial shock of the peace treaty that hardly any world at all existed for them. Those in England were only a few compared to the much greater number remaining in America, yet they who had gone to the mother country were, in a sense, representatives of all the Loyalists, for they spearheaded the pursuit of the claims. Some of those in London had been government officials, and upon these fell the duty of drawing up the petitions and memorials in behalf of the losses of all. In 1779, they formed an association to look out for their interests, and named Sir William Pepperell, grandson of the hero of Louisburg, as president. His huge Maine estate had been confiscated and he found himself almost penniless. The British government allowed him a pension of 500 pounds, which, with the sale of some of his personal property, enabled him to live rather well in his London home, but not approaching the baronial manner of his life in New England. For ten years, Sir William worked to further the interests of his fellow Tories.

Although this duty was somewhat of a sad one, there was solace in the gathering of key Loyalists who met at the Crown and Anchor in the Strand in London. Here at this favorite place of Dr. Samuel Johnson and his Boswell, the exiles from America planned the measures they would take, and appointed a committee of thirteen members, one from each colony, to prepare an address to the king. They made their fervent appeal to their sovereign in behalf of the suffering multitudes of their fellows. "Finally," they stated, "we make a melancholy appeal for the many families who have been banished from their once peaceful habitations; to the public forfeiture of a long list of estates; and to the numerous executions of our fellow-citizens who have sealed their loyalty with their blood." The situation was not helped by the fact that some of the exiles who had been in good circumstances were actually forced to become domestic servants, while there were others such as Judge Robert Auchmuty, formerly of Boston, who after he went to London found himself reduced to asking humbly for 100 pounds. No wonder a discouraged Loyalist wrote,

> "Tis an honor to serve the bravest of nations
> and be left to be hanged in their capitulations." [6]

One who did not give up hope was Joseph Galloway. He wrote in a pamphlet which was published in 1783 that the Loyalists were as much subjects of Britain as any man in London and reminded his readers that the exiles had been summoned by their king to defend the rights of the nation and that they responded with confidence that their sacrifices and losses would be made up by their mother country. It had been found necessary by the British government, Galloway continued, to acknowledge the independence of America without obtaining recompense to the loyal colonists, but the victims nonetheless expected proper restitution from their sovereign. Looking back from the present point of view, it is not difficult to understand that Britain felt she must await the action of the American states in this regard before she took final action to settle the Loyalist claims. Revealing is the report of Colonel Beverly Robinson, who wrote to Edward Winslow on April 29, 1784, from London, "The affair of the loyalists goes on but slowly. . . . The commissioners seem to take great pains and pay attention to our unhappy situation but they have a troublesome and difficult task to get through. Many extraordinary claims are put in such as you would be astonished to see. . . . As the matter is like to be so very tedious, the commissioners have recommended, I believe, that most that have applied for a temporary support receive from 40 to 200 pounds a year which is the highest they can go." [7]

One of these commissioners, Daniel Parker Coke, a member of Parliament, felt that they were doing very well by the Loyalists. He stated that the verdict of history upon the whole would be that "whatever may be said of this unfortunate war, all the world has been unanimous in applauding the justice and humanity of Great Britain in rewarding the services and in compensating with a liberal hand the losses of those who suffered so much for their firm and faithful adherence to the British government." Perhaps it seemed this way to an able and prominent official, but to an exile sad and in want of so many things dear to his heart, the situation was quite different indeed. It was not just that the loser was disappointed in not taking part of the spoils of war; the misery was intensified by the seeming suddenness of the blow contained in the treaty of peace.[8]

The commission classified the claimants under the following categories:

1. Those who had rendered service to Great Britain.
2. Those who had borne arms against the Revolution.
3. Uniform Loyalists.
4. Loyalists resident in Great Britain.
5. Those who took oaths of allegiance to the American states, but afterwards joined the British.
6. Those who armed with the Americans but later joined the British army or navy.

Compensation was not allowed for estates bought after the war, rents, incomes of office received during the rebellion, anticipated professional profits, losses in trade, labor, or by the British army, losses through depreciated paper money, captures at sea, or debts.[9]

Great Britain, on the other hand, did not wait until the war was over to start compensating the Loyalists. During the conflict, pensions were paid which totaled an annual bill of 70,000 pounds by 1782. The postwar claims were heard in both London and Canada. By states, the claimants were as follows: New York, 941; South Carolina, 321; Massachusetts, 226; New Jersey, 208; Pennsylvania, 148; Virginia, 140; North Carolina, 135; Georgia, 129; Connecticut, 92; Maryland, 78; Vermont, 61; Rhode Island, 41; New Hampshire, 31; and Delaware, nine, a total of 2,560.[10]

As far as the new United States government was concerned, on January 14, 1784, Congress issued a proclamation asking the states to restore all the rights and properties confiscated from British subjects, upon terms agreeable to the Americans who had purchased the property. But this recommendation had about as much effect as did the provision along the same line in the peace treaty. Most of the states continued to confiscate the Tory property, and in many localities, the Loyalists were tarred and feathered and driven from the towns. In Virginia, the legislature declared it would refuse to honor any such Congressional request, resolving instead that no private debt should be paid in England until that country had reimbursed Virginia to the extent of 500,000 pounds for the Negro slaves who had run away to the British forces during the war. This attitude toward debts was of special significance in this state, because many of the local planters were deeply in debt to English merchants, and had been accused of helping to foment the war in order to wipe out the obligations. George Mason wrote Patrick Henry that the question was frequently raised, "If we are now going to pay the debts due the British merchants, what have we been fighting for all this while?" [11]

Many state governments, hard pressed for funds, regarded the sale of Tory estates as one means of remedying this. But those who purchased the lands wished to be certain they had good title to them. In Virginia, for instance, with few exceptions, the property sold belonged to people whose actual residence was in England. Here, as elsewhere, the justification of forfeiture was the right of a government to dispose of an enemy alien's property. In some places, the exiles who chose to return to the new nation were regarded as British subjects and aliens who must be compelled to take out papers of citizenship. Massachusetts, for example, declared it ought to act with the greatest caution before it naturalized a set of people who had been declared outlaws, exiles, aliens, and enemies. A resolution of the commonwealth stated that as long as there were in America thousands of innocent people whose property had been destroyed by the British army, it would be unjust and cruel to allow estates to be restored to those who had abandoned their country. The town of Lexington, taking upon itself a large responsibility, passed a resolution that it was necessary for the peace and welfare of the United States that steps should be taken to prevent the return of the refugees and the recovery of the property that was formerly theirs.[12]

The tone of the sentiment in Massachusetts was set in its first confiscation act, passed on April 30, 1779: "An act to confiscate the estates of certain notorious conspirators," it stated, then cited by name all the leading officials of the royal government of the colony from Governors Francis Bernard and Thomas Hutchinson to Solicitor General Samuel Quincy. "These notorious conspirators against the government and liberties of the inhabitants of Massachusetts Bay had wickedly conspired to overthrow and destroy the constitution of government of the late province of Massachusetts, as established by the charter agreed upon by and between William and Mary and the inhabitants of Massachusetts Bay; and also to reduce the said inhabitants under the absolute power and dominion of the present king and parliament and had as far as in them lay aided and assisted the king and parliament in their endeavors to establish a despotic government over the inhabitants." So they "justly incurred the forfeiture of all their property." [13]

By April 19, 1780, when the court suspended sales of Tory estates in Suffolk County, Massachusetts—on the 15th anniversary of the battles of Lexington and Concord—the Suffolk sales alone had amounted to, in all, nearly 500,000 pounds in the depreciated currency. Thirty-five parcels of land, 18 in Boston and 17 in other Suffolk towns, formerly owned by eight Loyalists, had been sold to 18 merchants, three mariners, an attorney, a baker, a farmer, an upholsterer and an innkeeper. Proceeds from the sales went primarily to the creditors of the Loyalists. But in the frequent cases where the returns from a sale more than covered the creditors' claims, the excess went to the state. It has been concluded by one study that these Suffolk sales produced no dramatic democratization of land ownership. It remained for the vitriolic Samuel Adams to put the case into its strongest terms. "Shall those traitors who first conspired the ruin of our liberties," he asked, "those who basely forsook their country in her distress, and sought protection from the enemy, when they thought him in the plenitude of power, who have been ever since stimulating and doing all in their power to aid and comfort them, while they have been doing their utmost to enslave and ruin us,—shall these wretches have their estates reserved for them and restored at the conclusion of this glorious struggle, in which some of the richest blood in America has been spilled?" [14]

At the first opening of Parliament after the peace treaty, King George III spoke with feeling about the unfortunate Loyalists who had given up their property and professions, and he asked that generous attention be given to their claims. He had long shown a personal interest in the refugees, and in turn he seemed to most of them to be their lord and protector, After this initial meeting of Parliament, the Massachusetts association held a meeting at their London inn and requested Sir William Pepperell to present a petition of relief to Parliament. The cabinet officers were mixed in their reaction to this idea, but the petition was drawn up and duly presented. In Parliament it received enthusiastic support from both the government and the opposition. The next step was the appointment of the commissioners already discussed. This was done by Lord Shelburne, who made propitious choices in the persons of John Eardley Wilmot and Daniel Parker Coke, both lawyers and members of Parliament who, strangely enough in this age of venality, insisted that their work should not be paid for. (Could it be that they followed the example of their enemy, George Washington, when he refused to take pay for commanding the American armies?) Coke was at first not at all sympathetic to the claims of the Tories, but later on, after he had seen so much evidence of suffering among them, changed his mind entirely.

But there was little these remote commissioners could do about the Tory confiscation acts in America. As one historian has pointed out, these acts had one curious effect upon the development of American institutions: that is, the power of American courts to set aside laws for want of conformity to the Constitution. This is spoken of as a peculiar power of the United States Supreme Court and an invention of those who established our national Constitution in 1787. Such power was exercised in several instances in state courts before there was a Supreme Court of the nation. In a majority of these cases, the law against which objection was brought was one regarding the Tories. So antagonistic were the state legislatures that they went beyond what they were supposed to, in venting their spleen against them. Among the lawyers, therefore, there grew up the conception that courts might set aside laws if they conflicted with the constitution of the state.[15]

Bills of attainder were often used by the states as confiscatory statutes, sometimes when there seems to have been little justification for such. These attainder bills meant that the persons affected lost their civil rights and capacities. By using such laws, the legislators did not have to bother with fine distinctions about citizenship. Instead, they dispensed quick "justice" and made the rules as they proceeded. Most of these laws singled out persons of "a bad pre-eminence" in the eyes of the patriots, such as Mary Philipse and the royal governors. The fact that bills of attainder are specifically prohibited in the United States Constitution today speaks eloquently of the unfair nature of them, and this prohibition stems directly from the experience with these bills during and after the Revolution. They were found to violate the separation of powers, run roughshod over rules of evidence, deny trial by jury and put condemned persons in double jeopardy. A recent legal historian has summed up the situation succinctly: "Revolutionary settlements work great hardships on property owners who try to maintain neutrality or who choose the losing side. . . . Personal pique, politics and class animosity doubtless influenced decisions. Nevertheless, underlying these laws was the common principle that the validity of one's title to property depended on loyalty to the state. Such a policy was certainly no revolution-born innovation. These statutes created the dilemma of the Tory landowner. He could become an enemy alien or a traitor. Either way he lost his property." [16]

Perhaps the greatest opposition to the peace treaty provisions regarding the Tories was in the South, where many of the inhabitants were resentful over the escape of their Negro slaves with the British. The Tories also had savagely attacked their Southern neighbors, partly in retaliation for the assaults on them. General Anthony Wayne, a respecter of his adversaries, urged that Loyalists be treated leniently so that they could be reclaimed as citizens of Georgia. But those who had gone over to the British were allowed no political rights there until they had renounced their allegiance to the king and sworn allegiance to Georgia and the United States. Disaffected people from other states were prohibited from coming to the state and settling. Confiscated property helped to pay off war debts and those which followed the conflict. Some heroes were granted large land tracts; General Wayne himself was given acreage along the Savannah and Ogeechee rivers. So grateful were the Georgians to General Nathanael Greene for his strenuous efforts in the Southern military campaigns that they awarded him the extensive estate of the royal lieutenant governor, John Graham.[17]

The situation of the Tories in Georgia was unique, for this was the only colony in which the royal governor was restored during the war. In this case he was Sir James Wright, one of the best of these officials. He returned with British military successes in 1780, General Sir Henry Clinton winning, by the capture of Charleston, probably the most important British victory of the war. Not only did Wright resume his former duties in Georgia but he and his associates passed the Disqualifying Act of 1780, a sort of confiscation in reverse. Under this "Tory law," suits for debt were brought against rebel estates and the provost marshal could sell estates of absentees. Many such suits were filed until Cornwallis decided to move the main British army into Virginia in 1781. Taking advantage of this maneuver, the Americans moved back into Georgia and captured Augusta and then Savannah. These victories cut short the suits under the Disqualifying Act. When the British evacuated Savannah, most of the people who left went to East Florida or Jamaica, and a few to England. It has been estimated that about 5,000 people, whites and Negroes, left Georgia around this time because of their British loyalty. Yet a considerable number of Loyalists returned to Georgia from East Florida.[18]

Those who wished to buy confiscated land were not always able to do so. In fact, it seems remarkable, when the scarcity of money at that time is considered, that so many were able to purchase it at all. Some found that it was easier to buy than to put up security. Whigs offered themselves as security for each other for the interest owed the state. And there were individuals out of state who became interested in buying the Tory lands for the purpose of speculation. In November of 1783, an intensive campaign was begun to sell what Loyalist property was left in Georgia. Commissioners traveled about seeking personal property such as livestock and slaves, and when they did not find time to make the investigations themselves, authorized others to make the search for them. But even when the estates were selected for sale, it was not always easy to sell them, as many prospective buyers proved to be cautious; often, the same estates appear repeatedly in the advertisements set forth by the commissioners.[19]

As time went on and memories of the wartime strife grew less bitter, there was a softening of the confiscation laws of Georgia. Prominent political figures supported this more lenient attitude, men whose motives were of unquestionable integrity but who for reasons of their own favored a policy of moderation toward the Tories. Two of these were John Wereat and Joseph Clay. The former was state auditor during most of the 1780's and expressed his feelings in the sentence, "I agree to forgive everyone, now that the war is at an end."

Wereat furnished former Tory residents of Georgia with affidavits signifying the amount and value of property confiscated by the state in order to substantiate their claims for compensation from Great Britain. For his part, Clay, a businessman, all along had doubted the wisdom of the confiscation laws, for he was afraid they would cause such bitterness that proper reconstruction of the state would be hampered. So generous was his attitude that a number of Loyalists who were residing abroad appealed to him to help them return to Georgia or to help them dispose of their property there.[20]

In examining the financial records, it does seem probable that confiscation of the Tory lands did help to tide Georgia over during the period of adjustment after the war. The returns realized helped to liquidate the state's war debt, and for some time afterwards, income came into the treasury from this source. But the confiscation policy does not appear to have resulted in any appreciable redistribution of property from wealthy Loyalists to poor Whigs; nor did it, on the other hand, cause any greater concentration of property in the hands of a few. Many of the local Loyalists took the oath of allegiance to the king simply because the British controlled Georgia at the time. They were equally willing to take the oath to the United States after the British left. There seems little doubt that had the matter been left up to Georgia, the country would not have had a Revolutionary War.[21]

As it was, the situation in Georgia resulted in a national legacy. Two citizens of South Carolina, executors of a British creditor, brought suit in the United States Supreme Court, *Chisholm vs. Georgia*, 1793, for recovery of confiscated property. The Court rendered its decision in favor of Chisholm and the result was accompanied by elaborate opinions of the justices, especially John Jay and James Wilson, who maintained that under the Constitution, sovereignty was vested in the people of the United States. Chief Justice Jay said that the people established a "constitution by which it was their will that the state governments should be bound, and to which the state constitutions should be made to conform." But Georgia refused to permit the Chisholm verdict to be executed. The day after the decision, there was initiated congressional action which a year later resulted in the submission to the states of the Eleventh Amendment to the U.S. Constitution. It provided "The judicial power of the United States shall not be construed

to extend to any suit in law or equity, commenced or prosecuted against one of the United States citizens of another state,
or by citizens or subjects of any foreign state." Thus for the only
time in its history, the federal judiciary had its jurisdiction directly curtailed by constitutional amendment.[22]

Such ethical issues were usually secondary to more prag-
matic ones. Like the Loyalists of Massachusetts, those of North
Carolina who were living in London in 1783 held a meeting at
the London Coffee House under the chairmanship of James
Parker. Their purpose, of course, was to present the claims for
losses they had suffered. They also tried to help the commissioners to distinguish between worthy and unworthy claimants.
One such questionable case was that of Archibald Hamilton of
North Carolina, who went to England in 1777 rather than take
the patriot oath of allegiance. He claimed that he and his part-
ners had lost 85,813 pounds from their business. In England it
was learned that his firm owed debts to creditors in Scotland, so
Hamilton was compelled to sell his two farms in Scotland to
meet this payment. His claim for losses was denied. Among the
reasons given by the commission was one which stated, "This
man had no great merit on the score of loyalty. He admits that
in the plight of war, he meddled in no politics but took care of
his business. He acted like a sensible man, but he certainly has
not so great a claim upon government as if he had been a parti-
san." In other words, England also reasoned that if a man was
not for her, he was against her.[23] But fortunately for Hamilton,
this was not the end of the story. He had a brother, John, who
was a lieutenant colonel in the British army. This brother
brought the claim again, and this time Archibald was awarded
80 pounds a year. Three years later, the amount was increased
to 200 pounds a year. In 1784, 62 men and women from North
Carolina were receiving regular annual pensions, ranging from
16 pounds a year for Joseph Johnston to 500 pounds for former
Governor Joseph Martin. When these Loyalists died, payments
were made to their widows and heirs down to the year 1832.[24]

Difficult prospects of obtaining compensation did not prevent most of the eligible Tories from trying. Soon after the
signing of the peace treaty, Sir Robert Eden and several other
Tories returned from England to Maryland for the purpose of
regaining their property. Their attempts were met mainly with
resentment. In like manner, Henry Hartford, a proprietary,
sought to repossess his Maryland possessions. In answer to his

petition the assembly stated that since the war was a result of unwarranted aggressions of the British government and since Hartford had supported said government, he should rely upon the British for compensation of his losses. On June 21, 1783, a resolution of a Baltimore town meeting declared "that all refugees having opposed the establishment of the independence of America should not participate in the advantages thence accruing and ought not to reside among us." This resolution was said to be typical of the prevailing attitude of the patriots toward the Tories. In addition to their pre-emption of the property, the former felt that now that they were in power as leaders of the new community, they did not want the Tories to return and assume their former prominent positions. The merchants and agents having British connections who left Maryland and Virginia during the war owned property valued at three million pounds sterling and of course were eager to return. But when they tried to, they were met with orders to leave the states and laws preventing them from collecting their debts or recovering their property.[25]

Requiring what was probably the longest time to recover his property was Matthias Aspden, a merchant of Philadelphia, who fled from there in 1776, went to New York and then to Spain, on his way to England. His business in the Pennsylvania city had netted him a profit of 2,000 pounds annually. In 1785, Aspden returned to America at the urging of friends who had undertaken to obtain a pardon for him, but he fled again on hearing that his life was in peril. But in April of the following year, after a slow consideration of the matter, the Pennsylvania Assembly granted him a full pardon. He did not recover his house, wharf and warehouses in Philadelphia, however, because they had already been confiscated by the state four years before and given to its university. So in spite of his pardon, Aspden did not remain in America. In 1802, he was in France, in 1810 he was traveling in Italy, in 1815 he was in New York, and in July of 1817, the ubiquitous Tory left Philadelphia for England by way of Canada. He died in London on August 9, 1824, leaving a will which was said to have resulted in the most extraordinary suit ever filed under the confiscation acts of the Revolution. It was not finally decided until 1848, when his heirs in America secured a decree in the United States Circuit Court which gave them property valued at more than $500,000. The decree was sustained by the Supreme Court.[26]

While Pennsylvania was lenient in many of the property cases, it was a different story in the case of Joseph Galloway. Following his forced retirement to England in 1778 after ably championing the loyal cause in America, this active individual continued to support vociferously American loyalism by criticizing the military campaigns in the middle colonies, by elaborately discussing the provisions relating to the Loyalists in the treaty of peace, in his manifold services as agent for his fellow sufferers, and in his long continuing correspondence with many of the Loyalists who for one reason or another remained in America. Galloway's petition to the Pennsylvania Assembly was presented by his attorney, Thomas Clifford, and was terse and formal. It simply mentioned "the attainder of the said Galloway of high treason, and praying that the Council would be pleased to grant him a pardon of the said offense." But here the patience of the Pennsylvanians seems to have run out. When the petition was read the second time in 1790, its author was advised to withdraw it, which he did. Galloway remained in England and died there in 1803.[27]

There were those who were more fortunate. Many of the Pennsylvania Tories did remain in America, some did return, and a number did not even bother to obtain pardons. Among those who continued to reside in Philadelphia was Dr. Edward Shippen, the father of Peggy Arnold, the loyal wife of Benedict Arnold. She had been expelled from the state, and doubtless would have joined her husband anyway, but her father was so well thought of that he was not only permitted to remain but was elevated to the position of chief justice of Pennsylvania in 1799. He held this position until his death in 1806. Another individual who braved the storms of war and remained in Philadelphia was Robert Proud, teacher of Greek and Latin in the Friends Academy. He is remembered for his two-volume *History of Pennsylvania* which appeared in 1797 and 1798. Chief Justice Benjamin Chew, whose sturdy house defied the artillery of Henry Knox during the battle of Germantown, was sent into temporary exile for refusing to sign a parole in 1777. But this did not prevent him from re-entering the state or from being appointed president of the High Court of Errors and Appeals in 1790, a position ironical in its title considering his own circumstances. Judge Chew held this post for 16 years until it was abolished. He lived for four years more. Governor John Penn, an associate of Judge Chew in exile, left with his family for

England by way of New York in 1783. But Penn himself returned and died in Bucks County in 1795. As already noted, Reverend Jacob Duché, who was banished to England, also came back to his homeland, where he passed away in 1798.[28]

In New York there had been quite a stir ever since the peace was announced. Lord Cathcart wrote to Lord Carlisle on June 12, 1783, that "The town of New York by the end of April was full of Americans from all the states. The port, by order of Sir Guy Carleton, opened for all American vessels to load and unload. . . . Many estates belonging to people not mentioned in their acts of confiscation have in the month of April been located by persons possessed of certain certificates that had been given to the army as pay. These certificates have been bought up at nine shillings for the pound and are to be paid out of confiscated estates. It is impossible that this can ultimately be allowed of—but in the meanwhile it produces a confusion which your Lordship can easily figure to yourself. The object, however, which they really have in view is to get the Loyalist whose estate is thus low-rated to purchase the military certificate perhaps at ten shillings on the pound, and then to say he is well off in recovering half his property." [29]

At this time, the New York law discouraged the sale of such lands in large parcels. The estate of James De Lancey went to 275 persons, that of Roger Morris to 250. One of the largest estates in this region was that of Philip Skene of Skenesborough, located not far from Fort Ticonderoga. In his claim to the commissioners in 1784, Skene recounted that he had established this settlement at the suggestion of Lord Amherst in 1759, stocked it with livestock and slaves and settled there with his family. He had great prospects of success, he stated, until in May of 1775 his estate, improvements and family were seized upon by armed banditti, "to the unspeakable terror and anxiety of a helpless aged sister, who with his daughters were forced from their peaceful dwelling, under an armed escort, and obliged in this situation, to perform a journey of near 200 miles; in which, exclusive of their being prisoners to a lawless banditti, they suffered exceeding hardships from the mode of their travelling, being sometimes obliged to walk through the woods, and at other times carried in a cart drawn by oxen, without scarce a change of apparel, and exposed to every insult and mortification from a licentious people, by whom they were surrounded and threatened repeatedly."

Skene related that he was seized and after an examination—conducted by John Adams and a committee of Congress—was sent under a strong guard to Hartford, Connecticut. "Where, from his being particularly obnoxious on account of his principles, (which he did not conceal) he was frequently insulted and surrounded by numbers of armed people, assembled for that purpose; which did not deter him from encouraging and keeping up a correspondence with the friends of government. And from his zeal," he stated, "he did at his own expense send expresses to Canada, to the commander in chief at Boston and to the Secretary of State's office—some of which did not arrive. That at length he was thought too dangerous to be suffered at large, and accordingly was taken up and close confined in the common jail at Hartford, during the space of six months, in the criminals' cell; [William Franklin said Skene harangued the people from the prison windows.] where, from the heat of the climate in the summer months, and never being permitted to go out of his dungeon upon any occasion, he suffered greatly in his health; but being exchanged by Sir William Howe, at the conclusion of the year, 1776, and thinking his services would be more requisite with the northern army, he embarked for England." Upon his arrival there, Skene, "Understanding that an expedition was formed to penetrate by way of Lake Champlain through the country, lost no time in joining General Burgoyne upon Lake Champlain, and acted to the best of his abilities in his army, in several different capacities, without any pay assigned him; was in several actions in that campaign; was made prisoner, and remained with the army at Boston until late in the year 1778, and hopes his example of zeal was favorably looked upon." One who did not look very favorably upon some of Skene's zeal was John Burgoyne, who later accused him of routing the British army by way of Skenesborough instead of via Ticonderoga and thus contributing to the later defeat at Saratoga. This is thought to have been done by Skene partly to get a good military road built, which would later benefit his estate.

Skene further claimed that he had lost an income of 2,000 pounds annually and was reduced to poverty with a numerous family. He lists as losses, among other items, "a most complete bloomery for constructing bar iron, a very good saw mill, burnt in the engagement of July, 1777, a good grist mill, a framed mill dam, destroyed by order of General Burgoyne in 1777, spirituous liquors, linens, woolens, tea, gunpowder, an excellent stone barn and stables, 950 cords of wood, 2,000 sawlogs, 8,000 pipe staves, wagons, carts, ox teams, sledges, implements of husbandry, a strong built schooner of 40 tons, eight healthy Negro men and 20 cows." His estate totaled, he claimed, 56,350 acres. He was eventually awarded, by England, 22,000 pounds.[30]

The man to whom such Tories most owed their plight, George Washington, was, according to one historian, quite willing to relent his antagonism. Even before the peace, he alone among his contemporaries of high station stood ready to forgive the past for the benefit of the multitudes of Loyalists who had borne arms against the American cause. By the end of April, 1782, he had recommended to Congress the pardoning of the 75 or more regiments of Loyalists in British service, under proper restrictions.[31]

His chief lieutenant in the postwar years was another who felt merciful toward the Tories. Alexander Hamilton was disgusted with the vengeful measures taken against the Tories. His comments compared the exodus of these unfortunate people with the flight of the Huguenots from France a century before. Even Robert R. Livingston, who had told Benjamin Franklin that he wanted to see the Loyalists driven from the country, changed his mind and admitted that sordid personal motives were behind the actions of those who persisted in persecuting the Tories, one of which was the greed to gobble up their estates. Livingston now regretted the loss of the exiles and he considered them the principal victims of the war.[32]

As for Hamilton, even during the war he had refused to condone wholesale persecution of the Tories. Nothing was worse, he believed, than to impose penalties indiscriminately upon all suspected of loyalism. Theoretically, it would be better to exterminate them altogether than to embitter them against the government, leaving them with the power to do it injury, he said, paraphrasing an idea of Machiavelli. Unlike Governor George Clinton, Hamilton deplored the departure of the Tories as a great loss to the community, which now more than ever needed wealthy and conservative citizens. He wrote a series of newspaper articles under the signature of "Phocion" (an Athenian leader given to espousing the causes of those who differed with him, and who readily forgave and sought the recall of those who had been banished). In one of these letters, Hamilton pointed out that the fifth and sixth articles of the peace treaty asked the states to deal fairly with Loyalist property and promised that no future confiscations would be made after the conflict was settled. "Make it the interest of those citizens," he said, "who, during the Revolution were opposed to us, to be friends to the new government by affording them not only protection but a participation in its privileges, and they will undoubtedly become its friends." He cited the examples of Emperor Augustus and Queen Elizabeth, who forgave their foes, and concluded with the prophetic admonition, "Our government hitherto have no habits. How important to the happiness not of America alone but of mankind that they should acquire good ones." [33]

By thus championing them, Alexander Hamilton brought down upon himself charges that he was a Tory-lover. It was said that he swooned with joy whenever a blue-blooded monarch gave him a civil word. He was accused of being the bellwether of the flock of Loyalists and of being in British pay. Journalists speculated as to the number of pieces of silver he had sold his country for. If he were given a free hand, they warned, Hamilton would wreck the results of the Revolution. The New York state legislature refused to go along with him. In 1784 it enacted a law disenfranchising all who had voluntarily remained within the British lines, lumping them all together, innocent and guilty. Hamilton denounced this act as inquisitorial. Of course at heart he was an Anglophile, and doubtless he was sympathetic to the Tories, because many of them were prominent and conservative people to whom he looked for help against those who seemed to threaten the men of principle and property.[34]

In 1783 the New York legislature passed the Trespass Act under which Loyalists and British occupants of patriot property within the British lines were made legally responsible for all damages and accrued rents during the whole period of the British occupation of New York City and vicinity. Soon after the passage of this act, Mrs. Elizabeth Rutgers, a patriot widow, sued Benjamin Waddington, a British merchant, for rent of her brewery which he had occupied from 1778 to 1782. Hamilton defended Waddington. The case of *Rutgers v. Waddington* came to be regarded as one of far-reaching significance. Hamilton did not deny that the British had been guilty of atrocities. He did not dare do this in an American court at the time. But he quoted Emerich de Vattel that regardless of the justice or injustice of a war, the rights of the belligerents remain unimpaired. Hamilton declared that the treaty of peace between the United States and Great Britain had here been violated. To him it was a question of whether the states or the Continental Congress were to control foreign policy, so of course he pleaded for nationalism. He urged the judges of the Mayor's Court to void the Trespass Act as a violation of the Articles of Confederation and of international law, thus being one of the first Americans to invoke the judicial power as a brake upon the authority of the state legislatures. But this was asking too much of the court—so it thought. The court acknowledged that there were certain ambiguities in the Trespass Act which required judicial interpretation. It held that during the period when Waddington had occupied Mrs. Rutgers' property under the authorization of the British army, 1780 to 1783, he was not obliged to pay her any rent. But for the two years from 1778 to 1780, he was compelled to reimburse the widow Rutgers. In this way, the court upheld most of the points on which Hamilton had based his distinguished argument, although it did not go so far as to admit it held the power of judicial review. Finally, in 1788, partly as a result of Hamilton's efforts, all laws discriminating against Loyalists were removed from the statute books of the State of New York, and the treaty of peace could then operate here as in most of the other states, in letter as well as spirit.

In the same year, the board of Loyalist agents in London met once again at the Crown and Anchor Inn in the Strand. The meeting here beside the Thames in the midst of hotels, theaters, and business buildings in the center of the city was not an extremely happy one, but neither was it sad. Sir William Pepperell, the hard-working leader of these exiled Loyalists, again was in the chair. The main business this day was the preparation of an address of thanks to the king for the welcome provisions made in their behalf. On this significant occasion, Benjamin West was inspired to draw an allegorical sketch in which Religion and Justice held the mantle of Britannia, who with outstretched arms received and embraced the Loyalists hovering around the English throne. These stood in a group which represented Law, Church and Government and which also included an American Indian chief pointing with one hand to England and the other to a widow and orphans created by the war between Patriots and Tories. A Negro with his children were shown looking up to Great Britain with gratitude for emancipation from slavery—long before Lincoln—and in a cloud on which repose Religion and Justice were seen the geniuses of Britain and America binding up the broken symbols of the two countries, emblematic of the treaty of peace.

Here, far from their American homes, these men met for their last official business. Somehow, with heavy hearts but stubborn willpower, they had adjusted themselves to the inexorable loss they had undergone. In one way, they had come home, if that was what their motherland could be called; yet, they understood the words of a friend at the inn, Samuel Johnson, which were especially appropriate for their American experience on this historic occasion, "Patriotism is the last refuge of a scoundrel."

[7]

ISLANDS OF REFUGE

But early torn reluctant from their home
Amidst the tempest's roar condemned to roam
The scattered sons, a race of giant form
Whose souls at peril mock and brave the storm
At honest labor's call with fruitless pains
Are far disposed o'er Britain's wide domains.[1]

AMERICAN TORY REFUGEES SOUGHT SHELTER under the British in the Carribean islands and elsewhere southward during the early years of the Revolution. Several American families arrived in Jamaica in October of 1775, and by March of the next year, a number of Georgia Tories followed the example of Governor Sir James Wright. He fled to England, while they departed for the West Indies and the Bahamas.

Wright was the only royal governor who returned to his American post, but this was not for long, and in 1782 he was forced to flee again, this time from Savannah. He and some of the exiles disembarked at Charleston, many others going to East Florida. But almost half of these 7,000 refugees sailed to Jamaica in the wake of the frigate *Zebra*. Most of them were slaves. Governor Wright explained that he considered Jamaica the best market for such Negroes, who if they had been left behind would have been stolen by patriots. It has been estimated that some 5,000 slaves and 400 white families went to Jamaica in the exodus from Savannah alone.

That not all of these American Tories arrived directly from the new United States is borne out by the fact that some of the first settlers of Jamaica came from Honduras and the Mosquito Shore, where British colonists lived and worked at cutting hardwoods from the forests. The Spaniards considered these colonists aliens in Central America and drove them out during the later years of the American Revolution. Records indicate that they arrived in Jamaica during the year 1783, some of them Tories, accompanied by their slaves. In fact, Tories kept coming to this large island from both the northern and southern parts of the United States until the year 1788. Some of the refugees were from the ill-fated city of Shelburne. Partly as a result of such emigration, Jamaica showed a sharp increase in population between the years 1775 and 1787. From a population of 18,500 white people, 3,700 free colored and 190,914 slaves the figures increased in this period to 30,000 whites, 10,000 free colored and 250,000 slaves.

A huge convoy of Tories from Charleston arrived in Jamaica on January 13, 1783. That its members were welcome is attested to by the fact that within six weeks the law-making assembly of the island passed an act in behalf of all the former residents of North Carolina, South Carolina, Georgia, the Bay of Honduras, and the Mosquito Shore. These immigrants were exempted for seven years from payment of any taxes on Negroes who accompanied them. They were also released from all public services and duties except the requirement of serving in the militia; charges for patenting their lands would be borne by public expense. The act stipulated that persons claiming such benefits had to make affidavits before magistrates as to intended place of settlement, and the number of slaves they brought with them. As well, they were required to settle and plant their lands and improve them within two years from the date of such agreements. They were not exempted from quitrents on lands which they might purchase.[2]

The principal communities settled were Kingston, Port Royal, St. Thomas-in-the-East, St. Andrew, St. George, St. Catherine, St. Thomas-in-the-Vale, and Trelawney. According to one authority, 145 of these refugees arrived in Kingston while the remaining 18 went to the other places mentioned. Of the former number, 61 brought along 881 slaves from North America. Of the 18 latter, nine had slaves totaling 568. Over 200 Negroes were the property of Governor Sir James Wright of Georgia and more than 100 had been the property of William Bull, late lieutenant governor of South Carolina. Many of them engaged in public works and other menial tasks.[3]

Some of these loyal people came from Connecticut, Massachusetts, New York, and Pennsylvania, as well as Maryland,

Virginia, and other Southern states. Among them were a few surgeons, artisans, Quakers and widows as well as veterans of the war itself. Of course a large proportion of the exiles were planters. One of them received a grant of land in the parish of St. Elizabeth, where it was stated that the land was so swampy that "none but amphibious creatures such as fishes, frogs and Dutchmen could live." Ironically, the name of this Tory was Frogg.

One of the Tory families which settled in Jamaica was that of Dr. Lewis Johnston, former president of the King's Council in Georgia, and his son, Captain William Martin Johnston of the New York Volunteers. When their home town of Savannah was captured by the patriot forces in 1782, the Johnstons went to St. Augustine, Florida. Some of the ships carrying the refugees to St. Augustine were wrecked along the shore. The Johnstons remained in Florida for sixteen months, during which time fish was their main ration. When it was announced that East Florida had been ceded to Spain, Dr. Johnston and his family were granted transportation to wherever they wished to go in Great Britain. Being a native of Scotland, Johnston chose to return to that country. Captain Johnston, his son, had already fled to Scotland where he had begun medical studies in Edinburgh, and eventually became a doctor. The elder Johnston, along with his own and his son's families, embarked at St. Mary's River in Florida for Greenock, Scotland, where he remained for the rest of his life. The younger Johnstons, however, still liked America. In 1785 Captain William Johnston learned that General Alured Clark, the former commandant of Savannah, had been appointed governor of Jamaica, so the former, who had served under Clark, decided to go to that island also. His family followed him later. Johnston was amiably received by Clark and was attached to a local regiment so that he could receive foreign military pay, which amounted to 20 shillings a week for him, ten shillings for his wife and five shillings for each of his three children. There the younger Doctor Johnston remained, an important fighter of yellow fever, which came down to Jamaica from the Philadelphia epidemic in the early 1790's and "made great havoc among all newcomers and sailors," although it did not attack the natives of Jamaica or others who had resided there long enough to be acclimated. Dr. Johnston lived near Halfway Tree in Liguana, where he died in 1807. His wife and children then moved to Nova Scotia, where they lived with his wife's aged father near Halifax.[4]

Hardships which faced the Loyalists migrating to Jamaica included lack of food and other necessities. On April 8, 1783, a memorial was sent to Sir Guy Carleton in New York, signed by Sir James Wright and William Knox, among others, requesting a further allowance until they could find lands or employment in Jamaica, especially for their Negroes. Some of these Tories did obtain such employment for their slaves by hiring them out to labor on public works or sending them out "jobbing," which meant performing the heavy work on sugar and other plantations, such as digging the holes for cane and planting it. When they ran out of provisions, these displaced Tories called on the British authorities in the United States for replenishment, which usually was forthcoming. But such compliance was not always the case, so the exiles had to endure not only their individual hardships but also the famine and hurricanes which often struck during their early years on the island. In fact, there were such heavy hurricanes in 1780 and 1781 that starvation confronted the settlers. But these natural disasters were not the only cause of hardship. The American Revolution, to which they owed their banishment in the first place, continued to wreak its punishment. This time it was indirect. In retaliation, the British government had restricted the trade of its remaining American possessions with the United States. An Order in Council of July 2, 1783, limited the importation of products of the newly independent nation, such as livestock, grain and lumber, into the West Indies and to British vessels, and prohibited entirely the importing by them of American salt beef, pork and fish.

This policy of commercial hostility resulted in remonstrances and petitions being sent from the islands to the British Parliament, stating they were dependent on the United States for supplies. The legislature of Jamaica advocated that trade with the new country be free, as it was the only means of sustaining the estates on the island, of supplying families with their bread, and of averting ruin. As if to emphasize the dire forecasts, a violent storm struck Kingston, Jamaica, on July 30, 1784, and either sank, drove ashore, or dismasted every vessel in the harbor. The terrific gale blew down public buildings in and around the capital city and caused the loss of many lives. The situation became so bad that by the first week of August the local government, on its own initiative, suspended the British regulations and allowed foreign supplies to come in unrestricted for a period of six months. Encouraged by this action, the Jamaica planters increased their acreage of corn and similar products. But hardly had they gathered their crops when another hurricane hit the island on August 27, 1785. All food then had to be retained for local use and so the anticipated exportation was not allowed. "The climax of misery seemed to be reached" when still another hurricane "burst upon the land" on October 20, 1786. Many of the Tories as well as others felt as if this third disaster were some visitation of God.[5]

Out of these misfortunes, however, there did come a benefit. The islands came to depend more on themselves in raising their provisions and in making their own staves as well as other necessities. The Tories and their slaves contributed to the cultivation of coffee, an industry which was already catching on favorably when they arrived. Some of the refugees reportedly raised large quantities of indigo but found that this crop was unprofitable in the absence of government protection, although it was well suited to men with moderate means and few slaves. An attempt was also made to grow cotton in the North American manner, but the exiles found that this crop was only partially successful because of the variable climate.

All the settlers were not successful, as for example a Tory family which petitioned the governor of Jamaica for recompense in 1786: "That from the too pleasing expectance of this country," the petition read, "of being kept a British colony, they have been encouraged to make plantations and purchase houses and lands at pretty extravagant rates. The short notice of their removal from hence together with the knowledge of no indemnification being offered for their properties they will be obliged to leave behind. No provision to support their families in the unsettled state they must be in for six months after the embarkation, all these and many more conspire to make their situation wretched."[6]

The adventures of other Tories who sought refuge in the West Indies early in the war were such as to cause some of them to lament their attachment to the king. For instance, Owen Griffin, a tavern keeper of North Carolina, found it necessary to leave the state because his patriot neighbors swore his destruction. In February of 1776 he loaded his goods on a vessel and set sail. Yet his erstwhile "Carolina friends" were not yet ready to leave him alone. Griffin was pursued by 24 of them in two boats, but the wind enabled him to escape just in time. After a voyage of 26 days, he put into Dry Harbor in Jamaica. There he heard for the first time of the Restraining Act which forbade trade between the rebellious subjects and His Majesty's Dominions. He was advised to sell or make over his vessel and cargo or it would be seized. Knowing that he was a loyal subject, he refused to use any collusive subterfuges to save his property, but instead wrote to Charles Hamilton, the Collector of Montego Bay, and asked for the privilege of entering the harbor. Hamilton ordered the boat to be seized and brought into the bay.

Griffin produced affidavits about his ill treatment in North Carolina and the necessity of his leaving there. The collector was impressed by these, felt that Griffin was innocent, and so gave him a letter to His Majesty's Attorney and Advocate which allowed him to recover his vessel. Griffin then paid the required fees and obtained a permit to discharge and load. Having sold his cargo, he took on Jamaica products in exchange and started for Kingston. But he was soon overtaken and seized by the British ship *Squirrel* and escorted into Kingston, where, after a trial, his ship was declared a lawful prize. So, ironically, his vessel along with cargo, apparel and furniture was sold and the money divided among his captors. Griffin then went to England.

In similar manner, James Green of North Carolina received a pass from Governor Josiah Martin to go to Antigua. Green even agreed to bring back supplies for the British fleet at Cape Fear, but he no sooner had arrived in the harbor of St. Johns, Antigua, in March of 1776 than his ship was seized by the British ship *Lynx*. In the admiralty court, the seizure of his vessel and cargo was declared legal. Green likewise went to England.

A Carolina Tory named Richard Lang suffered even more hardships in his attempts to flee the country and set himself up southward. He reported that he was settled in the District of Ninety-Six on a 150-acre plantation with 12 head of cattle and seven horses as well as three Negro slaves. One of the slaves was stolen by patriots, Lang claimed, and another was concealed "on board of H. M. Ship *Cyrus* where after having obtained an order to receive him on board, I was treated in a manner too shocking to relate. The Negro, after my being grossly insulted on the quarter deck of the ship was given to me but had orders to take care of himself. An armed boat was dispatched after me, and when opposite me, the Negro upset me in my boat and every step was taken to deprive me of my life. The transport people were forced to take me up. They were armed with bludgeons and I was forced to remain up to my shoulders in the water, when the officer after many threats cast a large club and the oars at my head. . . . My Negroes, I have every reason to believe, were sent on to Jamaica or Dominica and there sold. . . . Chagrined exceedingly at such unheard of cruelty from the officers of that country for which I have sacrificed my all, long fought and freely bled. I determined rather to bear insult and injury from my enemies than be abused and robbed by my friends, I returned to South Carolina." [7]

So all the Tories did not find it worthwhile to leave home. An anonymous letter from one in Philadelphia, which appeared in the Kingston, Jamaica, *Weekly Advertiser* on October 16, 1779, stated that "The fears of our friends in this place, when they found themselves abandoned, were violent; yet their fondness for home and their despair of our cause led many of them to remain in the power of their rebellious countrymen." This statement was more generally true than has been realized.

As far as slavery was concerned, Jamaica had been a center of slave trade and use for over a century when the American Revolution occurred. At the time that slave trading was abolished in 1807, Jamaica ironically had reached its zenith in the production of native goods and commerce in them. In no colony did the system of slavery run more completely its baneful course than in Jamaica, and in none did it die harder. To a visitor in Jamaica today, this is difficult to realize, yet in the rhythm of the bongo drums and in the melodic voices of the people, both in talking and singing, one can sense still a hint of that plaintive cry against human bondage.

In the well-staffed West India Reference Library of the Institute of Jamaica in Kingston, there are yellowed copies of the *Royal Gazette of Jamaica* which appeared during the time of the coming of the American Tories. These newspapers are much like others of colonial days, with long stories from England about the state of the world, letters from readers who comment on the events of the day, and items of news colored by editorial opinion. In one issue dated May 11, 1782, there is an account of fighting between the patriots and Tories in America which puts them, for the time at least, ahead of the major forces in activity. The story tells of the brig *Belvidere* from New York carrying dispatches to the effect that "Some trifling skirmishes between the loyal refugees and the rebels, attended with various success but the main bodies of the two armies were totally inactive."

There follows in the same issue "the joyful account of the brave Admiral Rodney's ever memorable defeat of the French fleet on the 12th instant, was proclaimed here by the discharge of 21 guns from Fort Haldane, followed by 50 more from the shipping in the harbor, with the British flag displayed triumphant over the French, Spanish, Dutch and American colors."

In going through the files of the *Royal Gazette* one finds evidence of a distinctive problem of the time. In nearly every issue, there are short but colorful advertisements, placed there by Tory owners arrived from the United States, inquiring about their runaway slaves. Here are a few typical examples of these signs signaling the inevitable disappearance of slavery here and in the rest of the British Empire:

July 12, 1782:

A Negro named Bob, lately from Carolina and formerly the property of Peter Thomson of Charleston, 5 feet, nine inches high, 35 years of age and has a film over his right eye; was harbored by one, Dowson, formerly a servant in a Negro dram shop in Charleston, but now a constable or bum bailliff in Kingston. Five pounds reward offered for his return. Another Negro named Ovid, a stout made fellow, six feet high, pitted a little with the smallpox and has lost some of his front teeth, 24 years of age, from the colonies.
Same reward. W. Miller.

July 22, 1782

Ran away the night of July 4th [!] four North American Negroes the property of the late Colonel J. M. Prevost, a young waiting man named Prince, tolerably well made, pitted with smallpox and has a sore on his right hand from the kick of a horse—and three Negro women, all very short, one aged named Rose, the mother of the other two, who are named Patty and Esther, the first of whom is a fattish young woman, the other a little slight made girl about 14 years old. Reward offered by J. Johnson.

November 29, 1786

Run away this morning a mulatto boy named Alick, 16, stout, four feet and four inches high, grey eyes,

*brown hair, it curls very little and he generally wears
it tied. Born in Virginia, has been in New York and
speaks good English. Is often taken for a Spaniard or
a mixture of the Indian breed and by his looks,
few would take him for a slave. Five pounds reward.
H. Smith.*

Not so important as a Tory refuge as Jamaica but still of some
significance was the British West Indian island of Antigua, 300
miles east and south of Puerto Rico. Here, as we have seen, the
prominent Massachusetts lawyer Samuel Quincy went from his
exile in England and became an official of the Crown. Antigua,
along with neighboring islands, was discovered by Christopher
Columbus on his second voyage in 1493. Although at first uninhabited, by early 1787 the population of Antigua was 2,590
white people along with 37,808 slaves. Also listed in the same
census report are 1,230 "free, coloured and black" persons. At
English Harbor, Lord Nelson was later stationed with his fleet
and soon afterward began the voyage which took him eventually to Trafalgar and immortality.[8]

Among other West Indian islands to receive the Tory
emigres was that of Grenada, not far from Trinidad. Here had
come Mather Byles, Jr. in 1790, after he had left Nova Scotia
and gone to Barbados with a cargo of goods. Finding himself
not wanted there, Byles went on to Dominica, then Antigua,
thence to Grenada, in a pattern of testing the islands, as did
other Tories when they fled. "The weather since my arrival," he
wrote to his friend Edward Winslow from Grenada, showing
some of the humor of his famous pastor-father of Boston, "has
been very pleasant and the glass not above 86 which is a heat I
can very well bear. My health has been as good as I ever re-
member it and as I get a daily allowance of old Madeira or fresh
claret, I hope to preserve myself for some time against the whole
muster role of West India diseases. They are a pretty formidable
regiment and I was prepared for the worst by a medical book I
took up by accident at Dr. Allmons, which set out by gravely
remarking that in the West Indies, the inhabitants died of in-
flammatory disorders from October to June, and of putrid disorders from June to October."[9]

A more welcome atmosphere, but not without its draw-
backs, was found by the Tories in the Bahama Islands, just off

the coast of Florida. An investigation was made by the British governors in New York and Florida in 1783 and the first report on the Bahamas as possible places of refuge was not encouraging. One historian has described the original Bahamians as a rather sorry lot who were to resent the influx of Americans and who engaged mainly in the business of privateering. The official report ascribed the uncultivated condition of the lands to the indolence of the inhabitants, "who contented themselves with whatever nature produced by her unaided efforts. They took no trouble to clear the land but planted small patches of Guinea corn, yams and sugar cane, which they left without further care until the crops were ready to be gathered." This picture resembles that of William Byrd II describing the "lubberland" of the Carolinas half a century earlier.[10]

There were assets to be developed in the Bahamas, however, such as the growing of pineapples, oranges, lemons, limes, cocoa and other fruits common to the West Indies. True, the report continued, the islands were rocky and the surface rough, but three kinds of soil existed there, one adapted to the raising of cotton, another to the raising of vegetables of all kinds and a third to the production of sorghum. But such inducements were not the real cause of the movement of American Tories. Those who lived in Florida were not granted it as an asylum by the Peace Treaty of 1783. Instead, the loyal people there now had the choice of living under Spanish rule, which they greatly dreaded, or of preserving their fealty by withdrawing to some British possession. Most of them chose the latter course, taking the advice of Governor Patrick Tonyn of Florida to leave before the Spanish took possession.

King George III helped matters by instructing Governor John Maxwell of the Bahamas that "forty acres of land be granted to every person being master or mistress of a family for himself or herself and twenty acres for every white and black man, woman or child of which such person's family shall consist at the actual time of granting such warrant." Lord North followed this up with a promise: "For those who prefer the Bahama Islands, a considerable quantity of provisions has already been provided and dispatched and supplies will be sent to the West Indies, proportioned to the number who may desire to become settlers upon these islands."[11]

The number of desperate Tories who responded to the royal invitations is not definite, one authority giving it as 5,000, another as between six and seven thousand. That they went in considerable numbers there is no doubt, for the population of the islands trebled within less than five years after 1783. The *Bahama Gazette* stated on September 11, 1784, "This place bids fair to become a flourishing settlement from the number of refugees of property now settled and daily coming into these islands from New York, South Carolina, Georgia and Florida." Many of the Loyalists did not go to the Bahamas until they had tried other places such as England, Nova Scotia or the West Indies. Southern Tories virtually transplanted their plantations to the Bahamas, creating new parishes, churches, schools and private homes. They infused new life into the tropical islands. As the torrent of refugees poured in with their slaves, they took up land grants ranging in size from 15 acres on New Providence to 1,500 acres on the island of Abaco. By 1789, the population had reached 11,300, of whom 8,000 were Negroes. Of the 114 original landowners, nearly all their names can be found in a present-day list of Nassau merchants and members of government. The influx of so many Tories had a marked effect upon the commercial, agricultural and social conditions of the Bahamas. Towns grew and trade increased. Exports of cotton, salt, turtles, mahogany, dyes, woods and bark were sent to England and smuggled to the United States and the southern islands of the West Indies. And in turn, from these places, the Bahamas received supplies of livestock and provisions.[12]

These islands were also the subject of some misrepresentation on the part of American Tories. John Ferdinand Dalziel Smyth, whose career was as long and odd as his name, requested the British Privy Council in 1783 to grant him Yametta or Long Island in the Bahamas, but was turned down. The government had not yet purchased the islands from the original proprietors and his claim for compensation for the loss of thousands of acres of land which he claimed to have owned and lost was not believed.

According to Smyth's account, he was born in the highlands of Scotland in 1748 and emigrated to America in 1763, where he was a storekeeper and physician in North Carolina, Virginia and Maryland. He even wrote a book about his American experiences which was published in 1784. Apparently the account is basically true, but is embellished by exaggeration and doubtful anecdotes. Smyth swore that he lived in Charles County, Maryland, until 1775, but when one of his servants was killed by the patriot rebels and his own safety was endangered, he joined Lord Dunmore at Norfolk. The following November, according to Smyth, he was sent by Dunmore on a secret expedition to the Ohio Valley and Canada under the command of Lieutenant Colonel John Connolly. Its purpose was an attack upon Pittsburgh, but the force was captured at Hagerstown and imprisoned at Frederick, Maryland. Robbed in the prison, Smyth escaped after a few weeks and traveled through ice and snow over the Allegheny Mountains but was subsequently recaptured and returned to Frederick. Under heavy guard, he was transported to Philadelphia, where, he said, for three weeks he was confined in a fireless cell without a chair, a table, a bed, a blanket or straw and with little food and water. Then he was transferred to a cell which he shared with Connolly and another prisoner for six months, this confinement impairing their health.

Smyth further stated that fear the British might attack Philadelphia caused Congress in December of 1776 to order the removal of many Tory prisoners to Baltimore. So on bleeding feet and in irons, he marched 150 miles. When a servant girl in Newport, Delaware, expressed sympathy for the prisoners she saw passing, she was beaten by her master and mistress and thrown out into the cold, where she was abused by the prisoners' guards. In January of 1777, Smyth bribed his attendants to allow him to escape from confinement in Baltimore. In a small boat he sailed down the Chesapeake Bay and up the Nanticoke River. Near Princess Anne, some other Tories found him and concealed him in a woods. There he found that the Tories of Somerset County, Maryland, and of Sussex County, Delaware, were ready to stage an insurrection. But he believed that they would be defeated unless aided by British forces, so persuaded them to postpone the uprising.

In some way, Smyth made his way to New York, where, he related, he was given a commission as captain in the Queen's American Rangers. During 1777, he participated in an expedition to Danbury, Connecticut, and recruited 185 soldiers for the British army. By 1780, he had gone to England, where he received from the government an annual grant of 200 pounds for his services. Then he asked for the grant of land in the Bahamas. His numerous claims totaled 31,582 pounds, stating also that he had lost 60,000 acres of land along the Ohio and Mississippi rivers. For 25 years, Smyth tried to obtain a large compensation for his services. The result was an allowance of 90 pounds a year and a statement from the Loyalist Commissioners to the effect that "It is not only charitable but just to suppose that every man is innocent until he is convicted and therefore we conceive that we are perfectly consistent in this stage of the business in recommending an allowance adequate to his military situation." A recent historian has summed up the case with these words: "While he did perform some heroic services during the American Revolution, in most other respects he was conclusively demonstrated to be a liar, with an exaggerated notion of his own importance." [13]

Other Tories were more fortunate in their quest for a West Indian refuge. A traveler, David Schoepf, who accompanied a shipload of exiles from St. Augustine, Florida, to the Bahamas described the capital in vivid detail. In Nassau he found living space scarce and considered himself fortunate to locate a place in a carpenter's home a half mile from town, all the other houses being crowded with refugees and their possessions. Nassau is on the north shore of the island of New Providence and had only one principal street, now Bay Street. It was narrow and followed the shore, with houses and shops on one side and the open harbor on the other. Although the street was unpaved, this made little difference since the island was almost wholly rock.[14] There was an open-sided market called the Bourse where sales of all kinds were conducted, including the auctioning of slaves. Here buyers, sellers, ship captains and other such persons gathered for business or just to learn the latest news. Other public buildings included a church, a jail and an assembly house. The governor, John Maxwell, lived in a large house on top of a ridge, a house so conspicuous that it was a landmark for incoming ships. On this same hilltop, Mount Fitzwilliams, the present Government House was built in 1801.

Other Nassau buildings were constructed of wood and were simple and light in construction, most being of one thickness of boards nailed to a frame which was exposed in the interior. The better homes had ceilings to make them more ornate. There were no chimneys, and cooking was done over a wood fire in the separate kitchen, which was often a half-open shed. Rarely did windows have glass, but heavy wooden shutters were used to cover them at night and during bad weather. Cellars were unknown until the Tories built some. But the houses had spacious yards and individual gardens. At this time, New Providence

Island was overgrown with vines, trees, and shrubs, which served to conceal the rocks to some extent. But when the wild growth was cleared away, the difficulty of planting was obvious. There were no plows and few hoes. The favorite tool was a sharp stick. "An acre or a piece of arable ground here has indeed a fearful look," wrote Schoepf, "for there is to be seen hardly anything but rock, full of larger and smaller pits and holes, containing a pretty strongly reddish earth." [15]

A continual crop was that of yams, as well as watermelons, corn, and most of the common European vegetables. Noted among tropical fruits were papaws, limes, avocados, bananas, pomegranates, figs, oranges, soursops and pineapples. Sugar cane flourished but was used for syrup rather than sugar. Coffee also did well around Nassau and indigo flourished when there was enough water to moisten it. Cows and goats were kept for milk along with sheep and hogs, but there were not enough good pastures for much growing of livestock. Instead of beef, the natives ate turtles and iguanas, the latter being some three feet long and caught by trained dogs in the wild areas. These fearful looking animals could be stored alive for weeks by sewing their jaws together with needle and thread. The Tories had to accustom themselves to such hardy fare, which they did reluctantly.[16]

In the Bahamas, woodcutting was found to be an occupation in which almost everyone engaged at one time or another. When there was nothing else for slaves to do, their owners set them to cutting wood. Anyone had the right to cut wood wherever he found it, so by 1784 the islands of New Providence as well as its neighbors were pretty well cut over. Mahogany was found to be good for the construction of ships below the water line but too heavy for the superstructure. Pineapples were among the chief exports to Europe and illegally to the United States, with limes and yams being especially desired by people of the latter country. Meat, butter, rice, corn, wheat, utensils, and clothing were all imported from the United States and England.

As for the people of Nassau, Schoepf described them as "amiable, courteous and hospitable. They like to drink and dance the time away. One is puzzled to see most of the white inhabitants of Providence living well and yet going about in idleness; but they live by the sweat of their slaves. Even these serving people appeared to be happy, some of them paying their masters a small amount each week for the privilege of being let alone and allowed to do much as they pleased." [17]

This then was the sort of place and people which the Tories found when they entered the Bahamas. As one writer has said, the exiles were embittered by their losses, some with feelings of superiority toward the old inhabitants, whom they derisively called Conchs, and almost all of them with driving ambitions to remake their fortunes and obtain positions of leadership in the government. Because of this, a conflict was inevitable; and since the Tories outnumbered the old inhabitants almost two to one, they felt that they were certain to win. For a time they did. Yet in spite of their zealous work and their modern ideas about plantation management, the Tories who survived were the ones who came to accept the ways of those they found already living there and attuned to the easy-going environment. A casual attitude toward agriculture and a close dependence on the sea were found to be the key to adjustment in this balmy climate beyond the Florida coast.[18]

One Tory who did not adjust to the Bahamas was Colonel David Fanning of North Carolina, peerless guerrilla fighter, who seemed to the patriots at times to be almost a one-man army in himself, with his ruthless raids and what he called his eye-for-an-eye retaliation for patriot crimes. At the end of September, 1782, Fanning and his new wife—he took time out from fighting the rebels to marry her—were at Charleston, where ships were leaving for St. Augustine. He took charge of a shipload of refugees headed for Florida, but the vessel was forced to delay its landing for eight days because of the hostile situation. Eventually Colonel Fanning and his party did land, and he established a plantation. The next February, Fanning met Major Andrew Deveaux, who was collecting volunteers for an expedition to capture the Bahama island of New Providence. The two planned to collaborate in the adventure but somehow did not succeed in getting together. The dynamic Fanning was undaunted and instead set out for West Florida, from which he and a small party made their way to Key West. Here he found passage to New Providence, and landed at Nassau in early September of 1784. The Fannings evidently did not like this place, for they stayed only a month; then these restless Tories departed for Nova Scotia, where at long last they found a haven.[19]

It is not clear whether Fanning liked the royal government of the Bahamas or not, though he had stated that the American

Tories could no longer expect any worthwhile help from Great Britain. But it is certain that many of the refugees who went to the Bahamas were not looked upon with favor by Governor John Maxwell, nor did he relish their attitude. The coming of the Loyalists brought with it a factional feeling, the Americans soon denouncing Governor Maxwell, criticizing his administration, saying that he attempted to withhold from them the right of trial by jury, and accusing him of other conduct which they deemed tyrannical. They also disliked some of the local laws, which they said did not conform to those of the mother country, and demanded reform. In answer, Governor Maxwell sent a letter on May 17, 1784, to Lord Sydney in London, describing the Tories who had arrived in the Bahamas. One shipment of them from Florida consisted, he said, of 500 whites and 1,000 blacks.

"There are two classes of Loyalists," wrote Maxwell; "the first consists of farmers who have set themselves down on the out islands with huge families of ten, twenty or one hundred slaves. These, in my opinion, merit a particular attention, and I wish to show it to them. The second class is composed of the officers, merchants and people under a certain description, who hope to return to the American continent when they have made their peace there. Nothing can satisfy these people. Provisions ought to be immediately issued to them—lands and employments without number are what they tell me their merit entitles them to—such has been their behavior, that they can go but one step further, in my opinion, which is, to take the government from me. Flour, being very scarce, I have permitted the Americans to supply us, until it comes by its usual way. This, in their [Tories'] opinion, is a monstrous offence, some of them have attempted to tear down the American colors. If your Lordship sends them further supply of stores and provisions, I entreat your Lordship that I may have nothing to say to them or do in the matter; as they are the most tormenting, dissatisfied people on earth." [20]

Here was a case of American Tories, who had not gotten along with their new government back in the United States, not being happy or even satisfied with the royal government as exercised in the Bahamas, either. Events grew worse. Three weeks later, Maxwell was again complaining to Lord Sydney about the refugees. "They have not attempted rioting yet," he warned, "but have amused themselves in writing libels. If the remainder that intends coming here are of the same sort, civil government is in danger . . . for in my life I never met with so much ingratitude and abuse as I have within three weeks." In order to prevent riots on Sundays, the governor ordered that all masters and marines of American vessels stay on board and remain there until Monday mornings.[21]

The reply of Lord Sydney was reassuring but it also showed understanding. "It is not surprising," he said to Maxwell, "that men who have lived in affluence and experienced every comfort resulting from it, should in the disagreeable state in which many of the Loyalists upon the Bahama Islands are represented to be, feel the difference between their former and present situation and that their temper and disposition should be soured from that unpleasant change." He urged the governor to make allowances accordingly and to do his best to carry into effect the intentions of the king "by affording them every possible means within your power, for alleviating the distress to which they have been exposed."

The situation, instead of improving, deteriorated. Maxwell reported that on August 20, a riot took place during which the Tories "insulted several inhabitants at night. On the 21st, (this being Sunday) opposite the church door, they had drums beating the Rogue's March, so as to drive the people out of the church. They then possessed themselves of the church and during the night, amused themselves with ringing the bell as if the town had been on fire. Judge my situation, my Lord, with only one officer and 13 men." [22]

Some serious actions, however, did result from the meeting of the Tories. James Hepburn, chairman of one of the meetings, reported that the Loyalists passed resolutions to form themselves into a representative body, in order to adopt such measures which they might deem necessary to promote their general interest. They further requested that the Bahama Island government "afford a comfortable asylum to the American Loyalists" and stated "that the soil and climate are well suited to produce cotton, tobacco, indigo, fruit, provisions and other valuable articles." [23]

Evidently Maxwell paid little attention to the request, for soon afterward, Hepburn wrote him stating that a committee had been appointed to call upon the governor, and that they were met by a servant who said he had been ordered not to disturb Maxwell. The Tories were indignant and informed

Maxwell that they considered this "piece of conduct as unworthy of a person pretending to be the representative of a great sovereign, and as tending to cast a marked and very undeserved insult upon a large and deserving body of His Majesty's loyal subjects." Maxwell replied the same day, explaining that he was busy making up his dispatches for England but would see them at any time after that day. It is not known what was in the dispatches, but they must have concerned his feeling of desperation, for in a matter of months, Maxwell was recalled to England.[24]

Such political feuding went on between the Tories and the established colonial government for 13 years. The elections of 1785 gave the former some seats in the House of Assembly but the native population still remained in control. After more altercation, the Tories sent a petition to the Assembly asking for its dissolution. The reply of that body was to read the petition, which was then handed over to the common hangman and burned before the door of the House.

By the latter part of 1786, the American Tories had the upper hand as a political party, but this situation was changed by the arrival of the Earl of Dunmore as governor of the Bahamas. He had been the last royal governor of Virginia and had never given up the cause of the Crown, even resorting to arms and the stirring up of the Negroes of the former colony against the rebels. In the Bahamas, Dunmore managed to obtain a larger salary than his predecessor and to secure considerable grants of lands to augment it. He maintained the same policy as did Maxwell. Dunmore received petitions from New Providence, Abaco, Exuma and Cat islands asking that the Assembly be dissolved, but he declined. As a consequence, it lasted eight years more, or until the end of his administration.

Although Dunmore has been condemned by most American historians, there were voices raised in his behalf. Anthony Stokes, a Tory employed as an agent in London for the Bahamas, stated on October 23, 1788: "I expressed my concern that the American Loyalists were so much altered from what they had been; for although they found the Bahama Islands in peace, yet they had made it a point to quarrel with every gentleman who had been commander-in-chief of the colony, since they settled there. That Governor Maxwell whom they now acknowledge to be an honest man, had been recalled to make them easy; and that although Lieutenant Governor Powell who was one of their own corps, had succeeded Governor Maxwell, yet they treated him in such a manner as to hasten his end; and that they had acted by Mr. John Brown and Lord Dunmore in a similar manner. That I had been informed that when the emigrants were disappointed in accomplishing their views on the old inhabitants, some of them proceeded so far as to draw cannon to the summit which commanded the town and to clean and repair musketry, declaring that what they had failed to obtain by other means, they would enforce by firing on the old inhabitants of the town, which I observed would have been considered a very serious business in this country." [25]

In the same documents appears an unsigned statement of the time which may help further to explain some of the reputation of Lord Dunmore. It states: "The first appearance of uneasiness shown by the former malcontents after Lord Dunmore's arrival was occasioned by his Lordship's proclamation relative to the Negroes, inserted in the *Bahama Gazette*. From the time the proclamation made its appearance, the new inhabitants considered Lord Dunmore as a friend to the Negroes. This was a serious concern to many whose property consisted in Negroes, many of whom had been manumitted in America, in consequence of His Majesty's proclamation during the rebellion; others, it was said had been stolen and brought by force from America; some, after having been deluded under false ideas of liberty to leave America, and to bind themselves for one or two years, were now claimed as the absolute property of their masters. . . . The first attack upon the Negroes was made soon after the proclamation. The houses of the free Negroes were broke open in the night by a number of persons armed with guns, swords, etc. and several women were most wantonly wounded, and more dreadful consequences would most probably have ensued had not timely assistance been given by the governor, who had been called out of his bed and fortunately prevented further mischief to the Negroes." [26]

The reign of Dunmore was brought to an end in 1796 partly through the influence of a group known as the Board of American Loyalists. This group was composed of Florida refugees and was organized in Nassau in 1784 "to preserve and maintain those rights and liberties for which they left their homes and possessions." Among the members were James Hepburn, formerly of North Carolina, John Wood, William Moss, Peter Dean, John M. Tattnall, and John Wells, all of whom were to play important parts, as were their descendants, in the future business and political life of the Bahamas. Wells published the *Bahama Gazette,* the only newspaper in the Bahamas during colonial times, and through this medium the Tories could express their grievances. One writer in this publication on April 2, 1785, suggested a new motto for the islands: "By wrangling and jangling, a country prospers." He further suggested giving prizes to people "who by their violence, virulence, petulance, impertinence, partiality, locality, scurrility and personality are best calculated to keep up a true and laudable spirit of faction in this much neglected and unbefriended country."

In the opinion of some, one such prize might have been given to Adam Chrystie, a one-time wealthy Tory planter of East Florida. After fleeing that harassed province, he lived until 1790 in his native Scotland. Then he was appointed Secretary of the Bahamas and a member of the council there, in which capacity he served until 1812. When he got to Nassau, he wrote to George Chalmers, the agent for the Bahamas in London, saying: "When I arrived in the province, I found two violent and indecent factions, with which no honest man could at all times act, one headed by the governor and the other by the chief justice. They were agreed only in one thing, which was to do me all the mischief in their power and drive me out of the province if possible. I was therefore prosecuted, fined, imprisoned and my office rendered of no value." [27]

Lord Dunmore was the governor to whom Chrystie referred, and the chief justice was Stephen De Lancey of the well-known New York Tory family. Though he sometimes got along well with Governor Dunmore, Chrystie quarreled with him on at least one occasion, when Dunmore took the seal away from Chrystie because he would not apply it to a paper which the latter considered dishonest. Perhaps the best things said about Chrystie appeared in the *Royal Gazette* of April 19, 1812, which eulogized: "In this gentleman, to the acquirements of the accomplished scholar were added the greatest integrity in his official capacities and the most pleasing and agreeable manners in private life. His worth being generally known, his loss will be as generally regretted in this community."

Another Tory who made a mark in the islands was Alexander Wylly, at one time the speaker of the colonial assembly of Georgia. His property was confiscated and he fled with his family to the Bahamas. His grandson, George Anderson, became chief justice of the Bahamas. But the son of Alexander Wylly, William, was to become a controversial figure in the local politics. A former captain in the Carolina Rangers, William Wylly became attorney general of the Bahamas. Once, in order to protect himself from being arrested in a political controversy, he surrounded his elegant mansion with his slaves bearing arms. The Assembly had ordered his arrest because it was suspected that he was plotting with England to end slavery in the Bahamas. This arming of the slaves was regarded by some of his associates as a dreadful portent, for when Britain freed all slaves in the empire, the plantation system of the Bahamas also ended.

Even so, improvements were made in the production of cotton there, as they were in the United States. Joseph Eve and his brother, Oswell, moved to the Bahamas during the American Revolution, and became cotton planters on Cat Island. Cotton was then ginned in the primitive manner, being run through two parallel rollers spiked with nails, and turned in opposite directions by a hand or foot crank. Joseph Eve invented a cotton gin which operated by wind and advertised that he could make one to be turned by cattle or water power. The record of an estate in 1797 listed a "cotton machine of Eve's to go by wind or cattle" valued at 175 pounds. The inventor also had the idea of modern servicing, for he stated that once his machine had been sold, he would keep it in repair at the annual rate of four guineas. This machine could gin as much as 360 pounds of cotton in one day and was praised, for example, by a fellow planter, Charles Dames, as follows: "Preparing our cotton for market was formerly considered as the most tedious, troublesome and laborious part of the agricultural process in this country. To you," he told Eve, "we are indebted for its having been rendered pleasant, easy and expeditious." Oswell Eve died at Cat Island in 1793, and his brother, Joseph, the inventor, returned to the United States in 1800. Apparently there was then no one to repair the Eve cotton gins, for according to the account of one planter some years later, the ginning of cotton was again being done by hand.[28]

During the time when East Florida was the property of Great Britain, an important plantation there, named "Rollestown," lay on the east bank of the St. Johns river, and was owned by an Englishman named Denys Rolle. When Florida was evacuated after the war, Rolle hired a ship and moved his slaves, livestock, dismantled houses, and other belongings to Exuma Island of the Bahamas, where he established two other plantations, "Rolleville" and "Steventon." The latter name was derived from Lord Stevenstone in England, elder brother of Denys Rolle. In 1797, when Denys Rolle died in England, his son, John, became Lord Rolle and inherited the Exuma plantation. Upon the freeing of slaves by Great Britain in 1834, Lord Rolle gave this property to his Negroes and all of them took the surname of Rolle. Men marrying into this clan also took that name until now several thousand Bahamian Negroes, and their relatives who have moved to Florida, bear the name of Rolle.[29]

An even wider influence of the Tories was shown at the time by the *Bahama Gazette*. Its editor, John Wells, published the *East Florida Gazette* in 1783 and 1784 at St. Augustine. He was the son of Robert Wells, a Tory bookseller and publisher of Charleston, South Carolina, who had fled to London at the outbreak of the Revolution and remained there as a successful merchant. The sister of John, Louisa Wells, ran the Charleston publishing business after her father went into exile; she married one of her father's apprentice printers and later, as Louisa Aikman, wrote an interesting account of her voyage from Charleston to London as a Tory refugee. She seemed to understand the printing business almost as well as her husband. A brother of Louisa and John, Charles Wells, went to Europe, where he became a physician and scientist.[30]

The *Bahama Gazette* was published in Nassau by John Wells from 1784 until his death in 1799. It was a four-page paper and was issued twice a week. The paper was used by the editor to further the cause of the Board of American Loyalists, of which he was a member, to publicize government abuses, and to aid the Loyalists in their struggle for political rights in general. Apparently this newspaper had good coverage of European and American news, running frequent stories about the changes of government then going on in both of these places. It has been said to have been "a kind of sustained beacon of culture in an environment which had long been indifferent to the rest of the world." To the lonely Loyalists, far from their original homes, and especially those on the distant plantations, the *Gazette* was a welcome medium of communication with the outside world and with each other. Representatives took subscriptions in the main Bahama Islands, and the paper also circulated in Charleston, Savannah and Bermuda. John Wells opposed both governors, Maxwell and Dunmore, but somehow had the contract for government printing, the reason probably being that his were the only adequate facilities. Wells died on October 29, 1799, at the age of 47. He was eulogized by his friends as being "popular, benevolent and good-humored." His writings were characterized as "energetic and forcible as well as correct and elegant," his style even being compared to that of Edward Gibbon, the historian. Above the grave of John Wells in the churchyard of St. Matthews in Nassau is a stone bearing the words, "In him the public have lost a respectable and useful member of society." [31]

Just to the north of Nassau, where the newspaper was published, there was special interest in any such information pertaining to the Tories. This was on the large island of Abaco, where it is believed that more of the exiles settled than on any other of the Bahama group. Philip Dumaresq, one of these settlers, described the island as having a delightful climate, but he noted that the soil was so shallow that in a dry season the sun heated the rock beneath to the extent that vegetables which had been planted were burned up. Dumaresq also observed sardonically that an unusual drought had prevailed almost from the time the Loyalists had arrived there. He wrote that Guinea corn, potatoes, yams, turnips, and other garden vegetables would grow well on Abaco, as would fruits such as oranges, limes, and bananas. Cotton could be produced here too. But he complained that the settlers were all poor, did not have the strength to do much in the way of work, and regretted that he had seen no fresh meat except pork. But he was sure that poultry would do well on the island. Wild grapes there were in abundance, so he was certain that wines of good quality could be produced. But Dumaresq and his family did not find the people of Abaco friendly. He did speak in complimentary terms of the treatment he received from Governor John Maxwell.[32]

Despite such criticism—Dumaresq stayed only a year—there is present-day evidence that many of the Tories did find lasting new homes in and around Abaco, as, for example, on Green Turtle Cay, one of a long chain of smaller islands on the eastern side of the mainland. Here, in the village of New Plymouth, the descendants of the Tories live in a quaint and picturesque hamlet so like New England in aspect that it might be on a Massachusetts bay instead. This tidy little town is only 110

miles north of sophisticated Nassau, yet it is immensely different in character and appearance. As one writer exclaimed,
"New Plymouth is a study in simplicity and tranquility. It's a
joy to visit!" Names of the present-day families which go back to
Tory days include those of Key, Roberts, Lowe, and Saunders.
Members of these families all claim to be descendants of the
exiles and cherish their homes as much if not more than the
original settlers.

Peaceful in general, but more transitory, was the plantation system of the larger islands of the Bahamas. Cotton was
tried on a large scale and succeeded to a considerable extent up
to the time that slavery was abolished in 1834, some 30 years
before the same step was taken in the United States. But it was
not only the problem of working the cotton which caused its
decline. Insects were a prime factor, as was land unsuited for
cotton culture, injudicious and wasteful methods of clearing the
land and the exhaustion of the soil by continuous use. So after
1805, there was a decrease in the value of Bahama land as well
as slaves. A number of planters, seeing the handwriting on the
wall, took their slaves and left for various places where the institution of bondage was to last even longer. Some of them came
back to Florida, deserting their fine island estates, the remains
of which may still be seen, interesting relics of a far-off day.

The general impact of the Tory refugees on the life of the
Bahamas was increased by the fact that these Americans soon
outnumbered the older inhabitants and introduced their own
ways of life. It appears that both whites and blacks of those days
were on the whole people of exceptional energy as well as
mutual consideration. The planters assigned daily tasks to their
Negroes according to their strength and ability. If the slaves
were diligent enough to complete their assigned work at an
early hour, the rest of the day was given them for whatever
amusement or private activity they wished. Most of the estates
did not even have overseers of slaves, the master usually acting
as his own superintendent. So flogging was rare and discipline
was easier than on estates where direction of slaves was given
over to stern foremen who aimed at fulfilling their quota of
work regardless of the human cost. Bahama planters had the
power to do virtually as they pleased with their slaves, but did
not often find it necessary to exercise their power to extremes. As
the number of blacks increased in proportion to whites, the laws
regulating slaves became more severe. Fear on the part of the

ruling class was one cause, as shown in the legislation enacted in 1784, which provided for the punishment of assault on a white by a slave with death, other offenses to be dealt with by heavy fines or corporal punishment. The law also provided that whites could disarm not only slaves but free colored persons whom they found at large with arms in their hands. In trials, only Christian Negroes, mulattoes, mustees or Indians were allowed to testify against whites, and they only in suits for debt.[33]

As in Jamaica and elsewhere, many slaves ran away, and issues of the *Bahama Gazette* had notices of escaped slaves and offers for rewards for their return. So many of the blacks slipped away in New Providence that a law was passed ordering the registration of all free Negroes, mulattoes, mustees or octoroons, and Indians. If more than five runaways were reported at any time, free Negroes might be sent in pursuit of them, were given rewards for their return, and could even shoot fugitive slaves in self-defense. All blacks were excluded from service in the local militia until 1804, and much the same restrictions applied to jury service. After 1807, foreign slave trade could not be carried on openly in the islands, and subsequently, owners claimed that their slaves had lost much of their value because of this softening of the laws. Under the new provisions of the English Parliament, flogging of female slaves was to cease; instruction was to be given to Negroes in the principles of Christian morality and religion; the right to testify in courts was to be accorded them; the sacredness of the marriage tie was to be taught and fully protected; self-emancipation was to be encouraged, together with the accumulation of property by Negroes; and severe punishments were to be discouraged. The Bahama Assembly, composed largely of American Tories, opposed these measures for a long time, mainly because these exiles had a different view of slavery, based on their old ties. But in time, they too became more lenient and fell in step with the times.

By 1800, New Providence was producing 600 tons of cotton a year, according to E. W. Forsyth, a Tory descendant, and slavery was not so brutal here as in Jamaica or the United States because the Bahamas plantations were smaller. Forsyth could recall only one brutal slave owner, named Baillou, whose black men set dogs on him and when they caught him, placed his head under a large stone and crushed it into the ground until he was dead.[34]

The imprint made by these exiles lives on in some of

the names of places in the island, such as Dunmore Town or Harbour Island at the northern tip of the long and slender Eleuthera. Nearby are some of the finest beaches in the world, distinctive in their pink appearance, caused by the mixing of powdered coral by the waves which sweep upon the shores.

If in this land of the Loyalists there was a desire to build a living monument to beautiful simplicity, it has come about in the form of a village located on neighboring St. George's Cay. It is called Spanish Wells and is said to be so named because Spanish ships called there centuries ago to fill their casks with sweet water from the wells. Here is almost a modern Utopia, combining the best elements of a Brook Farm and New Harmony, the kind of place which Henry Thoreau seemed to have in mind.

These descendants of the Tories are happy and peaceful in Spanish Wells, although they are in many ways cut off from the world outside. Joseph William Pinder and his family are examples. He lives here and is a descendant of an American Tory, John Brice, who came to the region after the Revolution. How important the Pinder family is in Spanish Wells may be judged by the fact that of the approximately 800 people in this community, some 650 of them are named Pinder. For instance, Billy Pinder owns the local grocery store, Alphaeus is the automobile and boat mechanic, Mrs. Mattie Bell Pinder is the genial librarian, Mrs. Preston Sands, formerly a Pinder, represents the airlines, Carl Pinder works for the son of Lord Beaverbrook, and Reginald Pinder comes the closest to being wealthy of anyone on the island.

Joseph William Pinder goes by the name of "Dody Willie." How he got the nickname he did not recall, but perhaps it is because he is only one of eight Pinders who have the first name of Joseph. Numerous Negroes around the Bahamas also have the name of Pinder, a reminder of the connection with their former masters. Most of the Pinders and other Spanish Wells residents were farmers and yacht masters at one time, but these pursuits have gradually given way to catering to tourists.

Although some of the Pinders have intermarried, they were mostly distant cousins; hence there appears no evidence of inbreeding. Most of the family are Methodist in religion. There was no desire expressed by them of living anywhere else, although they of course have visited elsewhere, especially Miami. "Dody Willie" said that what he had found there was mostly "high taxes and noisy civilization."

The American Tories fled to the Bahamas for their lives. Yet their humble descendants have, in many ways, fashioned a better life than their more well-to-do forebears had on the American mainland. Spanish Wells is a place without juvenile delinquency, with no police force, no bars, few cars, and everybody happily knows everybody else.

The American Revolution touched but did not appreciably change the island of Bermuda, lying out in the Atlantic at a safe distance from the young warring nation and its irate British parent. There was little interest in the early phases of the conflict, for, the Bermudians were not recipients of the East India Company's tea. The coercive acts which roused the ire of Americans left the residents of the people of Bermuda rather cold.

The numerous and important Tucker family of Bermuda were exceptions to this attitude of neutrality. Henry Tucker, president of the Bermuda Council, thought the Bostonians were too violent in their reactions to the tax on tea. But he felt that the colonists and Britain should get together and reconcile their differences in a gentlemanly way. Nonetheless, he was concerned about Bermuda and had an answer ready at hand when he should be asked by the Americans why Bermuda did not cast in its lot with them: it was that the islanders were powerless in the face of the British navy. Henry urged his son St. George Tucker to take the same attitude, but this young gentleman and his brother, Thomas, made known their sympathy with the American cause early in the war. It was apparent that in 1775, Bermudians in general considered the Revolutionary dispute to be a temporary matter which could be settled as soon as the British ministry should abandon its claim to tax the colonists.[35]

A delegation from Bermuda, headed by Henry Tucker, was sent to Philadelphia in July of 1775 and presented an address to the Continental Congress. Its leader tried to make a good impression by praising the eminence of the members of Congress and beseeching them to show a kind attitude toward their small island-neighbor. He pointed out that Bermudians had always been good and loyal persons and felt that they should not interfere in the internal affairs of the United States. At the same time, Tucker expressed the hope that the Americans would in any circumstances continue to supply food to Bermuda, something that was much needed.

Congress was not in a very receptive mood toward the visitors. That body did, however, make it plain that Bermuda was included in a recent embargo on exports passed by Congress. A strong hint was given out that some gunpowder known to be at Bermuda might be exchanged for the necessary provisions. For quite some time, 112 barrels of powder had lain unguarded in the royal magazine of St. Georges, Bermuda, and the American rebels knew about this. The supply was even discussed with George Washington at Cambridge, Massachusetts, and he, in typical methodical fashion, wrote a letter to the people of Bermuda, urging them to send the powder to his aid. After pointing out the well-known arguments in favor of the American uprising, Washington wrote, "We are informed there is a very large magazine on your island under a very feeble guard. We would not wish to involve you in an opposition in which, from your situation, we should be unable to support you; we know not, therefore, to what extent to solicit your assistance in availing ourselves of this supply; but if your favor and friendship to North America and its liberties have not been misrepresented, I persuade myself you may, consistently with your own safety, promote and further the scheme, so as to give it the fairest prospect of success." [36]

Several other individuals were giving this project fair prospects of success, among them being Thomas Tucker at Charleston, South Carolina, and St. George Tucker, who before returning to Bermuda mentioned the powder to Peyton Randolph, president of Congress. The matter was referred to a committee on which were Benjamin Franklin and Robert Morris, the former taking on the negotiations for the powder. This put Henry Tucker in a difficult spot, but he concluded that the interests of Bermuda came first, so arranged with Franklin to trade the powder at St. Georges for an exemption from the American embargo. Accordingly, the sloop *Lady Catherine* and the schooner *Packet* were sent to Bermuda to obtain the valuable ammunition. [37]

After returning home, Henry Tucker, along with a cousin, James, asked Joseph Jennings to help steal the powder. Jennings, a Loyalist, refused. In the meantime, the American sailors had arrived on August 13 and were sneaking up to the magazine in small boats. Landing on St. Georges at midnight, they marched stealthily to the magazine on Retreat Hill just east of the Government House, and found it, as usual, without the semblance of a guard. Losing no time, the elated raiders broke through the top of the huge repository and lowered down to floor level one of their men, who proceeded without interruption to force open the doors and let his companions in. Evidently the intruders knew just what they were about, for they went at once to the store of powder—now increased by a recent addition —seized the barrels and rolled them out onto the beach, some of them actually being steered through the grounds of the Government House itself.

Dawn was now breaking and it was time to bring the operation to a close. Just as the raiders were making their last haul, they were seen by an early-rising old resident of St. Georges, who called out in alarm and notified his son that this "deed would be a dark cloud hanging over Bermuda." But the only clouds the robbers were interested in were those which showed them how the wind for their sails was blowing. Quickly they loaded the loot from the small boats on to the *Packet* and *Lady Catherine* and made their way across the horizon. It was an almost unbelievably clean getaway.[38]

The *Lady Catherine* reached Philadelphia on August 26, and the captain, George Ord, carried a letter from Henry Tucker to the Pennsylvania Committee of Safety about the powder. This cargo amounted to 1,800 pounds, but some of it had spoiled. The *Packet* reached Charleston, South Carolina, at about the same time and deposited her powder, which later was used in the guns of Fort Moultrie against the attack by Sir Peter Parker. It may have been a bit of this British explosive which cost Sir Peter his breeches in a direct hit during this battle.

Bermuda's Governor George Bruere had not discovered the theft of the powder until the morning after it had been committed. Even so, he was able to spot the *Lady Catherine* in the distance making her hasty way toward America. If laggard in detection, the governor was not in words. He issued a hurried proclamation with this appeal: "Save your country from ruin which may hereafter happen! The powder stole out of the magazine late last night cannot be carried far, as the wind is light. A great reward will be given to any person that can make a proper discovery before the magistrates." He summoned the council and induced it to order the parish magistrates to do all in their power to detect the persons taking part in "the atrocious act" and ordered the customs officers to search all vessels outward bound. He even convoked the legislature. This body, probably with tongue in cheek, voted a reward of 100 pounds to the finder of the perpetrators. But the reward was never claimed and exactly who took part in the robbery is still not clear, excepting the foregoing details. St. George Tucker of Virginia was in Bermuda at the time and probably had a hand in it, although American sailors did the actual work of removing the powder itself. Some Bermudians must have acted as guides for the raiders and pilots for their boats in that night adventure.[39]

After the Revolution ended, some of the Bermuda Tories tried to return to their homeland. A small item in the *Bermuda Gazette and Weekly Advertiser* of September 18, 1784, states that Thomas Crowell and Elias Barnes, two Loyalists, having been invited by the people of New Brunswick, New Jersey, went to Woodbridge instead, where Barnes had purchased an estate. Scarcely was their arrival known, when they "were waited on by their numerous *friends,* who after having congratulated them in the most seemingly friendly manner, introduced a bag of feathers and tar, stripped them and gave them a complete suit of it, and said this was the treatment usually given all Tories on their return. Several others have received like treatment."

Examples like this may have influenced other Tories to stay away from America. One who spent eight years in Bermuda certainly had a successful experience there. He was William Browne, who became governor of the islands, and whose descendants today are among the leaders of its important affairs. Browne was born in Salem, Massachusetts, in 1737, into one of the wealthiest and most socially prominent families in the big colony, descended from Governor John Winthrop of Massachusetts and from Governor John Dudley of Connecticut. William Browne was educated in the schools of Salem and then went to Harvard, where he was listed as Number Three in his graduating class. However, this was only a mark of social distinction. The fact that he was chosen valedictorian of his class on July 4, 1755, is a better indication of his high ability. After graduation, Browne studied law and returned to Salem to live. His father had died and left an estate of 104,000 acres of land and 5,000 pounds sterling. Browne married his cousin, the daughter of Governor Gideon Wanton of Rhode Island.[40]

When Browne was 25, he was chosen to represent Salem in the General Court. Two years later, he was appointed Collector of Customs for the ports of Salem and Marblehead. These duties came at an unfortunate time for him, as the unpopular Sugar Act was passed in 1764 and the hated Stamp Act the next year. Browne was in a dilemma. As a royal official he was charged with supporting the laws, but as a representative from Salem to the Assembly, he was instructed by his constituents to speak of the Stamp Act as "very injurious to liberty, since we are therein taxed without our own consent, having no representation in Parliament." Browne was unwilling to act against his native section in enforcing the Sugar Act so was dismissed from his customs post in 1766. He retained his place in the Assembly, but when that body voted two years later to oppose the orders of Britain to rescind their circular letter opposing the actions of Parliament, Browne voted with the minority to uphold the royal cause. He was in agreement with protests but opposed to outright rebellion. As a result, Browne was not re-elected to his post the next year.[41]

Thomas Hutchinson became governor of Massachusetts, and one of his first acts was to appoint Browne as Judge of Common Pleas for Essex County and colonel of the Essex militia. The latter was now definitely aligned with the conservative element of the colony. After General Thomas Gage was appointed to succeed Hutchinson following the Boston Tea Party, the new official arrived in Salem and was met by a delegation of citizens who presented him with an address of welcome signed by 48 members of the community, among whom was William Browne. Browne was soon after appointed a Justice of the Supreme Court, as well as a member of the new council of the colony. Such acts on the part of Gage caused violent reaction among the Massachusetts patriots. Browne was asked to surrender his official positions. This he steadfastly refused to do, stating that he intended "to give the King no cause to suspect my fidelity, to act with honor and integrity and to exert my best abilities." He now found himself an outcast. The officers of his regiment resigned their commissions and he became a colonel without a command. His position within the community became so unbearable that he went to Boston. At first it seemed safe to stay in that city, but when the British decided to evacuate it after the battles of Lexington and Concord, Browne was among those who decided to leave. With the thousand other Tory exiles, he embarked with General William Howe from Boston in the middle of March, 1776. The fleet stopped at Halifax, Nova Scotia, and disembarked many of the exiles, but Browne along with others went on to London, where he lived for a time at 11 Haymarket Street, the same address as that of another prominent Massachusetts Tory, Colonel Richard Saltonstall. Following the general pattern of other Tories, Browne left his wife behind in Massachusetts for two years. He was granted 200 pounds a year by the British government but found this hardly enough to live on, much less in the sumptuous manner to which he had been accustomed. There were fellow exiles such as Thomas Hutchinson and Samuel Curwen to commiserate with him but this was not a happy situation either. So he went to Wales along with other Tories and stayed for two years, now and then writing the government asking for employment. He was forced by circumstances, he said, to meditate on a journey to heaven sooner than one to London. "You will not wonder," he wrote a friend, "that haunted by the specter of past possessions and enjoyments and without consolation from any prospect of better days to come, I have fallen into that torpid, inanimate state which deprives one of all hope and rids one of all fear." But he was greatly heartened when his son, through the influence of Governor Hutchinson and General Gage, received a commission in a British regiment at Gibraltar.[42]

More good fortune came in 1780. One of Browne's friends was appointed to a position in American affairs in London and Browne thoughtfully wrote and congratulated him. As a reward for his courtesy, the former was offered the post of the governorship of Bermuda, a welcome opportunity which was quickly accepted. Lord North approved the appointment and Browne was officially designated governor in February, 1781. Lord George Germain, favorably inclined toward Browne because of the intercession in his behalf by a mutual friend, Benjamin Thomas, later Count Rumford, asked Browne to be conciliatory toward Bermuda so as to hold it fast to the Crown. This was agreed upon, but a new problem now confronted the governor. Women could not travel on warships, so Browne waited three months and then sailed with his wife in convoy by way of New York. There they were held up for seven more weeks for lack of further transportation. At length they boarded a sloop of war and landed in Bermuda on December 16, 1781.

Governor William Browne found Bermuda in an economic mess. There was a serious lack of food, especially bread, and prices were outrageously high. St. Georges, the capital, was crowded with Tories and others, and rents had advanced to an unprecedented figure. Smallpox and typhus were raging unchecked. As if these were not enough, Browne found the official residence in such a state of disrepair that it horrified him, and he showed convincingly that it could not be occupied soon. A kindly resident, Copeland Stiles, came to the rescue by offering his own town house for the governor's use. There were other problems, such as the hundreds of prisoners of war ashore, strolling about on parole and taking note of everything. Danger of attack by the Americans was a definite possibility, because Washington was looking to the growing Continental Navy as a decisive factor in concluding the war.

Browne found that Bermuda was moderate among the colonies regarding the American Revolution. The islanders seemed to their new governor to be a simple people wholly bewildered by the events and hardships which had been thrust upon them. They were impressed by the new chief executive, especially because he had already suffered so much for the royal cause, and responded quickly to his leadership. Browne told Lord North that the Bermudians had a new attitude, and instead of lamenting what they had lost, flattered themselves with the hopes of what they would gain. As a sort of climax to his career, Governor Browne in 1786 went to Halifax to look into the claims of American Loyalists which a commission from London was examining there. He also wanted to enter his own claim for the loss of his great estate in Massachusetts. During this trip, Browne visited his old home in Salem and was warmly welcomed there by friends. But he remained only seven weeks before returning to Bermuda, where he believed his people were united in their loyalty to the king. In 1788, Browne went to England, where he spent the rest of his life. His last recorded comment about his sojourn there was, "The prosperity of Bermuda will ever be near my heart."

H. T. Watlington, a distinguished business and civic leader and historian of present-day Bermuda and a descendant of Governor Browne, appraised him thus: "William Browne was the product of American life at its peak. With the Revolution, it was extinguished suddenly and completely and was replaced by a new order which professed to ignore degree, a new philosophy which was to precipitate the French Revolution, and its effect has not yet run its course in the twentieth century." [43]

Contemporary with Tory Governor William Browne and a

close associate of his in building the early life of modern Bermuda was another Loyalist, Daniel Leonard, also from Massachusetts. He became chief justice of Bermuda and remained in this important position for almost 30 years. Born in 1740 at Norton, Leonard was the son of wealthy Judge Ephraim Leonard of the Massachusetts Court of Common Pleas. His early schooling was casual but he was prepared for Harvard and was graduated, like Browne, Number Three in his class of 1760. He delivered a graduation address in Latin before a large audience which included Governor Thomas Hutchinson. The young scholar returned to Norton to practice law and to get married, but unfortunately his wife died a year later in childbirth. Leonard soon remarried and moved to Boston.

In the larger community, Daniel Leonard prospered in more ways than one. He was elected to the General Court and became, for some reason, a sort of dandy in his dress and travel. His hat had a broad brim with gold lace trimming and his cloak glittered, according to his friend John Adams, who also noted that Leonard traveled to and from home to his office in a coach drawn by two fine horses, something no other local lawyer did. For a time, Leonard was active with the Whigs and even served in 1773 as a member of the Committee of Correspondence. But the Boston Tea Party changed that. Leonard thought it was a disgrace and worse than witchcraft. He supported Governor Hutchinson and was one of the "Addressers" who signified this support in writing.

After the arrival of General Gage, Daniel Leonard was again elected to the General Court, but this body was soon dissolved and the latter chosen among others to advise the new governor. This was too much for the patriots. They gathered outside Leonard's house and showed noisy disapproval. As in so many such demonstrations, ardor outraced reason, and violence erupted. Shots were fired by the mob into the Leonard bedroom. This affront to a respected and prominent citizen would have been bad enough, but it so happened that Mrs. Leonard was pregnant at the time and the shock caused the baby to be born prematurely at the time of the violence. Already saddened by the death of his first wife in childbirth, Daniel Leonard was so profoundly stirred and dismayed by the cruel mob action that any doubts he may have had about aligning himself definitely on the side of the king and against such outrages vanished.

Boston appeared to be the haven of the Tories, so there Leonard remained until the city was evacuated by the British in March of 1776. But before he left, Leonard gave an active account of himself in behalf of the loyal side. He wrote letters to the *Massachusetts Gazette* which appeared under the name of "Massachusettensis" and were quite effective. Although Leonard did not sign his name to this Tory propaganda, many knew he was the author. John Adams thought the letters were "shining like the moon among the lesser stars" and at first attributed them to Jonathan Sewall. Adams replied with some similar missives, using the name "Novanglus." "These papers were well written," said Adams about those of Leonard, "abounded with wit, discovered good information and were calculated to keep up the spirit of their party, to depress ours, to spread intimidation and to make proselytes among those whose principles and judgment gave way to their fears." Leonard's letters were published in England as the ablest exposition of royal policy that had been produced in America. In them, Leonard took the view that the king was monarch not only of England but of the colonies as well because they were fundamentally part of the kingdom. Parliament and Crown were both sovereigns of the colonies, and the colonials, like all Englishmen, were British subjects. True, the colonies were being taxed without representation, but to remedy this, he advised that the representation system be improved. "May the God of our forefathers direct you in the way that leads to peace and happiness," Leonard warned, "before your feet stumble on the dark mountains—before the evil days come when you shall say, we have no pleasure in them." But neither side followed the advice of Daniel Leonard, and 16 days after this warning appeared, the battles of Lexington and Concord occurred. Now the decision was to be made by arms, not words. But if the wise words of this cultured American gentleman, reluctantly turned Tory, had been heeded, the Revolution might well have been avoided.[44]

Depended upon heavily by Gage, Leonard was appointed Solicitor for the Customs, his chief duty being to enforce the Boston Port Act, a most repugnant law to the patriots. After their army under Washington had occupied Dorchester Heights with the cannon brought from Ticonderoga by Henry Knox, the rebels got the upper hand and the British decided to leave. With them went Daniel Leonard, his wife and four children, a secretary and a nurse. After a stop at Halifax, they continued to

England. There he claimed 3,621 pounds for his property loss but typically received instead 915 pounds. However, he was pleased to learn in 1780 of plans for a royal colony in Maine, with himself as chief justice, even though the project fell through. The energetic Benjamin Thompson apparently brought the name of Leonard up again, for the latter in 1781 was appointed chief justice of Bermuda and was to depart at once with his family. His brother-in-law, Andrew Cazneau, another Tory, accompanied him and acted as judge of the Admiralty Court. Thus, Governor William Browne now had two high-placed loyal associates from Massachusetts to help him administer the affairs of the island, all of whom had suffered at the hands of the ardent patriots, who were called rebels instead.

Daniel Leonard was chief justice of Bermuda for three decades and made a definite mark upon its legal precedents and subsequent life. Although there do not appear to have been any sensational achievements by him in this long period, the records indicate a steady, able performance by this brilliant jurist who did credit to his past training and his adopted way of life. In him, the patriots lost a leading light. His descendants had a long connection with Bermuda, a daughter, Sarah, marrying John Stewart, who was collector of the customs. Their son became solicitor general.

Twice Daniel Leonard re-visited Massachusetts and on both occasions was a guest in his house which had been confiscated. His wife died in 1806 and he retired to England, where he became dean of the English bar and lived until 1829. His death was by gunshot administered by himself, but his family declared that it was accidental from a pistol he did not realize was loaded. At any rate, he was buried in St. Pancras Cemetery and not in unconsecrated ground, though far from his native land.[45]

His was the general lament of the American Tories: far from their homeland they were forced to live and not from reasons of their own choosing. Having been persecuted at home and pitied abroad, most of them lived out their latter days in parsimony and longing for cherished native hearths. Theirs was the lot of the loser, with some of them accepting it gracefully, others allowing the bitterness to overcome all else. And although theirs was a lost cause, what was righteous in it is well revealed in their heritage.

NOTES

1
A City That Was

1. North to William Knox, Aug. 8, 1778, *Knox Papers*, Clements Library, University of Michigan; Carleton to Parr, Dec. 22, 1782, *Shelburne Mss.*, Public Archives of Canada (hereafter known as PAC).
2. *Minute Book*, Port Roseway Association, Dec. 21, 1782, pp. 37-40, PAC.
3. Raymond, W. O., "The Founding of Shelburne," *New Brunswick Hist. Coll.* (Saint John, 1955) VI; Smith, T. Watson, "The Loyalists of Shelburne," *Nova Scotia Hist. Coll.* VI, 56.
4. "Benjamin Marston of Marblehead," *Collections of the New Brunswick Hist. Society*, No. 7, pp. 79–112; *New England Quarterly*, XV (1942), 625.
5. Edwards, J. P., "The Shelburne That Was and Is Not," *Dalhousie Review*, II, p. 179–197.
6. "Preliminary Steps to Be Taken, etc.," regarding Shelburne; Ms. in the Public Archives of Nova Scotia, Halifax; Edwards, 182.
7. *Marston Diary*, entry of May 18.
8. *Marston Diary*, entry of May 24.
9. *NBHS Collections*, Vol. 6–8, 219.
10. Parr to Carleton, July 25, 1873, *Winslow Papers*, NBHS, Fredericton; Edwards, 186. Edward Winslow was muster master general for the Loyalists under General William Howe. He came to Nova Scotia in 1783, later became its first solicitor general and supreme court judge. His uncle, General John Winslow, was in charge of exiling the Acadians in 1758.
11. *Marston Diary* as quoted in *NBHS Coll.* Vol. 6–8, 237–40.
12. Edwards, 187–88; Smith, 65.
13. Ward Chipman from New York to Jonathan Sewall in England, Oct. 6, 1782; Sewall Papers, PAC, M.G. 23, G. 10, Vol. 2. Chipman was a life-long friend of Winslow; Dole to Carleton, Sept. 19, 1783, *British Headquarters Papers*, ND 10, 172, New York Public Library; Carleton to Parr, Oct. 23, 1783, Public Record Office, London, CO 5, 111, 116.

14. Quoted in *NSHC*, VI, 66.
15. Owen, Daniel, "Loyalist Shelburne," *Canadian Magazine* (May, 1911), 68–69; Raymond, 247.
16. Raymond, 250.
17. McMurtrie, Douglas C., *The Royal Printers at Shelburne, Nova Scotia* (Chicago, 1933), 3.
18. *Marston Diary*, entry of April 5, 1784.
19. Marston to Edward Winslow, Feb. 6, 1784, *Winslow Papers*, NBHS, 164. This is an important collection of private and public papers containing 650 letters and documents, written by 170 persons between 1766 and 1820.
20. MacDonald, James S., "Memoir of Governor John Parr," *NSHS Collections*, XIV (1909), 46; Raymond in *NBHS Coll.* Vol. 6–8, 273–77.
21. Letter to Lord North. Jan. 3, 1784, *Sydney Papers*, 1750–85, M.G. 23, A3, PAC.
22. *Winslow Papers*, 264; *New Eng. Quarterly*, XV, 622.
23. Edwards, J. P., "Vicissitudes of a Loyalist City," *The Dalhousie Review*, II (1922–23), 314; Smith, 81.
24. Edwards, II, 318–19.
25. Robertson, Marion, "History and Folklore of Shelburne County," *The Coast Guard*, Nov. 1, 1962; visit with and letter from Mrs. Marion Robertson, Aug. 23, 1965; letter from Robert Pell, Oct. 26, 1965.
26. Edwards, 325; Smith, 85.
27. Edwards, 327.
28. McLeod, R. R., "Historical Sketches of the Town of Shelburne," *Acadiensis*, Jan. 1908; Bole, 70.
29. Campbell, G. G., *The History of Nova Scotia* (Toronto, 1948), 170; quote from Smith, 84; Van Tyne, Claude H., *The Loyalists in the American Revolution* (Gloucester, Mass., 1959), 304–05.

2
The Exodus Spreads

1. Smith to Adams, April 21, 1776, *The Adams Papers*, ed. by Lyman Butterfield (Cambridge, Mass., 1963), I, 373.
2. Abigail to John Adams, April 21, 1776, *The Adams Papers*, I, 390.
3. Van Tyne, 294.
4. Robinson to Clinton, Aug. 8, 1782, *Clinton Papers*, Clements Library.
5. *Winslow Papers*, 509; Creighton, Donald, *A History of Canada* (Boston, 1958), 170–71; Bartlett, W. S., *The Frontier Missionary* (Boston, 1853), 200–15.

6. *Ontario Bureau of Archives* (1904), 12–13; (1930), 81; *Winslow Papers,* 509; Wallace, W. S., *The United Empire Loyalists* (Toronto, 1922), 56; Sabine, Lorenzo, *Biographical Sketches of the Loyalists of the American Revolution* (Boston, 1864), I, 201–02; Wertenbaker, T. J., *Father Knickerbocker Rebels* (New York, 1948), 254–55.
7. *Rivington's Gazette,* Oct. 19, 1782.
8. Quoted in *Captain John Hatfield, Loyalist* (New York, 1943), 10.
9. MacDonald, 55.
10. All these communications went to the Society for the Propagation of the Gospel in London, where the originals remain. The church of which Dr. Inglis was rector still stands, active and picturesque, in the exquisite Annapolis Valley, and was visited by the author and his cousin Milton Callahan.
11. *Second Report of the Bureau of Archives for the Province of Ontario* (Toronto, 1905), 11; the *Grafton Magazine,* II, No. 3 (Feb. 1910), 186–87.
12. Callahan, North, *Royal Raiders: The Tories of the American Revolution* (New York and Indianapolis, 1963), 35–57.
13. Stokes, Kathleen, "The Character and Administration of Governor John Wentworth," unpublished master's thesis, Dalhousie University, Halifax, 1935.
14. Beverly Robinson to General Clinton, March 15, 1783, *Clinton Papers.*
15. Quoted in Egerton, Ryerson, *The Loyalists of America and Their Times* (Montreal, 1880), II, 186; Wrong, G. M., *Canada and the American Revolution* (Toronto, 1935), 412.
16. Chipman to Sewall, Sept. 6, 1783, *Jonathan Sewall Papers,* Public Archives of Canada, Ottawa, M.G. 23 G 10, V. 2.
17. Winslow to Chipman, April 26, 1784. *Winslow Papers,* 192–93.
18. Campbell, G. G., *The History of Nova Scotia* (Toronto, 1948), 169–72.
19. Stark, James H., *The Loyalists of Massachusetts* (Boston, 1910), 225–29; Newcomer, Lee N., *The Embattled Farmers* (New York, 1953), 76; *Rivington's Gazette,* Sept. 8, 1774.
20. Carleton to General Henry Fox, Sept. 5, 1783, PRO, CO 511.11; petitioners to Lord Sydney, Feb. 9, 1785, PRO, FO, 41.234.
21. MacDonald, 60–61.
22. Winslow to Watson, Nov. 12, 1784, Winslow Papers, 248; MacDonald, 64; *Nova Scotia Packet,* Jan. 1, 1787.
23. *Winslow Papers,* 337.
24. Sabine, 90–97.
25. Muir, Mary, "In the Days of the Loyalists," *Dalhousie Review* (July, 1932).

3
Home Is the Hunted

1. Quoted in Bradley, A. G., *Colonial Americans in Exile, Founders of British Canada* (New York, 1927), 120–21.
2. Sabine, 75–76.
3. Raymond, W. O., *The River St. John* (Sackville, N. B., 1943), 254.
4. Wrong, 431; Vesey, 642.
5. MacNutt, Stewart, Trueman, A. W., *New Brunswick and Its People* (Fredericton, 1963), 18.
6. Winslow to Chipman, July 7, 1783, *Winslow Papers*, 99.
7. Wright, Esther Clark, *The Loyalists of New Brunswick* (Fredericton, N. B. 1955), 65–66; MacNutt, W. S., *New Brunswick: A History: 1784–1867* (Toronto, 1963), 31–32; Raymond, 267.
8. Wallace, 74–75; Clark, 88; Raymond, 268; *Winslow Papers*, 443.
9. Gorham, R. P. (ed.), "The Narrative of Hannah Ingraham," typescript in the Bonar Law-Bennett Library, University of New Brunswick, Fredericton.
10. MacNutt, 37–38.
11. Winslow to Joshua Upham, July, 1783, *Winslow Papers*, 102, 509.
12. Cody, H. A., *The United Empire Loyalists* (Fredericton, 1933), 15–17.
13. *Journal of Stephen Jarvis*, which he kept from the age of 12 to 74, in the New York Historical Society; "Reminiscences of a Loyalist" by Stinson Jarvis in the *Canadian Magazine*, XXXI, No. 4 (Feb. 1906), 366–73.
14. Wrong, 438–39; MacNutt and Trueman, 19.
15. Sargent, Winthrop (ed.), *The Loyalist Poetry of the Revolution* (Philadelphia, 1857), 1–2; also quoted in Tyler, Moses Coit, *The Literary History of the American Revolution* (New York, 1957), 114.
16. Winslow to Ward Chipman, July 7, 1783, *Winslow Papers*, 95–96.
17. Wright, 163.
18. Arnold to the Commissioners of American Claims, April 26, 1875, PRO, AO 13/96; Sereisky, Jean, "Benedict Arnold in New Brunswick," *Atlantic Advocate Magazine* (March, 1963).
19. Lawrence, J. W., *Footprints: Or Incidents in the Early History of New Brunswick* (Saint John, 1883), 71.
20. Jonathan Sewall, Jr., to his father, Dec. 5, 1785, M. G. 23, G 10, Vol. 2, *Sewall Papers*, PAC.
21. Sereisky, 37.
22. Quoted in Wallace, Willard, *Traitorous Hero* (New York, 1954), 291.
23. Wallace, 292.

Notes

24. Memorial of Jonathan Ketchum, *American Loyalist Transcripts*, New York Public Library, Vol. 12, 305; Sereisky, 38.
25. Elizabeth to Jonathan Sewall, Sept. 6, 1789, and Oct. 1, 1789, *Sewall Papers*, PAC, M. G. 23, G. 10, Vol. 2.
26. Arnold to Bliss, Feb. 26, 1792, in *Odell Collection,* New Brunswick Museum, Fredericton.
27. Clark, Gerald, *Canada, The Uneasy Neighbor* (New York, 1965), 227.

4
From Island to Mainland
1. Batchelder, Samuel F., *Bits of Cambridge History* (Cambridge, Mass., 1930), 313.
2. Germain to Clinton, Sept. 7, 1778, *Clinton Papers;* Smith, Paul H., *Loyalists and Redcoats* (Chapel Hill, 1964), 176.
3. McLean to Germain, Aug. 26, 1779, Willcox, William B., (ed.), *The American Rebellion* (New Haven, 1954), 419–20.
4. Siebert, W. H., *The Exodus of the Loyalists from Penobscot to Passamaquoddy* (Columbus, O., 1914), 18; "Dispersion of American Tories," *Mississippi Valley Historical Review* (September, 1914); C. O. Paullin, quoted in Batchelder, 320.
5. Siebert, W. H., *Exodus, etc.,* 485–89; *Campobello Island, New Brunswick, Canada* (Campobello Board of Trade, 1964).
6. Wallace, 87–89.
7. Bureau of Archives, Ontario, *Second Report,* Pt. II, 1051.
8. *Haldimand Papers,* III, B. 138, 343.
9. Richardson, Rev. James, "Michael Grass, a Family Tradition," in *Kingston Before the War of 1812* (Toronto, 72–73).
10. Haight, C., *Coming of the Loyalists* (Toronto, 1899), 7.
11. Ibid, 8.
12. *Kingston Gazette,* Dec. 10, 1911.
13. Quoted in *Ontario Historical Society Papers and Records,* XXX (Toronto, 1934), 113.
14. Hadfield, Joseph, *An Englishman in America, 1785* (Toronto, 1933), 68.
15. Tucker, Rev. Bowman T., *The Camden Colony* (Montreal, 1908), 108–11; quoted in Talman, James J., *Loyalist Narratives From Upper Canada* (Toronto, 1946), xlix.
16. Cruikshank, E. A., *The Settlement of the United Empire Loyalists on the Upper St. Lawrence and Bay of Quinte in 1784* (Toronto, 1934), 46; Mathews to Major Campbell, July 29, 1784, *Haldimand Papers,* NA 21 B 63.
17. Stuart, E. Rae, *Jessup's Rangers as a Factor in Loyalist Settlement* (Ottawa, 1961), 103; Wrong, 456.
18. *OHS Papers and Records,* Vol. XXX, 115.
19. Waugh, John T., "The United Empire Loyalists" in the Uni-

versity of Buffalo *Studies*, IV, No. 3 (Nov. 1925), 111–12; *Historical Collections*, Michigan Pioneer and Historical Society, XVII (Lansing, 1910), 579.

20. Kirby, William, "The Hungry Year," from the *Centennial of the Settlement of Upper Canada by the United Empire Loyalists* (Toronto, 1885), 123.

21. Described from old records in Waugh, 96.

22. Callahan, *Royal Raiders*, 164–70.

23. *Proceedings*, New York State Historical Association, VII, 1907, 20.

24. Cruikshank, Ernest, "The Story of Butler's Rangers and the Settlement of Niagara" in *Lundy's Lane Historical Society Publication* (Welland, Ont. 1893), 112–14.

25. Charles Lindbergh, in a letter to the author dated May 6, 1966, states that he is "under the impression that it was John Land, not his father, Robert, who fought on the Loyalist side in the Revolutionary War and fled to Canada. . . . My grandfather descended from Robert Land through John Land. Also descended from Robert Land, through John Land, is my cousin, Admiral Emory Scott Land, who was Chairman of the Maritime Commission during World War II."

26. Williams, Fred, "A Vindication of Laura Secord" in the *Toronto Mail and Empire*, June 23, 1934; Wallace, W. S., *The Story of Laura Secord: A Study in Historical Evidence* (Toronto, 1932), 14–16. Wallace vigorously challenges the authenticity of the story. But J. Hitsman Mackay in *The Incredible War of 1812* (Toronto, 1965), 138–39, gives some credence to the account.

27. Fraser, Alexander, *Thirteenth Report of the Ontario Bureau of Archives, 1916* (Toronto, 1917), 58, quoting La Rochefoucauld; Talman, lx, lxii; Noyes, John P., *Canadian Loyalists and Early Pioneers in the District of Bedford* (Cowansville, Quebec, 1906), 3–4.

28. Tasker, L. H., *The U. E. Loyalist Settlement at Long Point, Lake Erie, OHS Papers and Records*, II (Toronto, 1900), 58; Noyes, 3; Talman, 109–148.

29. *Letter Book of Lt. Gov. John G. Simcoe, 1792–93*, in Huntington Library, San Marino, California.

30. McDonald, H. S., "Memoir of Colonel Joel Stone, etc.," *OHS Papers and Records*, XVIII (Toronto, 1920), 59–90.

31. Pierce, Lorne, "Doctor Solomon Jones: United Empire Loyalist" in *Queens Quarterly*, XXXVI (Summer, 1929), 438; McDonald, 75–76.

32. Letter from Mrs. Cameron to Mrs. Macpherson at Broadalbin, New York, May 15, 1785, in PAC, NG 23, H 11, 19.

33. Wallace, 110.

34. Taylor, Edward L., "Refugees to and from Canada and the Refugee Tract," *Ohio Archaeological and Historical Quarterly,* XII (July, 1903), 219–241.
35. Baker, William K., *The Loyalists* (London, 1903), 127.

5
In England

1. Committee of Secret Correspondence to Deane, Oct. 1, 1776, Peter Force, *American Archives,* Fifth Series (Washington, D. C. 1853), II, 821.
2. Jonathan Boucher, Jan. 8, 1776, in *Maryland Historical Magazine,* Vol. 8, 344.
3. *Egerton Mss.,* British Museum, London, 2672, f. 5.
4. Einstein, Lewis, *Divided Loyalties* (London, 1933), 202.
5. *Winslow Papers,* 13.
6. Curwen, Samuel, *Journals and Letters* (New York, 1845).
7. Hutchinson, Thomas, *Diary and Letters* (London, 1883), II, 240.
8. Tyler, II, 286; Einstein, 209–10.
9. Curwen, 563–64; Stark, 365.
10. Curwen, 567.
11. Letters of Samuel Quincy, typescript of which is in the University of London Library, A. L. 34.
12. Quincy to his wife, April 18, 1778, U. of London typescript.
13. Quincy to his wife, May 31, 1778, U. of London typescript.
14. Quincy to his wife, March 15, 1779, Mass. Hist. Society manuscripts.
15. Curwen, 574.
16. U. of London typescript.
17. Curwen, 575–76.
18. Curwen, 577.
19. Bristol Election Mss., New York Historical Society; "Letters of Jonathan Sewall," *Proceedings,* Mass. Hist. Society, 2nd Series, X, 420.
20. Hall, Edward H., *Philipse Manor Hall* (New York, 1930), 94–109.
21. Irving, Washington, *Life of Washington* (New York, 1869), I, 246.
22. Sabine, II, 107n and 224–25.
23. Quoted in Hall, 139.
24. *London Chronicle,* June 7, 1783.
25. Sewall to Chipman, *Sewall Papers,* NAC, M. G. 23, G 10, Vol. 2, 345–52.
26. Sewall to Chipman, 1781, *Sewall Papers,* PAC, 367–68.
27. From a report, "On board the Sally Transport," June 8, 1784, in the National Maritime Museum, Greenwich, England.

28. Hutchinson *Diary*, II, 40; I, 261.
29. Quoted in Einstein, 216.
30. Curwen, 408.
31. Jones, Thomas, *History of New York* (New York, 1879), I, 351.
32. *Continental Journal and Weekly Advertiser*, Boston, March 26, 1778.
33. *Winslow Papers*, 83–84; Jones, II, 86n.
34. Ibid, 209, 377.
35. *Wilmot Papers*, Records of Loyalist Commissioners, Library of Congress, II, 80.
36. Stevens, B. F. *Facsimiles of Manuscripts in European Archives Relating to America, 1773–1783* (London, 1889–95), IX, 850; Sachse, William L., *The Colonial American in Britain* (Madison, Wis. 1956), 197–98.
37. Harper, J. Russell, "Christopher Sower, King's Printer and Loyalist," *Collections* of the NBHS, No. 14, 67–108.
38. Ibid, 70.
39. Quoted in Harper, 74–75.
40. Van Schaack, H. C., *Life of Peter Van Schaack* (New York, 1842), 54–60.
41. Ibid, 129; Einstein, 264.
42. Van Schaack, 130–131.
43. Ibid, 147.
44. Ibid, 391–92.
45. Ibid, 300.
46. Ibid, 104, 300.
47. Jones, II, 573; Einstein, 266; Van Schaack, 379.

6
Recompense

1. "New Jersey Legislation Concerning Loyalists," *Proceedings of the New Jersey Historical Society*, LXXIX, No. 2 (April 1961), 91; Appendix to a Representation of Such Acts as Have Been Done by the U.S., etc. 1783–84, PRO.
2. Petition from Henry to Lord Rockingham, June 28, 1782, *Rockingham Papers*, III, Wentworth Woodhouse Muniments, Sheffield, England, City Library.
3. Debates in both houses of Parliament on the 17th and 21st of February, 1783, on the Articles of Peace, T. 50/53, PRO.
4. "A Brief Statement of the Case of the American Loyalists," Berkshire Record Office, Shire Hall, Reading, England; "Case of the British-American Claimants," and "Papers Relating to the American Loyalists," British Museum, London.
5. Robson, Eric, *The American Revolution, 1775–83* (London, 1955), 230.
6. Quoted in Sabine, 525; Einstein, 230–35.

Notes

7. Winslow Papers, 198.
8. Egerton, Hugh (ed.), *The Royal Commission on the Losses and Services of American Loyalists, 1783 to 1785* (London, 1915), xxxiii–lv.
9. *Second Report of the Bureau of Archives of the Province of Ontario*, 14.
10. Brown, Wallace, "The Loyalists of the American Revolution," *History Today* (March, 1962); Fraser, 21. Brown, in a book, *The King's Friends* (Providence, 1966), disagrees slightly with the foregoing numbers of Loyalists claims by states.
11. Henry, William W., *Patrick Henry: Life, Correspondence and Speeches* (New York, 1891), II, 187.
12. Morris, Richard B., "Class Struggle and the American Revolution," *William and Mary Quarterly* (Jan. 1962); Curwen, 385, 444.
13. *Acts and Resolves, Public and Private, of the Province of Massachusetts Bay* (Boston, 1869–1922) V, 966–67.
14. Adams to James Warren, Oct. 1778; Wells, William V., *Warren-Adams Letters, MSH Collections,* LXXIII (Boston, 1925), III, 49–50; Brown, Richard D., "The Confiscation and Disposition of Loyalists' Estates in Suffolk County, Massachusetts," *William and Mary Quarterly* (Oct. 1964).
15. Jameson, J. Franklin, *The American Revolution Considered as a Social Movement* (Boston, 1960), 35–36.
16. Chapin, Bradley, *The American Law of Treason* (Seattle, 1964), 80.
17. Nevins, Allan, *The American States During and After the Revolution, 1775–89* (New York, 1927), 647; Coleman, Kenneth, *The American Revolution in Georgia, 1763–1789* (Athens, 1948), 184.
18. Lambert, Robert S., "The Confiscation of Loyalist Property in Georgia, 1782–1786," *William and Mary Quarterly* (Jan. 1963); Coleman, 184.
19. Candler, Allen D. (ed.), *The Revolutionary Records of the State of Georgia* (Atlanta, 1908), II, 474.
20. *Georgia Historical Society Collections*, VIII (Savannah, 1913), 205–210.
21. Lambert, 89–92; Coleman, 185–86.
22. Warren, Charles, *The Supreme Court in United States History* (Boston, 1926), I, 93–94; Kelly, Alfred H., and Harbison, W. E., *The American Constitution* (New York, 1963), 191–93.
23. *Loyalist Transcripts,* New York Public Library.
24. DeMond, Robert O., *The Loyalists in North Carolina During the Revolution* (Durham, 1940), 202–09.
25. Nevins, 648; Luce, Melvin G., "The Southern Loyalists in the American Revolution," unpublished master's thesis, New York University, 1951.

26. Siebert, W. H., "The Loyalists of Pennsylvania," *Ohio State University Bulletin* (Columbus, 1923), XXIV, 83–84; Sabine, I, 186–90.
27. Siebert, 85–86.
28. Siebert, 87; Sabine, II, 483; Fraser, 669.
29. Cathcart to Carlisle, letter in Howard Castle, York, England, by courtesy of the present owner, George Howard.
30. "The Memorial of Philip Skene to the Honorable Commissioners, etc.," March 15, 1784, PRO, FO 4/3; Flick, 212.
31. Siebert, W. H., "General Washington and the Loyalists," *American Antiquarian Society Proceedings*, New Series, Vol. 43, April, 1933, 48; Ford, W. C., *Writings of George Washington* (New York, 1889), Vol. 9, 488–90.
32. Van Alstyne, Richard W., *Empire and Independence* (New York, 1965), 220.
33. Hamilton, Alexander, "A Letter from Phocion to the Considerate Citizens of New York on the Politics of the Day" (New York, 1784), 7–41.
34. Miller, John C., *Alexander Hamilton, Portrait in Paradox* (New York, 1959) 103–05.

7
Islands of Refuge

1. Hicks, F. C., "Bermuda in Poetry" in *The Bermudian* by Nathaniel Tucker (Hamilton, Bermuda, 1915), 6.
2. Siebert, W. H., *The Legacy of the American Revolution to the British West Indies and Bahamas* (Columbus, O. 1913), 35–36.
3. Ibid, 38.
4. Eaton, A. W. (ed.), *Recollections of a Georgia Loyalist,* by Elizabeth L. Johnston (New York, 1901), 12.
5. Gardner, W. J., *A History of Jamaica* (New York, 1909), 212–13.
6. PRO, C. O. 137/86.
7. Narrative of Richard Lang, Nov. 27, 1784, PRO, T1/622.
8. Oliver, Vere L., *History of the Island of Antigua* (London, 1894), cxxx.
9. *Winslow Papers,* 379.
10. Siebert, 19; letter from Mrs. Lydia Parrish, July 18, 1949.
11. PRO, C. O. 24/14; Lockey, J. B., *East Florida, 1783–85* (Berkeley, 1940), 178.
12. Craton, Michael, *A History of the Bahamas* (London, 1962), 162.
13. PRO, AO 12/101, 72–73; Hancock, Harold, "John Ferdinand Dalziel Smyth: Loyalist," *Maryland Historical Magazine,* Dec. 1960; Smyth, J. F. D., *A Tour in the USA* (London, 1784), 180.

Notes

14. Schoepf, Johann David, *Travels in the Confederation*, A. J. Morrison (ed.) (Philadelphia, 1911), 263.
15. Ibid, 267.
16. Ibid, 282.
17. Ibid, 272–74; Sir Etienne Dupuch, publisher of the Nassau *Tribune*, was personally of much help to the author while there.
18. Peters, Thelma, "The Loyalist Migration from East Florida to the Bahama Islands," *Florida Historical Quarterly*, XXX, No. 2 (Oct. 1961), 123–41.
19. "Narrative of David Fanning," in *Southern Historical Collection* at the University of North Carolina, 37–46.
20. Maxwell to Sydney, PRO, 23/25.
21. Ibid.
22. Maxwell to Sydney, Aug. 6, 1784, PRO, CO 23/25.
23. Maxwell to Sydney, Aug. 26, 1784, PRO, CO 23/25.
24. Copy of Resolutions for July 29, 1784, PRO, CO 23/25, Sept. 2, 1784.
25. PRO, CO 23/28.
26. PRO, CO 23/28.
27. Parrish, Lydia, "Records of Some Southern Loyalists," Mss. in Harvard Library, 205.
28. *Bahama Gazette*, Nov. 28, 1793, as quoted in Peters, Thelma, "The American Loyalists in the Bahama Islands: Who They Were," *Florida Historical Quarterly*, XXX, No. 3 (Jan. 1962).
29. Larrish Mss., 29.
30. Aikman, Louisa S., *The Journal of a Voyage from Charleston, S. C. to London, etc.* (New York, 1906).
31. Peters, 239–40.
32. Siebert, 25.
33. Siebert, 30; Northcroft, G. J. H., *Sketches in Summerland* (Nassau, 1900), 288; *Miami Herald Sunday Magazine*, Oct. 25, 1959.
34. Personal interview by the author.
35. Kerr, Wilfred B., *Bermuda and the American Revolution* (Princeton, 1936), 38–41; Bethell, A. T., *The Early Settlers of the Bahamas* (Norfolk, England, 1937), 205.
36. Washington to the Bermudians, Sept. 6, 1775.
37. Hunt, Gaillard (ed.), *Journals of the Continental Congress* (Washington, 1904–37), II, 174, 187, 239; St. George Tucker to Richard Rush, Oct. 27, 1813, *Virginia Magazine of History and Biography* (July, 1934), 211–21.
38. *New York Evening Post*, Feb. 24, 1904.
39. *Minutes of Executive Council*, Aug. 15, 1775, Bermuda Archives; Vergill, A. E., "Relations Between Bermuda and the American Colonies During the Revolutionary War," *Publications of Yale University*, XIII (July 1907), 57.

40. Stark, 449; Felt, Joseph B., *The Annals of Salem* (Salem, 1827), 424.
41. Felt, 464, 469; Bentley, William, *The Diary of William Bentley* (Salem, 1907), II, 425.
42. Stark, 131; Van Tyne, 35–38; Curwen, 505; Wilkinson, Henry, *Bermuda in the Old Empire* (London, 1950), 424–25; Jackman, S. W., "William Browne, Governor, 1782–88," *Bermuda Historical Quarterly*, XIII, No. 1 (Spring, 1956), 17–24.
43. From a special article in manuscript by Mr. Watlington, used with his kind permission. Terry Tucker, Bermuda author and librarian, was extremely helpful.
44. Quoted in Tyler, I, 357; Van Tyne, 49.
45. Jackman, S. W., "Daniel Leonard, 1740–1829," *Bermuda Historical Quarterly*, XIII, No. 3 (Autumn, 1956), 136–45; Gosling, Alice E., "Preserved in a Ginger Jar," *Bermuda Historical Quarterly*, Vol. IX, No. 4 (Nov. 1952), 345–50.

BIBLIOGRAPHY

Manuscripts

"A Brief Statement of the Case of American Loyalists," Berkshire Record Office, Reading, England

Adams Papers, The, Lyman Butterfield (ed.) (Cambridge, Mass. 1963)

Admiralty Records, National Maritime Museum, London

Bristol Election Manuscripts, New York Historical Society

British Headquarters Papers, New York Public Library

Buckinghamshire Papers, Marquess of Lothian, Melbourne Hall, Derby, England

Cannon Hall Muniments, Sheffield City Libraries, England

Clinton, Sir Henry, Papers, Clements Library, University of Michigan, Ann Arbor

Emmet Collection, New York Public Library

Germain Papers, Clements Library, University of Michigan

Haldimand Collection, Public Archives of Canada, Ottawa

Hartley Russell Papers, Berkshire Record Office, Reading, England

John Peters Papers, New York Historical Society

Knox, William, Papers, Clements Library, University of Michigan

Letter Book of Lieutenant Governor John Simcoe, 1792–93, Huntington Library, San Marino, California

Letter of Lord Cathcart to Lord Carlisle, Castle Howard, York, England

Letters of Samuel Quincy, typescript, University of London Library

Loyalist Souvenir, New Brunswick Historical Society, Fredericton

Luce, Melvin G., "The Southern Loyalists in the American Revolution," unpublished master's thesis, 1951, New York University, New York City

Marston, Benjamin, Diary, New Brunswick Historical Society

Massachusetts Historical Society Revolutionary Manuscripts, Boston

Minute Book, Port Roseway Association, Public Archives of Canada

Minutes of Executive Council, Aug. 15, 1775, Bermuda Archives, Hamilton

Miscellaneous Manuscripts of the American Revolution, Library of Congress, Washington, D. C.

Narrative of David Fanning, Southern Historical Collection, University of North Carolina, Chapel Hill

Narrative of Richard Lang, Public Record Office, London

Nova Scotia Historical Collection, Halifax

North Carolina State Records, State Archives, Raleigh

North, Lord, Manuscripts, Bodleian Library, Oxford University, England

Papers Relating to the American Loyalists, British Museum, London

Parrish, Lydia A., "Record of Some Southern Loyalists," Harvard University Library, Cambridge, Massachusetts; microfilm copy in Library of the University of Florida, Gainesville

"On Board the Sally Transport," voyage report in National Maritime Museum, Greenwich, England

Odell, Jonathan, Papers, New Brunswick Museum, Saint John

Peters, Samuel, Papers, New York Historical Society

Rockingham Papers, Wentworth Woodhouse Muniments, Sheffield City Library, England

Sewall, Jonathan, Papers, Public Archives of Canada, Ottawa

Shelburne, Lord, Manuscripts, Public Archives of Canada

Stokes, Kathleen, "The Character and Administration of Governor John Wentworth," unpublished master's thesis, 1935, Dalhousie University, Halifax, Nova Scotia

Sydney, Lord, Papers, Public Archives of Canada

"The Memorial of Philip Skene to the Honorable Commissioners, etc," Public Record Office, London

Bibliography

"The Narrative of Hannah Ingraham," typescript, Bonar Law-Bennett Library, University of New Brunswick, Fredericton

Webster, Deborah, "The Thomson House," Shelburne, Nova Scotia, Historical Society

Transcripts of the Manuscript Books and Papers of the Commission of Enquiry Into the Losses and Services of American Loyalists, held under Acts of Parliament of 23, 25, 26, 28 and 29 of George III, preserved amongst the Audit Offices Records in the Public Record Office of England, 1783–1790. Transcribed for the New York Public Library, 1899

Newspapers

Bahama Gazette
Bermuda Gazette
Chattanooga News-Free Press
Continental Journal and Weekly Advertiser
Kingston, Jamaica, Gazette
London Chronicle
Miami Herald Sunday Magazine
New York Evening Post
New York Times
Nova Scotia Packet
Rivington's Gazette
Royal Gazette
Toronto Mail and Empire

Books, Periodicals and Published Historical Collections

Acadiensis (Saint John, N. B., 1904)

Acts and Resolves, Public and Private, of the Province of Massachusetts Bay (Boston, 1869–1922)

Adair, Douglas, and Schutz, John A. (eds.), *Peter Oliver's Origin and Progress of the American Rebellion, a Tory View* (San Marino, California, 1961)

Adams, John, *Diary* (Cambridge, 1961)

Adams, John, *Works* (Boston, 1850–1856)

Adams, Randolph, *Political Ideas of the American Revolution* (New York, 1958)

Aikman, Louisa S., *The Journal of a Voyage from Charleston, S. C. to London* (New York, 1906)

American Antiquarian Society Proceedings, Vol. 43, April 1933

Andrews, Charles M., *The Colonial Background of the American Revolution* (New Haven, 1961)

Arnold, Isaac, *The Life of Benedict Arnold* (Chicago, 1880)

Atlantic Advocate Magazine, March, 1963

Bakeless, John, *Turncoats, Traitors and Heroes* (New York, 1959)

Baker, William K., *The Loyalists* (London, 1903)

Bancroft, George, *History of the United States from the Discovery of the Continent* (New York, 1882–1884), IV

Barnwell, Robert W., Jr., "Loyalism in South Carolina," unpublished master's thesis, 1941, Duke University

Bartlett, W. S., *The Frontier Missionary* (Boston, 1893)

Batchelder, S. F., *Bits of Cambridge History* (Cambridge, Mass. 1930)

Beloff, Max (ed.), *The Debate on the American Revolution, 1761–1783* (London, 1960)

Bemis, Samuel Flagg, *The Diplomacy of the American Revolution* (Bloomington, Ind., 1957)

Bermuda Historical Quarterly, Vol. V, No. 3; Vol. VI, No. 2; Vol. IX, No. 4; Vol. XIII, No. 1

Bermudian Magazine, Dec. 1943 and June 1942

Bethell, A. T., *The Early Settlers of the Bahamas* (Norfolk, England, 1937)

Boucher, Jonathan, *A View of the Causes and Consequences of the American Revolution in Thirteen Discourses* (London, 1797)

Bradley, A. G., *Colonial Americans in Exile, Founders of British Canada* (New York, 1927)

Brinton, Crane, *The Anatomy of Revolution* (New York, 1960)

Brown, Wallace, *The King's Friends* (Providence, R. I., 1966)

Callahan, North, *Daniel Morgan: Ranger of the Revolution* (New York, 1961)

Callahan, North, *Henry Knox: General Washington's General* (New York, 1958)

Callahan, North, *Royal Raiders: The Tories of the American*

Revolution (New York, 1963)

Campbell, G. G., *The History of Nova Scotia* (Toronto, 1948)

Campobello Island (Campobello, 1964)

Canadian Magazine, Feb. 1906; May 1911; Oct. 1914; Aug. 1928

Candler, Allen D., *The Revolutionary Records of the State of Georgia* (Atlanta, 1908), II

Captain John Hatfield, Loyalist (New York, 1943)

Centennial of the Settlement of Upper Canada by the United Empire Loyalists (Toronto, 1885)

Chapin, Bradley, *The American Law of Treason* (Seattle, 1964)

Chitwood, Oliver P., *A History of Colonial America* (New York, 1961)

Clark, Gerald, *Canada, the Uneasy Neighbor* (New York, 1965)

Clark, Walter (ed.), *State Records of North Carolina* (Goldsboro, 1886–1907)

Coast Guard, The, Nov. 1, 1962

Cody, H. A., *The United Empire Loyalists* (Fredericton, 1933)

Coleman, Kenneth, *The American Revolution in Georgia* (Athens, 1958)

Collections of the New Brunswick Historical Society, No. 14 (Saint John, 1955)

Craton, Michael, *A History of the Bahamas* (London, 1962)

Creighton, Donald, *A History of Canada* (Boston, 1958)

Cruikshank, E. A., *The Settlement of the United Empire Loyalists on the Upper St. Lawrence and the Bay of Quinte in 1786* (Toronto, 1934)

Curwen, Samuel, *Journals and Letters* (New York, 1845)

Dalhousie Review, July, 1932

d'Auberteuil, Hilliard, *Histoire de L'Administration de Lord North* (London, 1784)

Davidson, Philip, *Propaganda of the American Revolution, 1763–1783* (Chapel Hill, 1941)

DeMond, Robert O., *The Loyalists of North Carolina During the Revolution* (Durham, 1940)

Diary of William Bentley (Salem, 1907)

Dorson, Richard M., *America Rebels* (New York, 1953)

Eaton, A. W. (ed.), *Recollections of a Georgia Loyalist* (New

York, 1901)

Eddis, William, *Letters from America, Historical and Descriptive, Compromising Occurrences from 1769–1776* (London, 1792)

Egerton, Hugh (ed.), *The Royal Commission on the Losses and Services of American Loyalists* (London, 1915)

Egerton, Ryerson, *The Loyalists of America and Their Times* (Montreal, 1880)

Einstein, Lewis, *Divided Loyalties* (London, 1933)

Erskine, John, *Reflections on the Rise, Progress and Probable Consequences of the Present Contentions with the Colonies* (Edinburgh, 1776)

Fitzmaurice, Sir Edmund, *Life of the Earl of Shelburne* (London, 1912)

Flick, Alexander, *Loyalism in New York During the American Revolution* (New York, 1901)

Florida Historical Quarterly, XXX, Nos. 2 and 3, Oct. 1961

Force, Peter (ed.), *American Archives*, Fifth Series (Washington, D. C., 1853), II

Ford, W. C. (ed.), *The Writings of George Washington* (New York, 1889)

Fraser, Alexander, *Thirteenth Report of the Ontario Bureau of Archives, 1916* (Toronto, 1917)

Freeman, D. S., *George Wishington* (New York, 1949), II

Gardner, W. J., *A History of Jamaica* (New York, 1909)

Georgia Historical *Collections*, VIII (Savannah, 1913)

Gipson, Lawrence P., *The Coming of the Revolution, 1763–75* (New York, 1954)

Grafton Magazine, The, II, Feb. 3, 1910

Granger, Bruce I., *Political Satire in the American Revolution* (Ithaca, N. Y., 1960)

Greene, Evarts B., *The Revolutionary Generation* (New York, 1943)

Grimsby Historical Publications No. 1 (Grimsby, Ontario, 1950)

Guedalla, Philip, *Fathers of the Revolution* (New York, 1926)

Hadfield, Joseph, *An Englishman in America, 1785* (Montreal, 1908)

Bibliography

Haight, C., *The Coming of the Loyalists* (Toronto, 1889)

Hall, Edward H., *Philipse Manor Hall* (New York, 1930)

Hancock, Harold B., *The Delaware Loyalists* (Washington, 1940)

Harrell, I. S., *Loyalism in Virginia* (Durham, N. C., 1926)

Henry, William W., *Patrick Henry, Life, Correspondence and Speeches* (New York, 1891)

Hicks, F. C., *Bermuda in Poetry* (Hamilton, 1915)

History Today, March 1962

Hitsman, J. M., *The Incredible War of 1812* (Toronto, 1965)

Holliday, Carl, *The Wit and Humor of Colonial Days* (New York, 1960)

Hughes, Edward (ed.), "Lord North's Correspondence," *English Historical Review,* April 1947

Hutchinson, Thomas, *Diary and Letters* (London, 1883)

Irving, Washington, *Life of George Washington* (New York, 1869)

Jameson, J. Franklin, *The American Revolution Considered as a Social Movement* (Boston, 1956)

Jones, Thomas, *History of New York During the Revolutionary War* (New York, 1956)

Journals of the Continental Congress, ed. by Gaillard Hunt (Washington, 1904–1937)

Kelly, A. H., and Harbison, W. E., *The American Constitution* (New York, 1963)

Kerr, Wilfred B., *Bermuda and the American Revolution* (Princeton, 1936)

Knollenberg, Bernhard, *Origin of the American Revolution, 1759–1766* (New York, 1960)

Labaree, Leonard W., *Conservatism in Early American History* (Ithaca, 1959)

Lawrence, J. W., *Footprints or Incidents in the Early History of New Brunswick* (Saint John, 1883)

Lockey, J. B., *East Florida, 1783–85* (Berkeley, 1940)

Lossing, Benson J., *Field Book of the Revolution* (New York, 1850–1852)

Lucas, Reginald, *Lord North* (London, 1913)

Lundy's Lane Historical Society Publications (Welland, Ontario, 1893)

MacDonald, James S., "Memoir of Governor John Parr," Nova Scotia Historical Society *Collections*, XIV, 1909

Maclean's Magazine, August 26, 1961

MacNutt, Stewart, and Trueman, A. W., *New Brunswick and Its People* (Fredericton, 1963)

McIlwain, Charles H., *The American Revolution: A Constitutional Interpretation* (New York, 1958)

McMurtrie, Douglas C., *The Royal Printers at Shelburne, Nova Scotia* (Chicago, 1933)

Maryland Historical Magazine, December 1960

Massachusetts Historical Society *Collections*, LXXIII (Boston, 1925)

Michigan Pioneer Historical Collections, XVII (Lansing, 1910)

Miller, John C., *Alexander Hamilton: Portrait in Paradox* (New York, 1959)

Moore, Frank, *Diary of the American Revolution* (New York, 1860)

Moseley, Mary, *The Bahamas Handbook* (Nassau, 1926)

Nelson, William H., *The American Tory* (London, 1961)

Nevins, Allan, *The American States During and After the Revolution* (New York, 1927)

Newcomer, Lee N., *The Embattled Farmers* (New York, 1953)

Northcroft, G. J. H., *Sketches in Summerland* (Nassau, 1900)

Noyes, John P., *Canadian Loyalists and Early Pioneers in the District of Bedford* (Cowansville, Quebec, 1906)

Ohio Archaeological and Historical Quarterly, Vol. XII, July 1903

Oliver, Vere L., *History of the Island of Antigua* (London, 1894)

Ontario Historical Papers and Records, II, XVIII (Toronto, 1900)

Proceedings of New Jersey Historical Society, LXXIX, No. 2, April 1961

Proceedings of the New York Historical Society, VII, 1907

Queens Quarterly, XXXVI, Summer, 1929

Raymond, W. O., *The River St. John* (Sackville, N. B. 1943)

Bibliography

Richardson, James, *Kingston, Before the War of 1812* (Toronto, 1959)

Robson, Eric, *The American Revolution, 1763-1783* (London, 1955)

Rossiter, Clinton, *Conservatism in America* (London, 1955)

Sabine, Lorenzo, *Loyalists of the American Revolution* (Boston, 1864)

Sachse, W. L., *The Colonial Americans in Britain* (Madison, Wis., 1956)

Sargent, Winthrop, *Loyalist Poetry of the Revolution* (Philadelphia, 1857)

Schlesinger, Arthur M., *Prelude to Independence, the Newspaper War on Britain, 1764-1776* (New York, 1958)

Schoepf, J. D., *Travels in the Confederation* (Philadelphia, 1911)

Second Report of the Bureau of Archives for the Province of Ontario (Toronto, 1905)

Sibley, John L., *Harvard Graduates,* Clifford L. Shipton (ed.) (Boston, 1951)

Siebert, W. H., *The Legacy of the American Revolution to the British West Indies and the Bahamas* (Columbus, O., 1913); *The Loyalists of Pennsylvania* (Columbus, O., 1923); *The Exodus of the Loyalists from Penobscot to Passamaquoddy* (Columbus, O., 1914)

Smith, Paul H., *Loyalists and Redcoats* (Chapel Hill, 1964)

Smyth, J. F. D., *A Tour in the United States of America* (London, 1784)

Stark, James H., *Loyalists of Massachusetts* (Boston, 1910)

Stevens, B. F., *Facsimiles of Manuscripts in European Archives Relating to America, 1773-1783* (London, 1889-95)

Stuart, E. R., *Jessup's Rangers as a Factor in Loyalist Settlement* (Ottawa, 1961)

Talman, James J., *Loyalist Narratives from Upper Canada* (Toronto, 1946)

Thacher, James H., *A Military Journal During the Revolutionary War* (Boston, 1927)

Tiffany, Consider, "The American Colonies and the Revolution," Mss. in the Library of Congress

Trevelyan, Sir George Otto, *The American Revolution* (London, 1921)

Tucker, Boman T., *The Camden Colony* (Montreal, 1908)

Tyler, Moses Coit, *The Literary History of the American Revolution* (New York, 1957)

Van Alstyne, R. W., *Empire and Independence* (New York, 1965)

Van Schaack, H. C., *Life of Peter Van Schaack* (New York, 1842)

Van Tyne, C. H., *Causes of the War of Independence* (Boston, 1929)

Van Tyne, C. H., *The Loyalists in the American Revolution* (New York, 1959)

Virginia Magazine of History and Biography, July 1934

Wallace, Willard M., *Traitorous Hero* (New York, 1954)

Wallace, W. S., *The United Empire Loyalists* (Toronto, 1922)

Ward, Christopher, *The War of the Revolution* (New York, 1959)

Warren, Charles, *The Supreme Court in United States History* (Boston, 1926)

Watson, J. Steven, *The Reign of George III, 1760–1815* (London, 1960)

Wertenbaker, T. J., *Father Knickerbocker Rebels* (New York, 1948)

Wilkinson, Henry, *Bermuda in the Old Empire* (London, 1950)

Willcox, William B. (ed.), *Sir Henry Clinton, the American Rebellion* (New Haven, 1954)

William and Mary Quarterly, Jan. 1962, Jan. 1963, October 1964

Winslow Papers, W. O. Raymond (ed.) (Saint John, N. B., 1901)

Wright, Esther Clark, *The Loyalists of New Brunswick* (Fredericton, 1955)

Wrong, G. M., *Canada and the American Revolution* (Toronto, 1935)

INDEX

Index

Crown and Anchor Inn, 123, 128, 139–40
Cruger, John Harris, 90
Cummings, Samuel, 29
Curwen, Samuel, 90–93, 107, 109–10, 172
Customs revenue, Shelburne (1786–1787), 24
Cuyler, Abraham C., 72, 90
Cyclops, the, 8, 9
Cyrus, HMS, 146

D

Dames, Charles, 161
Danbury (Conn.), 50–53, 152
Dancing, 16
Dayton, Abigail, 85–86
Dayton, Abraham, 85
Dean, Peter, 159
Deane, Silas, 89
Declaration of Independence, 54, 83, 93
De Lancey, James, 135
De Lancey, Oliver, 90, 106, 121
De Lancey, Stephen, 47, 160
De Lancey's Brigade, 15, 45
De Lancey's Volunteers, 12
Delaware, 125
Delaware River, 79
Detroit, 78, 86–87
de Vattel, Emerich, 138–39
Deveaux, Andrew, 155
Diana, 16
Disqualifying Act (1780), 130
Dobbs Ferry (N.Y.), 104
Dole, James, 2, 11
Dominica, 147, 149
Dorchester (N.S.), 36
Dorchester Heights, 175
Dresden (Me.), 30
Drummer, William, 31
Dry Harbor, 146
Dryden, John, 120
Dublin, 121
Duché, the Rev. Jacob, 93–94, 135
Dudley, John, 170
Duke of Cumberland's Regiment, 12
Dulany, Lloyd, 93
Dumaresq, Philip, 163
Dundas, Thomas, 39
Dunmore, Lord, 152, 158–60, 163
Dunmore Town, 166
Durfee, Joseph, 2
Dutch, descendants of, 36
Duties, import, 13

E

East Florida, 130, 141, 143, 160, 161
East Florida Gazette, 162
East India Company, 167
Eastport (Me.), 61
Eden, Sir Robert, 132
Edinburgh, 143

Egbert, Anthony, 60
Egbert, Mary, 60
Eleuthera Island, 166
Elizabeth I, Queen, 138
Elliot, Andrew, 90
England, Loyalist refugees in, 89–119
English Harbor, 149
Ernestown (Que.), 74
Espionage, 112–14
Eutaw Springs, Battle of, 45
Evangeline (Longfellow), 31
Eve, Joseph, 161
Eve, Oswell, 161
Exchange Coffee House, 60
Exiles, Loyalist, former homes of, 35–36
Exuma Island, 158, 162

F

Fairfield (Conn.), 85
Falconer, William, 108
Fanning, David, 155–56
Fanning, Edmund, 70
Finucane, Andrew, 49
Finucane, Bryan, 48, 49
Fishing industry, 21, 26, 31; *see also* Whaling
FitzGibbon, James, 82, 83
Florida, 150, 151, 155, 156, 159, 161–62, 164; *see also* East Florida
Flucker, Thomas, 90, 97
Forsyth. E. W., 165
Fort Clinton, 45
Fort Edward, 85
Fort Frontenac, 72
Fort Haldane, 148
Fort Howe, 43, 45, 59
Fort Montgomery, 45
Fort Moultrie, 169
Fort Niagara, 78–79
Fort Oswegatchie, 84
Fort Stanwix, 77, 84
Fort Ticonderoga, 135
Fox, Charles James, 48, 88, 118
Fox, Henry, 54
France, 133, 137; *see also* French and Indian War; Paris
Franklin, Benjamin, 101, 112, 115, 137, 168
Franklin, William, 136
Fraser, the Rev. Hugh, 15
Frederick, Prince, 21
Frederick (Md.), 152
Fredericksburg (Ont.), 74
Fredericton (N.B.), 12, 47, 50, 54, 55, 60, 62, 67
Freemasonry, 22
French-English war (1793), 25
French and Indian War, 37, 83, 105
Freneau, Philip, 55
Friends Academy (Philadelphia), 134
Frogg, Mr., 143

Index

Index

Wanton, Gideon, 170
War of 1812, 81–83
Washington, George, 10, 29, 40, 53, 55,
	59, 93, 104–6, 113, 114, 128, 137,
	168, 173, 175
Water Street (Shelburne), 4, 14, 16, 22
Waterloo Row (Fredericton), 60
Watlington, H. T., 173
Watson, Brook, 29–30, 39, 57, 115
Wayne, Anthony, 40, 129
Weather, Shelburne, 3; see also Climate
Weekly Advertiser (Kingston, Jamaica),
	147
Wells, Charles, 162
Wells, John, 159, 160, 162–63
Wells, Louisa, 162
Wells, Robert, 162
Wentworth (N.S.), 36
Wentworth, Sir John, 18
Wentworth, Paul, 111–12
Wereat, John, 130–31
Wesley, John, 92
West, Benjamin, 91, 139
West Canada Creek, 78
West Florida, 155; see also East
	Florida; Florida
West Indies, 19, 24, 36, 38, 57, 60–62,
	98–101, 141, 144, 145, 149–51, 153
West Point, 40, 104
Westchester (N.S.), 36
Westchester County (N.Y.), 121
Westminster Abbey, 117

Westminster Hall, 118
Westmoreland Road (St. John), 60
Whaling, 21; see also Fishing
White, Alexander, 71
White, Gideon, 4
White family, 4
Wilkins, Isaac, 90
William and Mary, 127
Williams, the, 23
Wilmot, John Eardley, 128
Wilson, James, 131
Winslow, Edward, 19, 35, 39, 44–45, 47,
	49, 54, 56, 57, 59, 63, 111, 124, 149
Winthrop, John, 170
Wood, John, 159
Wood Creek, 77
Woodbridge (N.J.), 170
Worcester (Mass.), 38
Wright, Sir James, 121, 129–30, 141,
	142, 144
Wylly, Alexander, 160–61
Wylly, William, 161
Wyoming Valley (Penna.), 78

Y

Yametta Island, 151
Yarmouth (N.S.), 20
Yonkers (N.Y.), 103
Yorktown (Va.), 28, 45, 114

Z

Zebra, the (frigate), 141